GREATEST GAMES
MANCHESTER UNITED

GREATEST GAMES
MANCHESTER UNITED

ROB CLARK

First published by Pitch Publishing, 2014

Pitch Publishing
A2 Yeoman Gate
Yeoman Way
Durrington
BN13 3QZ
www.pitchpublishing.co.uk

© Rob Clark

A CIP catalogue record is available for this book from the British Library.

ISBN 978-1-90962-640-9

Typesetting and origination by Pitch Publishing

Printed in Great Britain

CONTENTS

INTRODUCTION

WITH some clubs, writing a book about their 50 greatest games is a case of picking out the odd league or cup win, perhaps a stoic battle against relegation or a triumphant promotion season, a game where a star player put in a top performance, or the team scored a hatful of goals.

Choosing Manchester United's 50 greatest games is a different task altogether.

Just writing a chapter each on the trophies we have won would take you to 42, and that's without the FA Charity Shield/Community Shield. There are the three European Cup/Champions League triumphs, the 20 Football League/Premier League titles – a record, of course – the 11 FA Cups (another record) and the four League Cups. Not to mention various sundry other one-off cups and trophies.

Then there are the great players: Arthur Albiston, David Beckham, George Best, Steve Bruce, Martin Buchan, Nicky Butt, Roger Byrne, Eric Cantona, Bobby Charlton, Andy Cole, Eddie Colman, Steve Coppell, Paddy Crerand, Duncan Edwards, Patrice Evra, Bill Foulkes, Ryan Giggs, Mark Hughes, Paul Ince, Denis Irwin, Roy Keane, Brian Kidd, Denis Law, Brian McClair, Paul McGrath, Gordon McQueen, Billy Meredith, Charlie Mitten, Kevin Moran, Gary Neville, Gary Pallister, Bryan Robson, Cristiano Ronaldo, Wayne Rooney, Jack Rowley, Peter Schmeichel, Paul Scholes, Teddy Sheringham, Ole Gunnar Solskjaer, Jaap Stam, Alex Stepney, Nobby Stiles, Tommy Taylor, Ruud Van Nistelrooy, Robin Van Persie, Nemanja Vidic, Dennis Viollet, Norman Whiteside, Ray Wilkins, Dwight Yorke. Pick just one game from each of their stellar careers and there's your 50 – and there are some very good players missing from that list.

Arguing over who are United's greatest players is a discussion for another time and another book but some years ago I was working with a team of journalists on selecting United's 50 greatest players – it was a task which took many days and numerous meetings. Enjoyable days, but long ones nonetheless as good-natured argument flowed between us over the relative importance of players in different positions doing different jobs across different eras.

How good would Duncan Edwards and Eddie Colman have become? Should David Beckham have stayed at the club? Was Bryan Robson a more complete midfielder than Roy Keane? Was Eric Cantona's influence on the younger players more important even than his impact as a player in his own right?

One eminent football writer, who I shall allow to remain anonymous, was of the opinion that Cristiano Ronaldo should not figure in the top 50 players who have played for the club – five years after he left he has just been voted the world's best player, and the Stretford End still sings his name at every home game.

Not just players then. OK, how about the matches when we scored six goals or more? Nope, we've done that on more than 50 occasions since the Second World War as well.

You can see it's an almost impossible task, so what I've tried to do here instead is combine the obvious with the less obvious. I make no apology for the fact that I have included two games from some seasons, such as the Treble of 1998/99 – frankly I could have written almost the entire book on that season as we notched up significant victory after significant victory.

As that momentous campaign drew to a climax, Peter Schmeichel and Dwight Yorke shared an ongoing joke which had begun when United beat Liverpool in the fourth round of the FA Cup, 'Hey Yorkie, 27 games left – 27 more wins and we've had an unbelievable season.' As the number got smaller and smaller, so the impossible dream became a reality.

Any list of our greatest games has to include, at the very minimum, both *that* goal by Ryan Giggs in the FA Cup semi-final replay and the Champions League Final itself. I know all United fans will already have every detail of these matches burned into their souls, but it never hurts to be reminded of exactly how they both unfolded, does it?

Elsewhere I have tried to include a number of 'firsts' – our first match as Manchester United after changing our name from Newton Heath; the first time the Busby Babes took the field; the first time Bobby Charlton, Denis Law and George Best played together; the Class of 92 winning the FA Youth Cup; the debut of one Wayne Rooney; and, of course, the first match with Alex Ferguson (as he then was) in charge.

I have had to include some of the wins over Liverpool – the 1977 FA Cup Final ranks highly for me as it prevented the Scousers winning the Treble that year. It was also the first trophy I saw United win live, having become a fan the previous year when we lost in the final to Southampton. Nor could I possibly omit the 4-0 drubbing in April 2003 during a run of nine wins and a draw from our final ten games of the season which saw us regain our title.

The last word on Liverpool was John O'Shea's stoppage-time header at Anfield on 3 March 2007 which all but confirmed another league title. Three wins over Liverpool, but frankly I could have written a whole book about that too except that Ivan Ponting got there first with his excellent history of games between the clubs entitled *Red And Raw*.

What about the rivalry with Manchester City, I hear you ask. To which I reply that those noisy neighbours haven't really *been* rivals for most of our history. I have chosen a couple of games against them, but for other reasons. There is the 1991 victory which marked Ryan Giggs's debut. Oh, and he scored the winner. And there's the early December 1992 win which marked the debut of a certain Monsieur Cantona.

Great European nights have also become, if not commonplace, hardly a rarity at Old Trafford. Even those of us who have been fans for decades still get a frisson, a thrill, when one of Europe's giants comes visiting. From Sir Bobby Charlton's cathartic hat-trick in Germany against Borussia Dortmund in 1964, via the European Cup Winners' Cup Final against Barcelona in 1991, to the Wayne Rooney hat-trick on debut against Fenerbahce in 2004. Ever since Sir Matt Busby rightly insisted that United enter the pan-European competition, the Red Devils have loved pitting their wits against the best and the brightest from all over the continent.

Of course the three European Cup triumphs are in here too, but if I had to pick a favourite moment it would be the one when all four corners of Old Trafford rose to applaud one of the most incredible solo performances our great ground has ever witnessed – that of Ronaldo for Real Madrid in 2003. That we are able to appreciate an opponent's brilliance even in the moment of being knocked out of the world's premier club competition tells you everything you need to know about United's fans.

So first and foremost this one is for fellow fans. I know you won't agree with every one of my selections, that's the nature of books like this. But one of the best things about a book on United's 50 greatest games is that we are spoilt for choice in a way no other club in England is.

Rob Clark

ACKNOWLEDGEMENTS

A S is always the case with books like this, I am indebted to those who have gone before and done such a sterling job in detailing various aspects of the glorious history of Manchester United.

Among the excellent reference books which have provided invaluable information and the opportunity to double-check my own memories and notes are: *Manchester United in the Sixties* by Graham McColl; *Manchester United in Europe* by David Meek and Tom Tyrrell; *Always in the Running: The Manchester United Dream Team* by Jim White; *The Unique Treble* by Alex Ferguson; *Sons of United* by Steve Hobin and Tony Park; *The Man in The Middle* by referee David Elleray; *United We Stood* by Richard Kurt; *The Day a Team Died* by Frank Taylor; *Duncan Edwards: A Biography* by Iain McCartney and Roy Cavanagh; *The Tommy Taylor Story* by Brian Hughes; *Manchester United Almanac* by Dean Hayes; *Red and Raw: A Post-War History of Manchester United v Liverpool* by Ivan Ponting; *The Great Derby Matches: Manchester United Versus Manchester City* by Michael Heatley and Ian Welch; *You'll Win Nothing With Kids* by Jim White; *Best XI: Manchester United* by Sam Pilger; *Not Nineteen Forever* by Sam Pilger, Zac Hann, Rob Smyth and Doron Salomon; *The Manchester United Opus*; *Wayne Rooney: My Decade in the Premier League* by Matt Allen; *Champions Again!* by Aubrey Ganguly and Justyn Barnes; *Alex Ferguson: My Autobiography*.

Long-running fanzine *United We Stand* and the superb Stretford End website were also useful sources of information and statistics. Thanks to the National Newspaper Library at Colindale, to Peter Holme at the National Football Museum, to Tony Brown at ENFA (English National Football Archive), to the *Manchester Evening News* and to a whole host of our national newspapers and their journalists, whose reports I have sometimes quoted from.

A personal thanks to a few people who have provided support and advice along the way: Matt Allen, Justyn Barnes, Martin Cloake, Sue Grey, Sam Pilger, Tim Turner, Mark Wylie. Also to Paul Camillin at Pitch Publishing for taking a punt and letting me write this book, and to Gareth Davis for his proofreading and editing.

Thanks also to people whose interest lies mainly in other clubs for giving their time so freely and generously to allow me to get my facts right concerning their teams: Barry Richmond, Kilmarnock FC's biggest fan, who tracked down some details for me on United's visit to Kilmarnock for a friendly match in October 1953; Darren Bentley and Ray Simpson of Burnley FC who between them provided information on the Manchester United v Burnley double-header on 26 and 28 December 1963; and Martin Brodetsky, Oxford United's programme editor, who supplied his club's line-up for the November 1986 match at the Manor Ground which was Alex Ferguson's (as he then was) first game in charge of United.

Thanks to my wife, Sarah, and my children, Matt and Ellie.

Finally thanks to The Gaslight Anthem and Gin Blossoms whose music, along with strong fresh coffee, has kept me going late into the night when deadlines were approaching.

DEDICATIONS

To Matt and Ellie

—◆—

To United fans everywhere

—◆—

To Sir Alex Ferguson for putting us
back where we belong

v Blackburn Rovers 3-4

1

3 September 1892
Football League First Division
Ewood Park
Attendance: 8,000

NEWTON HEATH	BLACKBURN ROVERS
Jimmy Warner	Rowland Pennington
John Clements	John Murray
James Brown	John Forbes
George Perrins	Willie Almond
Willie Stewart	Geordie Dewar
Fred Erentz	Jimmy Forrest
Alf Farman	Harry Chippendale
Jimmy Coupar	Nat Walton
Bob Donaldson	Jack Southworth
Adam Carson	Coombe Hall
William Mathieson	Charlie Bowdler
Coach: Alfred Albut	*Coach:* Thomas Mitchell

THIS was the first official league game for Newton Heath, and in keeping with the nature of a club style that was destined to be based around aiming to score one more goal than the opposition, it produced goals galore. Unfortunately for the nascent club it ended in defeat after a seven-goal thriller, but the outfit that was to become Manchester United some ten years later had been born, and so too had an enduring legend begun.

In truth, the club was founded 14 years earlier in 1878, but Newton Heath LYR (Lancashire and Yorkshire Railway) was initially established as no more than a means of allowing railway workers some light relief from a hard day's labour. They played numerous games against other railway companies but such matches were rarely reported in the newspapers and hence are not often a matter of record. However, it seems safe to say that the club nickname of 'The Heathens' owed something to the club's quick accumulation of local victories.

By 1892 formal ties with the railway company had ended, although the majority of the players at that time were still its employees, so the LYR appendage had been dropped. With the Football League being expanded to two divisions on account of growing interest in the sport, Newton Heath were duly elected to the First Division.

It was not a success. Of course the mighty Blackburn Rovers were scarcely likely to provide a gentle introduction to league life – already five times FA Cup winners and one of the most notable teams in the country, they raced into a 3-0 lead inside ten minutes with goals from the prolific Jack Southworth (who scored 97 goals in 108 games for Rovers, and represented England on three occasions) and two from Coombe Hall. United fought back, however, with centre-forward Bob Donaldson pulling a goal back and James Coupar making it 3-2 to Blackburn at half-time.

In the second half honours were even as Alf Farman scored for Newton Heath and Harry Chippendale for Blackburn. It certainly wasn't a disgrace for the new boys against one of the country's top teams, and in front of 8,000 or so fans at Ewood Park.

The fact was, though, that Newton Heath were not quite ready for league football and they gained only a handful of victories in their first season. In fact they ended the season at the foot of the table, but with no prior arrangement having been made for relegation and promotion it was decided that the bottom three teams would play the top three teams from the Second Division and Newton Heath duly beat their near-namesakes Small Heath (later to become Birmingham City), winning a replay 5-2 after the first match had finished 1-1. That at least secured their place in the First Division for another season.

What the opening game of the season did do, though, was to display the fighting spirit and the never-say-die attitude which was to become synonymous with the club over the ensuing years. An interesting postscript to the season was that their first league victory was an almost unbelievable 10-1 win over a Wolverhampton Wanderers team which went on to lift the FA Cup at the end of the season. For all the goalscoring heroics of Tommy Taylor, Bobby Charlton and Wayne Rooney down the years – in much more successful teams – this remains United's biggest league victory.

Hat-tricks were scored by Bob Donaldson and Willie Stewart, and further goals were added by Adam Carson, Alf Farman, James Hendry and William 'Billy' Hood.

Hendry was making his debut that day and indeed made only one more appearance for the club. Hood was more successful, staying at the club for two years and featuring on 38 occasions; however, his record of just six goals did not warrant a longer tenure.

Donaldson, however, was to become the club's first great goalscorer, amassing 66 goals in 147 appearances. Although more than half his goals were scored when the club were in the Second Division, Donaldson nevertheless boasts a similar goals-to-games ratio in the higher division and his FA Cup record is even better, with ten goals in 16 games.

If on the pitch the 1892/93 season marked the arrival on the football scene of the club destined to become the greatest in the land, off it there were some major obstacles to be overcome. First of these was that the club were informed they had to vacate their home on North Road. it wasn't much of a home, admittedly, as it didn't even boast changing rooms – players, both Newton Heath and visitors, had to trudge to the Three Crowns pub, half a mile away instead.

Nevertheless, the football club had bought two stands which were able to hold 2,000 fans, and these had to be left behind; in fact, it has been suggested that the club's practice of charging fans for entry broke the terms of their lease and may have been the cause of their being asked to leave. Alternatively, it may just have been that the cricketers, with whom they shared the ground, got fed up playing on a mud patch.

The club officers did well to find a new ground, in Clayton, before the start of the 1893/94 season and although it was some three miles from Newton Heath, they managed to attract 7,000 spectators to their first match, a 3-2 win over Burnley. The location of the new ground was perilously close to chemical works, and some visiting fans went so far as to claim that it gave the Heathens an unfair advantage as they were used to the noxious fumes and the smells which assaulted the senses.

But if Newton Heath's first match was inauspicious, the advent of the club itself was anything but.

v Gainsborough Trinity 1-0

(First match as United)

6 September 1902
Football League Second Division
The Northolme
Attendance: 4,000

MANCHESTER UNITED	GAINSBOROUGH TRINITY
Jimmy Whitehouse	Jim Bagshaw
Harry Stafford	William Thompson
Bert Read	Harry Davies
Billy Morgan	William Jenkinson
Billy Griffiths	Arthur Pycock
Walter Cartwright	Frederick Johnson
Charlie Richards	Eddie Gettins
Dick Pegg	Tommy Tierney
Jack Peddie	Jack Dixon
Fred Williams	Hugh McQueen
Daniel Hurst	Fred Barnard
Coach: James West	*Coach:* Unknown

ALTHOUGH Newton Heath had survived in the First Division in their first year, by virtue of that play-off win over Small Heath, the respite was destined to last but one season. At the end of 1893/94 they finished rock bottom and this time the play-off saw them relegated. To make matters worse, it was defeat by Liverpool, of all clubs, that condemned the Heathens to the Second Division, the Merseysiders winning 2-0 at Ewood Park.

By the turn of the century, Newton Heath had become established as an average Second Division team, finishing fourth on three consecutive occasions from 1898–1900. They slipped even lower in 1901/02, dropping down to 15th out of 18 teams. The financial situation was fast moving from bad to dire but the following season their fortunes took a turn for the better thanks to one of the more unusual fundraising events in sporting history.

It came about in bizarre fashion, with a bazaar. Team captain Harry Stafford was accustomed to using his dog, a St Bernard called Major, to gather in donations by way of a barrel attached to its collar. Major was one of the main attractions at the bazaar, but when the dog went missing it was found by local businessman John Henry Davies, who was chairman of the local brewery, Walker & Homfrey – and later of the Manchester Brewery Company – making him a wealthy man in his own right. Not only that, he was also married to Amy, heiress of the Tate & Lyle Group. Davies and his wife were philanthropists noted in particular for their support of sport in the Manchester area, and he quickly agreed to invest in and take over the club.

So it came to pass that in 1902 Stafford was able to announce that he had found four businessmen (of whom Davies was one) who were prepared to invest £500 each as long as the directors gave them direct involvement in the running of the club. Whether the directors were in favour of such a move, or whether they were forced into it by the club's creditors, is not entirely clear, but the agreement paved the way for Davies's beneficial input.

At the start of the following, 1902/03, season, Newton Heath were renamed Manchester United. Manchester Central had been the early favourite but was dismissed as sounding too much like a railway station. Manchester Celtic was also considered, but rejected on the grounds that the club did not want to be seen to ally themselves too closely with any Celtic organisations. In the spirit of change, Davies also decided that the club should have a new strip, and they duly adopted the now-famous strip of red shirts and white shorts.

Stafford was put in charge of playing matters, not to mention being given the licence for one of Davies's pubs, though this was probably just reward for his part in saving the club from financial ruin, and he it was who led the team out for their first match in their new guise.

It was at Gainsborough Trinity's ground and United won it with a goal from Charlie Richards – his only league goal (he also scored one in the FA Cup) of the only season he spent at the club. It is easy to see why United signed him, in light of the three years he had spent at Grimsby Town where he scored 42 goals in 80 appearances. It was a strike rate which had played a major part in Grimsby's push for promotion and in 1901 the small seaside town won the Second Division, though Richards himself had little time to revel in the success, moving to Leicester Fosse in June of that year.

In a little over a year he was at Manchester United, but despite having only turned 27 that summer, Richards's best days were already behind him. Within eight months he had moved on to Doncaster Rovers, and he only remained there until the end of the season, whereupon he retired. But he will always have a place in United history as the first man to score after the team adopted their famous name.

Benefactor Davies had not previously shown much interest in football, preferring to lend his financial muscle to bowls and cycling, but he quickly showed that he was not going to be a sleeping partner. The club's financial difficulties dated back to their eviction from their North Road ground and although secretary James West had had an impact, Davies realised more needed to be done – and urgently.

Delighted though he was over United's first victory as United, he saw the need to attract large crowds to the Bank Street ground. In this, he was an instant success, drawing 20,000 to the first home game of the season, another 1-0 victory, over Burton Albion, secured by forward Daniel Hurst. Over the season, United's average crowd more than doubled from the 4,500 or so who used to watch Newton Heath, to over 10,000 in the club's first season as Manchester United.

A lot of those new fans, however, also expected to see instant success on the pitch, and while United improved from 15th position to fifth, they remained 13 points adrift of a promotion place which went to Small Heath in second spot. Even more gallingly, the league was won by Manchester City.

They did at least get the better of their city rivals in the league, drawing 1-1 at home and winning 2-0 away. United also enjoyed knocking Liverpool out of the FA Cup in February, when a double strike from Jack Peddie sent the Merseysiders home with their tails between their legs.

Peddie proved to be a stalwart of the team that year, making 36 appearances (the most of any player) and scoring 15 goals; regular strike partner Dick Pegg made only one appearance fewer and scored 13 times. A good return from the two men up front, but elsewhere it was not hard to see where the problems lay: 33 different men played for United in 1902/03, up from 21 the previous season. It was a huge number for that era, especially as 15 of them did not make it into double figures in appearances.

United never lost badly – no team defeated them by more than two goals all season, home or away, but they just didn't score enough. Eight of their 17 opponents in the division scored more goals than United did, a telling statistic, and one which Davies swiftly moved to correct.

A footnote to the career of Harry Stafford, who had played such a big part in the club's survival. Shortly after the club became Manchester United, Stafford was found guilty of making illegal payments to players and banned from football until 1907. Stafford admitted there might have been the odd 'irregularity', though his defence was that it was never done in order to line his own pockets, but to benefit the club.

He further claimed that the only 'crime' he was actually found guilty of was paying a Scottish player his wages in advance, before he had been registered with the club, a fairly minor matter in days when financial probity was rare. Satfford declared, 'Everything I have done has been done in the best interests of the club.' That is indisputable, and clearly Davies felt the same as he stood by Stafford.

Once his ban had been served, Stafford returned to Bank Street as a director of the club and doubled as the groundsman, though seemingly not entirely successfully as the pitch was frequently castigated by home and visiting players alike as resembling a mudbath. After the First World War, Stafford finally severed his long-serving ties with the club, emigrating to Canada where he opened a hotel in Montreal and also returned to one of his first loves: dogs.

If Stafford's defending on the pitch was occasionally somewhat agricultural in nature, his defence of the club off the pitch should never be discounted, and nor should his role in its preservation.

v Liverpool 4-0

(First League title)
7 September 1907
Football League First Division
Bank Street
Attendance: 24,000

MANCHESTER UNITED	LIVERPOOL
Harry Moger	Sam Hardy
Dick Holden	Percy Saul
Herbert Burgess	Alf West
Dick Duckworth	Maurice Parry
Charlie Roberts	George Latham
Alex Bell	James Bradley
Billy Meredith	Arthur Goddard
Jimmy Bannister	Charles Hewitt
Alex Menzies	Joe Hewitt
Sandy Turnbull	Sam Bowyer
George Wall	Jack Cox
Manager: Ernest Mangnall	*Manager:* Tom Watson

A FORTUITOUS side-effect of Harry Stafford and secretary James West being forced to step aside from playing and managing team affairs owing to 'financial irregularities' was that John Henry Davies was forced to look around for a new secretary. And so it was that the highly respected Burnley secretary Ernest Mangnall was persuaded to take over at Manchester United.

Mangnall was, as had already become apparent, a master promoter, both of himself and of whichever club he was working for. Taking charge of the club, Mangnall demanded – and got – complete control of the playing side, making him in effect the first professional manager of the club. The Jose Mourinho of his day, Mangnall liked only one thing more than being asked for his opinion – giving it.

In his defence, however, it should be pointed out that Mangnall was hugely successful, and makes a good case for being included in a triumvirate of brilliant Manchester United managers alongside the better-known Sir Matt Busby and Sir Alex Ferguson. Under the guidance of these three men between them, United claimed all of the club's league championship titles and eight of their 11 FA Cup triumphs. Not only that, but Mangnall looked towards Europe too.

If it took the persuasion and determination of Busby to take United into pan-European competition, it was Mangnall who first saw the possibilities. In 1908 he was to embark on the club's first continental tour – to Prague, Vienna and Budapest. A riot in the last of these great cities did give him food for thought, but United had shown that they were willing to go beyond the usual frontiers to seek out, if not new life, then at least new frontiers.

But all that was still in the future on the day that Alex 'Sandy' Turnbull scored Manchester United's first league hat-trick and it came against, joy of joys, none other than Liverpool. It was the second matchday of a season which had started with a 4-1 win away at Aston Villa, but it was Turnbull's performance in a demolition of United's fiercest rivals which made the rest of the league sit up and take notice.

Turnbull was to prove a somewhat controversial figure, but his goalscoring prowess was never in doubt. Born in Hurlford in Scotland, Turnbull scored 53 goals in 110 appearances for Manchester City, then added a further 101 in 247 games for United. And it was Liverpool that he particularly enjoyed scoring against, recording nine goals in his ten matches against them – the most he scored against any other team. Turnbull was very different from most of the 'all-action' strikers of his day; rather he would conserve his energy and only burst into life when he had a genuine opportunity to affect play, which frequently meant getting on the end of one of Billy Meredith's many crosses.

The season after his goals had taken United to their first league triumph, he also scored the winner in their first FA Cup victory. In those days the FA Cup was a much more prestigious trophy than the league, and United's succession of wins over Everton, Blackburn Rovers, champions Newcastle and Bristol City – all teams which finished above them in the league – was lauded far and wide. The final against Bristol City was a scrappy match played out in front of over 71,000 fans at Crystal Palace and decided in the 22nd minute when a Harold Halse shot came back off the crossbar and Turnbull was the quickest to the rebound.

Towards the end of a match lacking in clear chances, Vince Hayes was forced off with a cracked rib. In the days before substitutes this meant United having to reorganise to hold out for the win.

Turnbull, who had already been implicated in the Manchester City scandal which resulted in the entire team being suspended from playing, was later found guilty of match fixing and in 1915 received a lifelong ban from football.

In fact, Turnbull did not play in the match in question (a 2-0 win over Liverpool), but evidence that he had been part of a United 'delegation' which had twice met with Liverpool captain Jackie Sheldon was enough to condemn him. However it was to have little relevance as Turnbull joined the army and became a lance sergeant in the East Surrey Regiment. He was presumed killed in action at Arras, in France, on 3 May 1917. His body was never found but he is commemorated on the famous Arras memorial. Turnbull was posthumously reinstated in 1919, in recognition of his war service.

Modern-day United stars owe Turnbull a greater debt than just as a goalscorer, however. He, along with other United players, was instrumental in founding the Players' Union (the PFA as it is today) in 1907. Meredith had seen two friends from his Manchester City days die and their families not be given any compensation, so when 25-year-old team-mate Thomas Blackstock collapsed after heading a ball during a reserve game it was to prove the final straw. Turnbull and Meredith, possibly on account of their mining backgrounds, were the prime movers in establishing a Players' Union at a meeting at The Imperial Hotel, Manchester, on 2 December 1907.

Meredith eloquently summed up his stance, saying, 'I have devoted myself to football and I have become a better player than most men because I have denied myself much that men prize… If football is a man's livelihood and he does more than others for his employer, why is he not entitled to better pay than others?'

A year later the PU stated its aims as abolishing the maximum wage, establishing the right of players to more freely between clubs and for players themselves to receive a percentage of any transfer fee that was paid. The FA tried to make a stand and suspend any players who refused to resign from the union, but the United players were no fools and Charlie Roberts arranged a photoshoot with the players holding up a board reading 'The Outcasts FC'.

Concerned about the real possibility of a breakaway league forming, the FA backed down and recognised the union, allowing it to negotiate wages on its members' behalf. The union activists did pay a personal price, though, in that none was picked to represent his country again.

The rout of Liverpool that Turnbull inspired was the start of a glorious season for United. After one season of consolidation in the First Division, when they finished eighth out of 20 teams, they blazed their way through the 1907/08 season. At the halfway point they had lost just twice – at Middlesbrough and at Sheffield Wednesday, both of whom finished the season inside the top six. Just as significantly, they had scored four goals or more on nine separate occasions: this was the Manchester United its fans grew to love in all its swashbuckling glory.

Turnbull was to finish as the top scorer, with 27, though George Wall wasn't far behind with 22 and Jimmy Turnbull and Meredith both got into double figures.

Ironically, the success of United that season was due in large part to the demise of Manchester City, coupled with the astute business dealings of Mangnall. Mangnall had often seemed to be one step ahead of rival managers and in the days before scouting had become a recognised part of the football world, he always had an ear to the ground and a number of 'spies' reporting back to him and enabling him to subtly alter his style and tactics to suit specific opposition.

It was his ability to stay one step ahead of the pack which enabled Mangnall to pull off his biggest and most daring coup.

City had already been investigated by the Football Association for financial irregularities, and when Aston Villa captain Alec Leake claimed Meredith had offered him £10 to throw the game between the two sides, Meredith was fined and suspended from playing football for a year. When City refused to provide financial help during that period, Meredith decided to lift the lid on goings-on at the club and said that they did not adhere to the rule stating that no player should be paid more than £4 a week. The FA was obliged to investigate again and this time discovered that Meredith was correct, and the players had been receiving illegal payments.

Part of the draconian punishment imposed on Manchester City was that they were forced to sell their players, and to that end an auction was arranged at the Queen's Hotel in Manchester. All the top clubs of the day turned up expecting to be able to bid for the City stars, only to find that Mangnall had pre-empted the public auction and already signed not just Turnbull but Meredith, Jimmy Bannister and Herbert Burgess – four-fifths of the most feared forward line in the country. As United already boasted a steely defence of Dick Duckworth, Alex Bell and Charlie Roberts (signed for a then-astronomical £600 from Grimsby Town to captain his side), United now had a team to challenge the best.

The City transfers were all free and the signing of Meredith in particular was akin to Ferguson's casual enquiry of Leeds as to whether Eric Cantona might be available.

Meredith was the first superstar of the sport, the first in a long line of dancing, dazzling wingers who are so much a part of the United story. Down the pits in north Wales by the age of 14 (as was Sandy Turnbull in Scotland), Meredith escaped thanks to his footballing talent, though he continued to work as a ponyman for some time thereafter, until City officials deemed it an inappropriate way for him to spend his free time.

Meredith was already 33 by the time he made his United debut, but was still going strong eight years later when, in 1915, competitive football was suspended for the war. He put his longevity down to a combination of natural fitness (which must surely have been complemented by his extremely physical work in the pits) and chewing tobacco.

Whatever his secret, Meredith was there again in the autumn of 1919, ready to pick up where he had left off, and he continued to be worthy of his place for a couple more seasons. In 1921, as a result of arguments with the club over payments from his benefit matches, coupled with annoyance at being dropped when new manager John Bentley wanted to try out Jackie Sheldon, Meredith returned to City, for whom he played out the final two seasons of a long and illustrious career.

A Manchester United programme for their Boxing Day fixture against Woolwich Arsenal in 1910 summed up Meredith's worth when it said, 'Had he lived in an earlier age, Meredith would have been the subject of an epic poem and been immortalised with Achilles, Roland and the Knights of the Round Table. The pen of a mere football commentator cannot do justice to his genius.'

Two years later, United claimed their second league title, possibly inspired by their show of unity over the establishing of a Players' Union. It was to be their last league title for over 40 years.

v Millwall 2-0
(Avoided relegation to third tier)
5 May 1934
Football League Second Division
The Den
Attendance: 24,003

MANCHESTER UNITED	MILLWALL
Jack Hacking	Duncan Yuill
Jack Griffiths	Jack Walsh
Tom Jones	Jimmy Pipe
William Robertson	Lem Newcomb
George Vose	Bobby Turnbull
Bill McKay	Jimmy Forsyth
Jack Cape	Jimmy McCartney
Hughie McLenahan	Stan Alexander
Jack Ball	Jimmy Yardley
Ernie Hine	Harry Roberts
Tom Manley	Laurie Fishlock
Manager: Scott Duncan	*Manager:* Bill McCracken

A S Manchester United lined up for the most important match in their existence, only full-back Tom Jones and forward Ernie Hine remained from the 11 who had taken the field at Millwall 14 months earlier. In March 1933, United had travelled to The Den and lost 2-0. Although it was a disappointing result, it mattered little as United finished the season in sixth place on 43 points, with Millwall finishing one position lower on the same points total but with a one-goal worse goal difference.

Wind on to May 1934, however, and the scenario was a very different one. Both teams had endured poor seasons, and on the last day it was a winner-take-all match, again at The Den to see which side would drop into the third tier of English football. A repeat of the previous season's result would have seen United relegated to the Third Division North, but despite an early injury to Hine which left him limping and of limited use in the game, United reversed that scoreline and goals from Jack Cape and Tom Manley saw then home.

United thus avoided the ignominy of relegation to the Third Division – the closest they ever got to that happening – by the skin of their teeth. The *Sunday Express* reported the next day, 'Manchester deserved to succeed because they were quicker on the ball and better together as a team ... The United forwards were a more cohesive force and certainly more dangerous near goal,' while the *Daily Mail*, on the Monday after the game, reported, 'There was more thought behind the Manchester work and more resource and better covering in their defence.' It might not go down as one of United's greatest games in terms of the performance, but the result was everything to a team which had struggled to build on its pre-war successes.

The Great War had seen many changes. Not only was Sandy Turnbull killed in the trenches, but many other United players were now some way past their prime, or no longer interested in playing football. Billy Meredith was, but he wanted to follow United's iconic manager Ernest Mangnall across the city and play for the 'other' Manchester club. Which, after a certain amount of haggling over a transfer fee (Meredith said he didn't want to be traded, like a piece of meat), he did.

Just as serious as the losses on the playing side was that of chairman John Henry Davies, who had saved the club from going bankrupt many years earlier. Davies was into his 50s by the time the war ended, and no longer wished to be involved with the club on a daily basis. In fact, by 1924 he was quite ill and he died in 1927, leaving as his most lasting legacy the Old Trafford ground with which the club has become synonymous. And on 17 April 1926, it hosted its first international when Alex Jackson scored the only goal as Scotland beat England in front of 49,000 spectators.

On the managerial front, John Robson had given way to John Chapman who in turn was replaced by Clarence Hilditch, briefly, before Herbert Bamlett took over. Hilditch, in fact, was United's only player-manager in their history, but he was only ever intended as a stop-gap appointment.

But whoever was in charge, United were consistent only in their inconsistency, regularly suffering heavy defeats and with just one FA Cup semi-final to alleviate the gloom. Even then it was something of a mixed blessing as wins over Port Vale, Spurs, Sunderland and Fulham were brought to an abrupt halt when United were beaten 3-0 by Manchester City at Bramall Lane (Sheffield United's ground).

The only consolation was to be found in the facts that firstly, City didn't go on to lift the trophy (they were beaten by Bolton Wanderers) and secondly, their cup run led to City taking their eye off the First Division, from which they were relegated.

The rest of the 1920s was forgettable for Reds fans, though there was plenty of action off the field to excite them, most notably in the boardroom where A.E. Thomson, one of the directors, was forced to resign after his daughter, Betty, eloped with one of the players, Neil Dewar. Despite scoring 14 goals in his 36 appearances for United during 1933, Dewar swiftly moved to Sheffield Wednesday, taking young Betty with him.

The other main concern in the 1920s and early 1930s was the lack of funds. Stripped of their benefactor and not performing well enough on the pitch to draw large crowds, United were living beyond their means. It all came to a head in the week leading up to Christmas 1931 when the players were told that there was no money available to pay their wages. Of course the Depression was a difficult time for all, particularly those in the cotton industry which had virtually collapsed, and few had the spare money to go and watch a not-very-good football team.

Manchester United's Greatest Games

For a second time, however, a successful businessman/sporting enthusiast came to the rescue. James W. Gibson, whose main source of income was as a clothes manufacturer who specialised in uniforms, was persuaded to invest £30,000, and additionally to pay the unpaid wages and settle a few outstanding debts. Gibson was an astute businessman, however, and insisted on his own terms for saving the club – namely, that not only would he become chairman but he would be able to elect people to the board. As occurred later in United's history, the club got worse before it got better, but at least under Gibson's careful chairmanship the club's financial position started to improve.

Any footnote to the most trophy-free period in United's history must include a mention of Joe Spence. Not many players have turned out over 500 times (510, to be precise) for Manchester United without winning a single trophy. Over his 14 seasons at the club, Spence scored 168 goals and his crossing created many more chances for others. He twice scored four goals in a match, in a 5-1 win against Crystal Palace in 1924 and a 4-2 win over West Ham in 1930, though his hat-trick against Liverpool on the last day of the 1927/28 season will have given many United fans the greatest pleasure.

Spence was born in the Northumbria coalfield area that produced so many great footballers; down the mine at 13, fighting in the trenches on the Western Front at 17 he undoubtedly knew what real life was and when given the opportunity to make his living playing football he grabbed it with both hands.

At least Spence benefited financially from his commitment to the cause, receiving not one but two testimonials, in 1924 and 1929, though a trophy or two would have been even more welcome.

v Blackpool 4-2

5

24 April 1948
FA Cup Final
Wembley
Attendance: 99,842

MANCHESTER UNITED	BLACKPOOL
Jack Crompton	Joe Robinson
Johnny Carey	Eddie Shimwell
John Aston	John Crosland
John Anderson	Harry Johnston
Allenby Chilton	Eric Hayward
Henry Cockburn	Hugh Kelly
Jimmy Delaney	Stanley Matthews
Johnny Morris	Alex Munro
Jack Rowley	Stan Mortensen
Stan Pearson	George Dick
Charlie Mitten	Walter Rickett
Manager: Matt Busby	*Manager:* Joe Smith

WHEN Manchester United strode out on to the Wembley turf for the 1948 FA Cup Final, they saw lined up against them two of the all-time greats: Stanley Matthews and Stan Mortensen. Neither needs any introduction, but with the 'Wizard of the Dribble' on the wing (or outside-right as it was more commonly known in those days), and Mortensen – at centre-forward – being the primary beneficiary, to the tune of 197 goals in 317 matches for Blackpool, it was clear they would be a match for any team.

Indeed, Blackpool had already drawn 1-1 at Old Trafford in the league meeting between the two sides, and an early penalty from Eddie Shimwell put them ahead in the cup final. The first of Jack Rowley's two goals for United brought them level, but Mortensen put Blackpool back in front in the 35th minute, a lead they held for over half an hour.

Rowley eventually drew United level again in the 70th minute and spurred on by that, Stan Pearson put them in front for the first time ten minutes later. A mere two minutes after that, in the 82nd, John Anderson made it 4-2, and the game was up for Blackpool. Although Mortensen maintained his record of scoring in every round, he and Matthews would have to wait another five years before finally getting their names on the old trophy.

Matthews said after the final, 'When we were leading 2-1 I really thought it was our day, but Manchester United were inspired after their second goal. We did what we set out to do, played our best and cannot complain because we were beaten by a great team.'

In truth, despite the presence of Matthews and Mortensen, United had started the match as favourites. They were second in the league that season –

the second of three consecutive campaigns when they finished in that position – and their cup run had involved comfortable wins over Aston Villa (who finished sixth), Liverpool (11th), Charlton Athletic (13th), Preston North End (seventh) and Derby County (fourth). Furthermore, the four goals they scored in the cup final took their total (in league and cup) up over the hundred mark – to 103.

It was a far cry from the disappointment of the 1920s and 1930s, not to mention the destruction wrought on the main stand during a German bombing raid in 1941. But while the club were yo-yoing between the top two divisions of the Football League under the largely unsuccessful management of Scott Duncan, one hugely significant development took place in 1937.

In that year Walter Crickmer re-took the reins as manager and together with his chairman, James Gibson, he established the Manchester United Junior Athletic Club. Born partly out of financial necessity (money was so tight that it was essential for the club to start producing their own players), it quickly became a policy. With the youth team scoring an inconceivable 223 goals in its first season in the Chorlton Amateur League, Crickmer's first act as manager was to bring in some of the younger players.

An equally important though less well-known figure was one Louis Rocca. Rocca's parents had brought their ice cream business to the Newton Heath area of Manchester in the 1870s, and Rocca started his long and varied involvement with the club while still a teenager in the 1890s when he got a job as tea boy at the club's Bank Street ground.

Rocca always claimed – and dined out on the tale – that he was the one who came up with the suggestion of 'Manchester United' as the club's new name. There is no documentary evidence for this, but what is beyond doubt is that in the 1920s he had an unofficial role as the club's chief fixer, which later evolved into the more official capacity of chief scout.

Rocca cleverly employed his Catholic connections to establish a scouting network, even using some priests whose involvement in the everyday life of local families put them in the perfect position for a bit of talent spotting. Probably the best-known players who Rocca's scouting system were responsible for spotting are Johnny Carey and Stan Pearson, the former a local boy who Rocca reportedly saw as a 16-year-old playing for Adelphi Lads Club, the latter a Dubliner. In an echo of what was later to happen with Wayne Rooney, Rocca had gone to Ireland to watch a completely different player but was so struck by Carey's performance that he signed him on the spot, reportedly for £250.

Jack White, who was with MUJAC in the 1938/39 season, survived the war but was robbed of his chance to represent the first team which might otherwise have come. In the excellent *Sons of United*, a book by Steve Hobin and Tony Park which traces the history of Manchester United youth football, White recalls, 'We all went for trials and they narrowed it down to 20 boys, all more or less the same age, around 16. We went down to The Cliff once a week for training and our home games were played there. We had no money but the club paid our bus fares.'

The club would continue to support their junior players, and rightly so when they could have the kind of impact that Carey and Pearson did. Carey went on to make over 300 appearances for the club despite losing almost half his professional career to the war, and after the war was club captain from 1946–53. Carey had a successful coaching career after his retirement as a player, first spending five years with Blackburn Rovers and gaining them promotion into the First Division, then moving to Everton and guiding them to their highest league finish – fifth – since the war. In spite of that club director John Moores (who founded the Littlewoods chain of shops and after whom Liverpool John Moores University is named) famously sacked him in the back of a taxi.

As an aside, this is thought to be the origin of that crowd favourite 'Taxi for xxxx', aimed at any player or manager who opposing fans feel is facing the sack. It was most famously chanted at Inter Milan's Brazilian star Maicon after Gareth Bale (then still with Tottenham Hotspur) had given him the runaround in November 2010.

Carey also managed Leyton Orient and Nottingham Forest, not to mention serving as the Republic of Ireland's manager from 1955–67, albeit at a time when the actual team was selected by a committee.

Pearson also played in over 300 games for the club between 1936 and 1954 and his 148 goals in league and cup has him 12th in the list of United's all-time top goalscorers. It was Pearson's movement off the ball which enabled him so often to be in the right place at the right time for what appeared to be a simple tap-in. If he did nothing else in his United career, Pearson would still have been adored by the club's fans for scoring a hat-trick (one of five he notched in league and FA Cup) against Liverpool on 11 September 1946.

Although nominally a home game for United, the club were using Maine Road due to the bomb damage at Old Trafford and in front of a crowd of 41,657 they destroyed Liverpool 5-0. It was the last hat-trick by a United player against Liverpool until Dimitar Berbatov in 2010. Annoyingly for the United faithful they still ended the season one point adrift of their rivals despite scoring 11 more goals (95 to 84), on account of drawing too many games (12 to Liverpool's seven).

The following season, 1947/48, United finished ten points clear of Liverpool, scoring 15 more goals than them, but a slow start, when they lost five of their first 12 league matches, gave them too big a gap to claw back on eventual winners Arsenal. As the FA Cup loomed ever larger, United were in solid, sometimes spectacular, form in the spring but it was too late, and the Gunners claimed the titles by seven points.

Pearson scored 26 goals that season, though his intelligent passing was just as important as he often laid on chances for fellow striker Jack Rowley, who was much more in the mould of a traditional centre-forward: rough, tough and good in the air. After moving on from United, Pearson spent three years at Bury, adding a further 56 goals in 121 appearances to his tally. His two years as a player and two as manager of Chester were less successful, however, and Pearson retired in 1961.

Louis Rocca, meanwhile had one further part to play in the United story, and it was a massive one. In 1930 he had recommended a 21-year-old Manchester City winger named Matt Busby to the club, but United couldn't find the £150 transfer fee City demanded. Rocca and Busby stayed in touch, however, through the Manchester Catholic Sportsman's Club. When Rocca heard that Busby was thinking of calling time on his playing career and moving into management at Liverpool, he wrote to him and convinced him to come to United instead.

Even then chairman James Gibson needed a bit of convincing, as Busby quickly made it clear that he wanted complete control over team affairs, including training, team selection and which players he wanted bought and sold. All this at a time when such a level of involvement was extremely unusual; fortunately for the club, Gibson had the foresight to agree.

Between his appointment in February and Busby's start at the club, one further fortuitous event occurred. That spring Busby was in Bari, in Italy, for an Army football match and heard Welshman Jimmy Murphy, a former West Bromwich Albion player, give a motivational speech to the team. Busby later recalled, 'I could see how he was communicating his passion for the game and I found myself saying to him, "Jimmy, would you like to join me at Old Trafford as my assistant when you're demobbed?"'

Murphy didn't hesitate and the two men shook hands on it there and then. With a man like Busby, a handshake was a done deal, and the new management team was in place.

Busby reported for his first day of work on 1 October 1945 and a new era began. If the glorious 1948 FA Cup Final triumph was the start of it, it most assuredly was not the end.

v Arsenal 6-1

6

26 April 1952
Football League First Division (last day of season)
Old Trafford
Attendance: 53,651

MANCHESTER UNITED	ARSENAL
Reg Allen	George Swindin
Tommy McNulty	Walley Barnes
John Aston	Lionel Smith
Johnny Carey	Joe Mercer
Allenby Chilton	Arthur Shaw
Henry Cockburn	Alex Forbes
Johnny Berry	Cliff Holton
John Downie	Reg Lewis
Jack Rowley	Peter Goring
Stan Pearson	Freddie Cox
Roger Byrne	Don Roper
Manager: Matt Busby	*Manager:* Tom Whittaker

WHEN Matt Busby was offered the job of manager of Manchester United, chairman James Gibson presented him with a three-year contract; Busby asked for five years, telling Gibson it would take that long to put everything in place for the revolution he envisaged. He was half right – it took only three years for Busby to land the club's first trophy since 1911, but seven to claim a first league title.

Busby's impact was felt immediately, as a club which had spent much of the 1920s and 30s going up and down between the top two divisions became much more established, finishing runners-up in 1947, 48, 49 and 51.

As we have seen they also landed the FA Cup in 1948 and probably should have retained it the following year. In the event, however, they lost a semi-final replay to an 86th-minute winner by Wolverhampton Wanderers' Northern Irish international Sammy Smyth (who had also scored in the first match between the sides). Wolves went on to beat Leicester City comfortably, 3-1, in the final, with Smyth scoring the third.

The 1951/52 season started with United looking like they meant business, in particular Jack Rowley, who scored a hat-trick on the opening day in the 3-3 draw with West Bromwich Albion at The Hawthorns, and followed that up with another just four days later in the 4-2 defeat of Middlesbrough in the first home game of the season.

Rowley was always a prolific goalscorer, notching more than 20 goals a season on five separate occasions. But this was to be his best season of them all, recording 30 goals in just 41 matches including four hat-tricks – those first two games of the season and another in the 4-0 win over Stoke City on 8 September.

Manchester United's Greatest Games

In all, Rowley had scored 22 times before the end of 1951, and though he experienced something of a lull in the New Year, he saved his best until last.

On Saturday 26 April 1952 a vastly experienced United team took the field at Old Trafford against Arsenal knowing that their opponents needed to win by seven goals if they were to snatch the title. Rowley and Johnny Carey by this point had well over 300 appearances each to their name, with Rowley just ahead by 331 to 307. In addition, Stan Pearson (288), Allenby Chilton (269), Henry Cockburn (230) and John Aston (227) were all well over the 200 mark. A team with such big-match experience were never going to let Arsenal score hatfuls against them, but it was still a surprise to see United decide to go on the attack from the word 'go'.

To be fair to Arsenal their manager Tom Whittaker and captain Joe Mercer had sent congratulatory telegrams to Old Trafford in the wake of United's penultimate game, a 3-0 defeat of Chelsea, acclaiming the champions-elect. And they were right to do so – Rowley's hat-trick, two from Pearson and one from new boy Roger Byrne led to a 6-1 thrashing. This not only wiped out any chance Arsenal had of snatching the title for themselves, but even pushed them down into third place behind, of all teams, hated rivals Tottenham Hotspur (the previous season's champions) on goal average.

As fans streamed on to the pitch to celebrate a first title triumph since 1911, *The Sunday Times*'s Roland Allen wrote, 'Manchester United are worthy champions. They played delightful football, serene, controlled, immaculate and supremely efficient.'

The *Manchester Guardian*'s leader writer added that the title had 'never been better earned' and that Busby had displayed an 'uncannily brilliant eye for young local players' possibilities.

'By eschewing the dangerous policy of going into the transfer market whenever a weakness develops,' it continued, 'and giving their chances instead to the many local citizens on the club's books they have made it likely that this club will persist, since the club today is a Manchester one not in name only but in fact as far as most of its players are concerned.'

One such was Roger Byrne. The 23-year-old had made just 24 league appearances for the club when he started the decisive final game against Arsenal, but he was on a decent scoring streak and quickly showed the attributes which had prompted Busby to promote him to the first team. Byrne was something of an enigma as a player – neither his tackling nor his aerial ability were particularly striking, but his excellent reading of the game and sound positional sense meant that he was in the right place at the right time much more often than not.

And if he wasn't quite in the right spot, he was quick enough to get there – Busby once declared that 'there was never a faster full-back' and claimed that he had never seen the attacking genius of either Tom Finney or Stanley Matthews ever prosper against Byrne.

The other quality Byrne had a surplus of was charisma. A born leader, he is still often credited as one of United's greatest captains despite being only 28 when he died in the Munich air disaster. 'He had a wonderful confidence,' Sir Bobby Charlton said of Byrne, 'and he passed that on so effortlessly. You only had to see him at work to see a surge of belief spreading through the team.'

Byrne's elevation wasn't without hiccups, however, and although he made a success of playing on the left wing, he didn't enjoy it. To the extent that he actually submitted a transfer request, whereupon he was returned to his favoured position of left-back. From there he happily roamed forward in the manner of a modern full-back – which was in itself quite unusual at the time – but he preferred to be in a starting position at the back.

Byrne himself echoed the views of the media, declaring, 'One of the secrets of Manchester United's success is that nearly all of us grew up together as boy footballers. We were knitted into a football family.' It was a family which was about to take the footballing world by storm.

v Chelsea 6-5

16 October 1954
Football League First Division
Stamford Bridge
Attendance: 55,966

MANCHESTER UNITED	CHELSEA
Ray Wood	Bill Robertson
Bill Foulkes	John Harris
Roger Byrne	Stan Willemse
Don Gibson	Ken Armstrong
Allenby Chilton	Ron Greenwood
Duncan Edwards	Derek Saunders
Johnny Berry	Eric Parsons
Jackie Blanchflower	Johnny McNicol
Tommy Taylor	Roy Bentley
Dennis Viollet	Seamus O'Connell
Jack Rowley	Jim Lewis
Manager: Matt Busby	*Manager:* Ted Drake

SATURDAY 16 October 1954 seemed like an unremarkable day, towards the start of the 1954/55 season, but the game that took place that day between Chelsea and Manchester United was anything but unremarkable. Already it seemed likely that the teams which had finished fourth and eighth the previous year were going to mount a more sustained challenge this time around, and indeed Chelsea were to finish champions for the first, and only, time until the Roman Abramovich revolution began in 2003.

United faded into fifth place but their own revolution was gathering strength, and its full force would be unleashed the following season. In 1954/55 they had to content themselves with doing the double over the league champions-in-waiting, although the 2-1 win at Old Trafford (goals by Albert Scanlon and Tommy Taylor) came on the last day of the season, after the title was already won and lost.

Former Arsenal and England centre-forward Ted Drake became the Chelsea manager in 1952 and started modernising the club in many small but significant ways – improving the youth set-up, changing the club crest and logo and signing talented players from the lower leagues, including future England manager Ron Greenwood and striker Roy Bentley. United built a lead thanks to a hat-trick from Dennis Viollet, a double from Taylor and one from Jackie Blanchflower. Chelsea fought back late on, however, with Seamus O'Connell matching Viollet's hat-trick with one of his own.

O'Connell had only joined Chelsea from Middlesbrough that season and he was making his debut against United. His hat-trick seemed to presage great things for the 24-year-old but after just one further season with Chelsea he decided to give up professional football and return to work on the family cattle farm in Cumbria. Described by team-mates as a 'skinny guy with curly hair', O'Connell scored 12 goals in 17 games for Chelsea but often missed games because he went to farmers' markets on Thursdays.

As for the match, after Viollet had put United ahead, home fans watched their team go 2-1 up in 35 minutes through O'Connell's first and Jim Lewis only to be back level three minutes later through Taylor. Viollet gave United a 3-2 lead at half-time, which Taylor (47) and Viollet (57, completing his hat-trick) extended before the hour mark. Ken Armstrong then brought the deficit back to two goals, only to see Blanchflower almost immediately stretch United's lead to 6-3. O'Connell's hat-trick brought Chelsea back to 6-5 and what *The Guardian* described as 'a rather shaky United defence' were left holding on to reward the display their brilliant attacking had looked likely to make much more comfortable.

Even as United had won the 1952 league title, Busby knew that his side was ageing and he would have to start to break up the club's first great post-war side. At the start of the 1952/53 season United, as defending champions, had won just three of their first 11 matches, and any hope of retaining the title had already vanished. Busby was not dismayed, however, he had anticipated the situation and was putting in place the building blocks for his next team.

In March 1953 United acquired Tommy Taylor from Barnsley for a fee of £29,999. Legend has it that Busby, not wanting to burden Taylor with the label of being a £30,000 player, gave a £1 note to the lady serving teas in the boardroom at the time of the signing.

Whatever the fee, though, Taylor was quick to start repaying it – on his debut on 7 March he scored twice in the 5-2 win over Preston North End. Taylor played in all remaining 11 league games that season (United had been knocked out of the FA Cup by Everton in February) and by the end of it had notched seven goals despite being familiar with neither the tactics nor his team-mates.

In October that year Busby took his team to Kilmarnock for a friendly (a more frequent occurrence in those days), to mark the installation of floodlights at Killie's home ground of Rugby Park. The match, on 28 October, marked a watershed as Busby decided to omit Stan Pearson and Jack Rowley in favour of Dennis Viollet and Jackie Blanchflower. United took only three minutes to open the scoring and went on to enjoy a comfortable victory.

'I played half a dozen of the youngsters,' Busby recalled later. 'They did well and we won 3-0. As I walked the golf course over the next few days, I pondered whether the moment had come to play them all in the league team. One or two had already come into the side and I decided that I would go the whole way with the youngsters.'

Henry Cockburn, who had opened the scoring at Kilmarnock, had picked up a facial injury after just 20 minutes, and into the team in his place came one Duncan Edwards. Killie pensioner Eddie Bircham, who went to the game, said,

'I remember it being a very entertaining and interesting game. We were well beaten by a tremendous side, which as well as Duncan Edwards also included Tommy Taylor, who was superb. It was after this game I remember Matt Busby saying that Duncan Edwards would never be out of the first team because he had played so well.'

Kilmarnock FC historian John Livingston was a mere eight months old when the game was played. 'I remember my dad telling me that Tommy Taylor was the best centre-forward he had ever seen. It was a terrible tragedy what happened just a few years later. The game at Rugby Park was significant because it was after that Matt Busby decided to go with the young players, so you could say that Killie fans witnessed the birth of the Busby Babes that day.'

After a couple of days staying at Troon, United travelled to their league game at Huddersfield Town where they earned a creditable 0-0 draw at a team who were to finish the season in third place. The 17-year-old Edwards played, and Busby was true to his word with the teenager featuring 24 times between then and the end of that season.

If Edwards was to become the shining star, however, it was the 22-year-old Taylor who was to have the most stunning immediate impact.

Surprisingly little has been written about Taylor, but the bald facts are that he scored 131 goals in 191 appearances for Manchester United. This places him 14th in the list of all-time top United goalscorers. But Taylor was just 26 when he died; if he played four more seasons (and would still have only been 30) and continued to score at a similar rate, he could well have surpassed Sir Bobby Charlton and Denis Law at the very top of the club's scoring charts. As Taylor also scored 16 goals in 19 international appearances for England, we are clearly talking about a goalscorer par excellence.

Born on 29 January 1932 in an area of Barnsley called Smithies, Taylor had taken some enticing out of his home town where he had played as a youngster for the local coal mining team at the colliery where he worked from the age of 14. In July 1949 he had signed for Barnsley and combined playing with them (44 appearances, 26 goals) with his National Service.

Taylor wasn't at all sure he wanted to leave Barnsley, but his home-town club badly needed the money his transfer fee would bring, and at least Manchester wasn't too far from his home. Having checked with Busby that his mother and father would be given tickets to come and watch him play, the unassuming Taylor duly signed on the dotted line. 'There was a certain kind of magic atmosphere about Old Trafford in those days,' recalled Viollet, 'and Tommy's signing seemed to trigger it all into action.'

Jackie Blanchflower said much the same, 'From the day he joined the club, Tommy was a first-team regular and he never lost his place other than through injury or being on duty for England. He was the best thing that happened as far as United's fortunes were concerned. He had a few rough edges when he arrived but he was a wonderful trainer, he used to practise for hours.'

John Docherty agrees that Taylor's arrival was a seminal moment, 'The signing of Tommy Taylor was a major step. I played against him at Barnsley in a reserve game and he was immense, strong and quick. He was quick as lightning, fantastic in the air and knew how to hold the ball up on the front line – all precious qualities in a striker.'

On 21 November 1953 Manchester United beat Blackpool 4-1. Tommy Taylor scored a hat-trick, his first for the club as a young United team ripped apart a good Blackpool side in front of nearly 50,000 at Old Trafford. It was a promise that Busby's next great team was about to be born.

Dubbed the 'smiling executioner' by George Fellows, a leading sportswriter of the time, Taylor, despite playing with a smile on his face, was in pain a lot of the time. Bobby Charlton recalls that Taylor periodically said to him 'feel my knee' and when he did it felt like 'floating ice'; Taylor also struggled with an ankle injury which he picked up in a game against Arsenal on 27 March 1954 and which proved so troublesome that there was even a possibility of it ending his playing career.

In his definitive book on Taylor, entitled *The Tommy Taylor Story*, Brian Hughes quotes Viollet as saying, 'Tommy suffered from this nasty injury for quite some time. He was getting treatment daily, of course, sometimes twice a day but it wouldn't seem to clear up. He took a lot of unfair criticism after the ankle injury, and could justifiably have used it as an excuse, but he never said a word. I knew deep down Tom was very concerned about the damage.'

Blanchflower added that he felt sorry for Taylor. 'He was in constant pain with this ankle problem. He played a lot of games while in agony but he never complained. Ted Dalton, our physio, worked overtime trying everything to relieve the pain. Eventually he was taken to London where the Queen's surgeon x-rayed the ankle and there was a small piece of floating bone in it. Once they operated and removed it, Tommy was a different man.'

It wasn't always apparent to those watching how important Taylor was to that developing side. To a team-mate, however, it was obvious. 'If you were under pressure on the ball, you knew you could hit a long one and Tommy would get on the end of it and hold it up for you,' said Doherty. 'When a team-mate can do that he goes right to the top of their list of people they like playing with!'

Bobby Charlton remembers, 'Tommy Taylor and Dennis Viollet did get injured a lot, and that gave me my chance, but by God when Tommy was right he was so fast, and he was great in the air!'

The 1954/55 season might have belonged to Chelsea, but this high-scoring away win for United both set the tone for the style of play they were going to adopt and showed that they were assembling a team for all seasons, a team set to take the world by storm.

v Tottenham Hotspur 2-1

8

31 August 1955
Football League First Division
White Hart Lane
Attendance: 27,453

MANCHESTER UNITED	TOTTENHAM HOTSPUR
Ray Wood	Ted Ditchburn
Bill Foulkes	Mel Hopkins
Roger Byrne	Charlie Withers
Jeff Whitefoot	Harry Clarke
Mark Jones	Danny Blanchflower
Duncan Edwards	Ernie Walley
Colin Webster	Tony Marchi
Jackie Blanchflower	George Robb
Eddie Lewis	Len Duquemin
Dennis Viollet	Sonny Walters
Albert Scanlon	Alfie Stokes
Manager: Matt Busby	*Manager:* Jimmy Anderson

ON 24 August, just a week into the 1955/56 season, Tottenham Hotspur travelled to Old Trafford and the home team were unable to force a win, drawing 2-2 through goals from Johnny Berry and Colin Webster.

Their first match of the season, away at Birmingham City, had also finished 2-2 thanks to a double from Dennis Viollet but United knew they needed to turn these draws into victories if they were to improve on their fifth-placed finish the previous season.

In one of those vagaries of the fixture lists that often occurred in the days before everything was computerised, United travelled to White Hart Lane a week after the teams' first meeting. Spurs clearly fancied their chances in light of their away draw, and that's when Duncan Edwards decided to take control of the situation. Just two minutes into the game Edwards scored at the Park Lane end with a left-footed drive from the edge of the area; on 41 minutes he added a second as he fired a piledriver past Spurs keeper Ted Ditchburn from fully 30 yards.

United were 2-0 up at half-time, but with Viollet struggling with an injury, they shut up shop in the second half and concentrated on possession football which allowed Spurs few chances to get back into the game. Spurs did eventually pull a goal back with a couple of minutes remaining through Harry Clarke, who headed home a George Robb corner, but it was too little, too late for the home team.

It was a most un-United-like victory but it displayed a steely resolve which spoke of a desire to win at all costs, even when their buccaneering approach was not quite on song.

It is often forgotten that at the start of the 1955/56 season Edwards was still on National Service. Lance Corporal Duncan Edwards declared he was finding Army life 'not too bad', but the travelling – from Shrewsbury, where he was based – to wherever United were playing was often arduous. After scoring those two goals at White Hart Lane to give United a priceless victory he requested an early morning call from the night porter at the hotel where the United team were staying after the game – he needed to catch the 5.55am train back to his unit.

Edwards, of course, was the key, as he so often was that season. Bobby Charlton, so often the choirmaster leading the chorus of praise for Edwards, said, 'He was so good, when he was around you thought anything was possible. He was more than a great player, sometimes it seemed he was a great light in the sky.'

Born in Dudley, in the West Midlands, on 1 October 1936, legend has it that Edwards could kick a ball before he could walk; indisputably he could be found kicking a ball along the streets on his way to school. Although Edwards was never to grow taller than six foot or weigh in at more than 13 and a half stone, he was a big boy for his age, and his size and strength, as well as his talent, enabled him to play with boys several years older than himself, and even men.

But despite being physically imposing, Edwards was light on his feet, an attribute which briefly looked like it might take him a different direction altogether. 'He was a member of the school morris dancing team and the school sword dancing team,' recalled Reg Baxter, the music master at Wolverhampton Street School.

So much so that he was due to take part in a national festival in Derby on the day of the England under-14 international trial at Oldham. Music remained a passion throughout Edwards's tragically short life, in particular that of Perry Como and Pat Boone, and he often asked team-mates back to his digs to listen, but the lure of football was too strong, and Edwards not only went to the trial but was selected to play against Ireland. Edwards was 12.

Jimmy Murphy said of Edwards, 'From the first time I saw him as a boy of 14, Duncan looked and played with the assurance of a man, with legs like tree trunks, a deep and powerful chest and an unforgettable zest for the game. He played wing-half, centre-forward, inside-forward and centre-half with the consummate ease of a great player. He was never bothered where he played. He was quite simply a soccer Colossus.'

Edwards signed amateur forms for United in June 1952, and less than a year later made his first team debut, on 4 April 1953, at just 16 years and 185 days. It wasn't an auspicious occasion as United lost 4-1 to Cardiff City, at Old Trafford, but journalist George Follows wrote, 'When he heads the ball it is not a flabby flirtation with fortune, it is a bold, decisive soccer action. When he tackles it is with a man trap's bit. And when he shoots, with either foot, not even Jack Rowley, the pride of Old Trafford, is shooting any harder. Add to this the body swerve, and bravery and the sixth sense in a tight corner that distinguishes the truly great player and you have "the boy who has got the lot". And if you think this is a lot to write about a lad of 16 I can only say, "You obviously haven't seen this boy Edwards." Though nobody can tell exactly what will happen when Edwards explodes into First Division football, one thing is certain. It will be spectacular.'

Edwards hadn't been expecting to make his debut that day, but with Henry Cockburn already on the sidelines, Jackie Blanchflower had picked up an injury the day before, in the 2-2 draw at Charlton Athletic.

Nevertheless, Edwards was not fazed by the prospect and is quoted in *Duncan Edwards: A Biography* by Iain McCartney and Roy Cavanagh as saying, 'The thought of making my Football League debut was not terrifying after having played twice at Wembley before I was 15. On leaving school I did not have to face the difficulty of finding a job, like some youngsters, as football was my future. I thought my future would be better away from the Midlands.

'United had a great reputation for giving plenty of opportunities to young players and treating them in the best possible manner. I found it very easy to settle down and make friends. I went to the ground one Friday morning and was called to Matt Busby's office. He quietly told me I was selected for the first team. All I could think about was letting my parents know the news.'

Despite becoming a fully-fledged member of the first team, Edwards continued to play for the United youth team. It was suggested that now Edwards was also a full international (he made his debut in April 1955, in the 7-2 defeat of Scotland at Wembley), he shouldn't really be eligible to carry on playing in the FA Youth Cup. Matt Busby used his regular column in the *Evening Chronicle* to say, 'To suggest that because of his exceptional talent he should not play in youth games is, in my opinion, ridiculous. He is eligible and he is keen to play. I don't doubt that if other clubs had the opportunity they would willingly include him in their youth side.'

Edwards himself said that the 'only relaxation I wanted from football was to play more football, and that, I feel sure, is the only way to learn this, the greatest game in the world.'

Busby set great store by the FA Youth Cup. Ever since he decided that youth was the way to go at United, he saw that it was the perfect opportunity to give younger players the chance to gain experience in a meaningful competition. After their league championship triumph of 1952 he had said, 'In my opinion the young players on the United books are worth hundreds of thousands of pounds. In a couple of years' time we shall have wonderful young material when it is most needed.'

Many a prophetic word… The FA Youth Cup was inaugurated in 1953, and United won if for five straight years. Using players of the calibre of Eddie Colman, Billy Whelan, David Pegg and Albert Scanlon alongside Edwards, United swept all before them, beating Wolves in the first two years of the competition, followed by West Bromwich Albion, Chesterfield and West Ham United. It was only a semi-final in the wake of the Munich air disaster that saw United taste defeat.

Managed by assistant manager and Busby's right-hand man, Jimmy Murphy, the youth team regularly drew crowds of over 20,000 to their games and the astonishing sequence of victories gave United a level of belief which manifested itself throughout the club. On a Tuesday in November 1952 they recorded a 23-0 win over Nantwich, with Edwards, Pegg and Doherty each scoring five goals.

Wilf McGuinness, who was another key member of the youth side in the early 1950s, and who was later to manage the club himself, said of Edwards, 'How good was he? Well if you take Roy Keane, Bryan Robson, and Steven Gerrard rolled into one you'd have a Duncan Edwards. He did everything right. Amongst a lot of great players coming through, he was special.'

Another team-mate, John Doherty, who won a league title alongside Edwards in 1956, considered him unusually gifted both physically and in his feel for the game. 'Duncan was great,' he said. 'God alone knows what he would have achieved in another ten years. Playing at the highest level with your back to goal isn't so much a talent as an art.'

How good was Edwards? 'I totally believe he was the best player I ever saw or am likely to see,' said Bobby Charlton. 'He was unstoppable, literally unstoppable. He was a superb passer of the ball – crossfield passes of 50 yards were no problem, and this was with a heavy ball remember. Over the years I have seen, played with and against many world-class players. Pele and Di Stefano were marvellous players, but they needed help to play. Duncan could do it all himself. Yes I know all about Maradona, Best, Law and the others but if you asked great players like Tom Finney and Stanley Matthews who was the greatest, they would tell you, as they did me, they hadn't seen anything like Duncan.'

Matthews, the only footballer to have been knighted while still playing, said of Edwards, 'You can play him anywhere and he would slot into that position as if he'd been playing there season after season. When the going gets rough, Duncan is like a rock in a raging sea.'

Murphy, his manager through all those Youth Cup triumphs, was even more effusive, 'When I used to hear Muhammad Ali proclaim to the world that he was the greatest, I used to smile. You see, the greatest of them all was an English footballer named Duncan Edwards. If I shut my eyes I can see him now. Those pants hitched up, the wild leaps of boyish enthusiasm as he came running out of the tunnel, the tremendous power of his tackle – always fair but fearsome – the immense power on the ball. In fact the number of times he was robbed of the ball once he had it at his feet could be counted on one hand. He was a players' player. The greatest: there was only one and that was Duncan Edwards.'

Despite all the praise, Edwards was never anything other than grounded. He didn't drink and his few interests away from football were largely solitary ones, including fishing and playing cards. At the time of his death at the age of 21 he had already made 173 appearances for United, scoring 21 goals, and 18 for England, scoring five goals, but he was still living in lodgings in Stretford.

He once said, 'There is a playing field near my lodgings in Stretford and I go out there and watch the school matches. Do you know, I think I would rather watch them than any other kind of football, they give it everything. Who ever heard of a kid not trying on the football field?'

Edwards himself always tried his heart out and his team-mates always felt no cause was lost while Edwards was on the pitch.

The last word must go to Charlton, 'Duncan had everything a footballer could ever want. I always felt so lucky to have played with him.'

v **Real Madrid** 2-2

9

25 April 1957
European Cup semi-final second leg
Old Trafford
Attendance: 65,000

MANCHESTER UNITED	REAL MADRID
Ray Wood	Juan Alonso
Bill Foulkes	Manuel Torres
Roger Byrne	Marquitos
Eddie Colman	Rafael Lesmes
Jackie Blanchflower	Miguel Munoz
Duncan Edwards	Jose Maria Zarraga
Johnny Berry	Raymond Kopa
Billy Whelan	Enrique Mateos
Tommy Taylor	Alfredo Di Stefano
Bobby Charlton	Jose Hector Rial
David Pegg	Francisco Gento
Manager: Matt Busby	*Manager:* Jose Villalonga

I T is hard to imagine now, but in the first year of European competition, the Football League wasn't in favour of English clubs entering. Fearing disruption to their domestic league, and not wanting to be overshadowed by a glamorous new pan-European tournament, English champions Chelsea withdrew from the inaugural competition. Joe Mears, whose family had founded Chelsea and built Stamford Bridge, was chairman of the Football League and appeared to bow to pressure from the formidable league secretary, Alan Hardaker. Hardaker was happy for English clubs to remain in glorious isolation.

However, the Scottish FA were only too happy to allow their champions, Hibernian, to take part – and they acquitted themselves well, too, losing in the semi-finals to eventual runners-up Reims – and Matt Busby duly took note. Not only had it been a great adventure for the Scottish champions, it had also netted the club somewhere in the region of £20,000, a huge amount in those days.

When United won the league in 1956, Busby quickly indicated that he had a much wider vision of where his club was going and told his board that he thought United should accept the invitation to enter, telling them, 'Football has become a world game and this is where the future of the game lies.'

The Football League remained implacably opposed to the idea and even wrote to the club 'forbidding' them to enter. However, the Football Association secretary Stanley Rous – later Sir Stanley, president of FIFA – shared Busby's broader outlook and encouraged United to accept the invitation to play.

David Meek and Tom Tyrrell's excellent book *United in Europe* quotes Busby as saying, 'When I led Manchester United into Europe in 1956 in the face of league opposition, some people called me a visionary, others a reactionary, while a few thought me just plain awkward and stubborn. Certainly I was eager to be part of this new European challenge.

'There was money to be made for the club, there was a new kind of adrenalin-inducing excitement for the players and there was the opportunity for the spectators to enjoy the skills of continental players. It always seemed to me the logical progression that the champions of England should pit their abilities against the best of Europe. You cannot make progress standing still.'

Busby enjoyed the full support of chairman Harold Hardman, a football man through and through who despite being an amateur had won an FA Cup winner's medal with Everton and was to serve as a director at United for an astonishing 50 years.

United duly entered the European arena, and quickly showed they belonged with a 12-0 aggregate win over Anderlecht. Busby was immediately proved right is his feeling that European football would prove attractive to the fans – 75,598 of them gathered at Maine Road on 17 October 1956 to watch United beat Borussia Dortmund 3-2. A hard-fought 0-0 draw in Germany was an untypically austere United performance but it took them through to the quarter-finals and a tie against Spanish champions Athletic Bilbao.

On a pitch which captain Roger Byrne described as a swamp, United did well to keep the first-leg deficit to 5-3 in blizzard conditions in the middle of January. A superb solo goal at the death from Billy Whelan, who picked the ball up in his own half and dribbled past four men before thumping the ball into the net, just about kept United in the tie. Despite Bilbao manager Ferdinand Daucik telling reporters that he didn't believe his team could be beaten by three goals, United proceeded to do just that, overturning the Bilbao lead by winning 3-0 at home.

And another of Busby's feelings about European competition was proved correct when the club were congratulated by the Foreign Office following the tie in Bilbao for how well they had acted as unofficial ambassadors for their country.

So to the semi-finals, and Real Madrid. Spain had two representatives in the competition by dint of Madrid having won the inaugural European Cup. A 3-1 defeat in Spain in front of 120,000 at the Bernabeu gave United a mountain to climb back at home, and a fortnight later the mountain became insurmountable as first Raymond Kopa and then Jose Hector Rial scored the first-half goals which extended Madrid's lead to an aggregate of 5-1 at half-time. Alfredo Di Stefano made the first after 25 minutes with a sublime back-heeled pass to put Kopa in to flick the ball past United goalkeeper Roy Wood.

Eight minutes later Madrid increased their lead still further when the startlingly quick Francisco Gento was released down the right wing. His cross was touched home by Jose Hector Rial to put the result of the tie beyond doubt. Real Madrid were experienced, and talented, enough not to fall into the same trap as Bilbao had done by inviting United to attack them. Instead they used their pace and skill to defend solidly and pick United off on the break in what today would be termed an impressive display of counter-attacking football.

United, however, showed glimpses of what they could do with a spirited second-half fightback. Tommy Taylor pulled a goal back shortly after the hour mark, as David Pegg made a great run down the left and pulled the ball back across the area where it bobbled around before Taylor stuck it in.

After constant pressure on the Madrid goal, and several good saves from Juan Alonso, Bobby Charlton pulled United level on the night with five minutes left on the clock. United got frustrated by some of Madrid's time-wasting tactics, and feigning injury – in one instance they even tried to carry off 'injured' Madrid player Manuel Torres, while his fellow Spaniards tried to carry him back on to the pitch. Of course, it was no surprise that the English game was considerably more physical than that of the Spaniards and United at times felt the Madrid players were tumbling a little too easily.

There had almost been a major incident before the second leg had started. Busby, alarmed by the pace and close control of Madrid in the first leg, in particular their front line, had ordered the Old Trafford pitch to be heavily watered in an attempt to negate the speed of the likes of Di Stefano and Gento. A newspaper photographer unwittingly took pictures which showed surface water lying on the pitch – and the sprinklers still on! When the Madrid officials saw the picture, they demanded that the watering stop, even threatening not to play if it was.

Madrid weren't above a little gamesmanship either, though. Concerned about the runaround which Pegg had given their regular right-back Jose Becerril in the first leg, they had taken renowned hard man Torres on loan specifically to nullify Pegg. That coupled with the constant fouling and Madrid's habit of booting the ball away into the crowd every time United were awarded a free kick led to a less than edifying spectacle.

Although Duncan Edwards and Byrne both spoke afterwards of how rough the match was, the *Manchester Guardian*'s match report declared simply, 'The better team won, and should have won more easily.'

Desmond Hackett of the *Daily Express* was not alone in rhapsodising over Di Stefano, 'We were left without words to use for that odd man out among the continentals, Alfredo Di Stefano from the Argentine.'

Charlton said, 'Even though we were on the receiving end, you couldn't but feel it a privilege to be on the field with men like Di Stefano and Gento and Kopa. They had skill and breathtaking speed and as the game unfolded you kept thinking to yourself that this is the best football can be, that this is what we have to achieve. I still feel a thrill when I think of that night.'

United had also had to cope with three league matches in the week leading up to the second leg, with home and away games against Burnley and a home game against Sunderland. At least the travelling wasn't too arduous, and with

United winning all three they could take a lot of confidence into the match knowing that they had already clinched their second consecutive league title.

Although well beaten overall, United could take pride in the fact that they had drawn with Europe's leading club (Real Madrid won the first five European Cups and in 2014 claimed *le decima*, their tenth title). Furthermore the belated installation of floodlighting had enabled them to play the home leg at Old Trafford for the first time, following three consecutive 'home' legs at Maine Road. Huge crowds had shown a clear appetite for European competition among the fans, and also served to make the club money from gate receipts.

Madrid went on to take their second European crown with a comfortable 2-0 win over Italian champions Fiorentina, while Busby declared himself content with United's first foray into Europe, declaring that their time would come. After all, his team had an average age of 22 whereas that of Madrid's was 29. Undoubtedly the insistence of Busby that his team enter European football had been fully vindicated.

v Arsenal 5-4

10

1 February 1958
Football League First Division
Highbury
Attendance: 63,578

MANCHESTER UNITED	ARSENAL
Harry Gregg	Jack Kelsey
Bill Foulkes	Stan Charlton
Roger Byrne	Denis Evans
Eddie Colman	Gerry Ward
Mark Jones	Jim Fotheringham
Duncan Edwards	Dave Bowen
Kenny Morgans	Vic Groves
Dennis Viollet	Derek Tapscott
Tommy Taylor	David Herd
Bobby Charlton	Jimmy Bloomfield
Albert Scanlon	Gordon Nutt
Manager: Matt Busby	*Manager:* Jack Crayston

UNITED had not started the season particularly well as they went looking for their hat-trick of league titles, and Matt Busby had had to change the team around somewhat in an attempt to recapture the fast-flowing football which was their trademark.

Busby introduced Bobby Charlton, Eddie Colman and Kenny Morgans and United had started to buzz again. After three consecutive away draws, to Luton Town, Manchester City and Leeds United, the Red Devils had celebrated a return to Old Trafford with a 7-2 hammering of Bolton Wanderers. A Charlton hat-trick, two from Dennis Viollet and others from Duncan Edwards and Albert Scanlon had produced a surge of belief, so it was a confident side that travelled to Highbury on 1 February 1958.

Arsenal were in something of a rebuilding phase and were a solid mid-table team at the time, though one capable of some good football. But with just ten minutes gone, 18-year-old Morgans weaved his way down the right flank and picked out a charging Edwards who slammed it home without breaking stride. A few minutes later, Scanlon did much the same on the other flank, Bobby Charlton the beneficiary of his accurate cross. A third goal came before half-time with progress down both flanks before the ball was centred by Morgans for Tommy Taylor to score.

The second half was a different story, however. United, perhaps complacent after their irresistible first-half showing and with thoughts possibly turning to their midweek trip to Belgrade for the second leg of their European Cup quarter-final against Red Star, sat back a bit. Arsenal took full advantage with David Herd and a Jimmy Bloomfield double bringing them level. Three goals in six minutes and the home fans were elated. Arsenal were using their wings too, with Vic Groves remarkably enjoying considerable success against United captain Roger Byrne.

Some teams may have decided to defend in depth after seeing a three-goal lead vanish if such a fashion, but United, as they always have and always will, responded to the threat to seeking more goals of their own.

Arsenal had been forced to open the game up in an attempt to get back into it, and while they had succeeded admirably in that aim it also played into United's hands. Scanlon was playing havoc with the Gunners' defence and another of his crosses saw Viollet head home for United's fourth to put them back in front. Taylor then restored the two-goal cushion with a fierce shot from a tight angle and the game seemed up. Not on this day, though, as Arsenal kept battling and a superb through-pass from Groves put Herd through on goal. He selflessly drew Harry Gregg in the United goal then squared to give Derek Tapscott a tap-in.

With 15 minutes still to play, Arsenal poured forward in search of the equaliser, with Tapscott and Herd both going close, but were just unable to find it before time ran out.

All those present knew they had witnessed a classic encounter in what has since become one of football's classic rivalries, and as the Highbury faithful applauded United, the players left the pitch together.

David Clifford told arsenal.com, 'I was fortunate as a 15-year-old boy to witness this great game. I have always thought that this was one of the best matches I have ever seen, not because of the subsequent tragic events, but because of the actual game itself. The sheer excitement following our unbelievable second half comeback in front of the North Bank after being three down at half-time.

'The standard of football played by both sides on a mudbath of a pitch and, despite losing, the feeling on walking down the terraces at the end of the match that it would be a very long time before I would ever see such a game again.'

United had climbed up to third in the table but were still six points adrift of leaders Wolverhampton Wanderers, and knowing that Wolves had already beaten Leicester City 5-1 earlier in the day meant that the pressure was on them not to let the gap get any wider.

A nine-goal thriller on a heavy pitch probably wasn't quite the energy-sapping sort of a game which Busby would have wanted, but it was impossible not to praise such a match.

The *News of the World*'s Frank Butler certainly took that view, 'Never have I seen Manchester United greater – nor have I seen such superb fighting spirit in an Arsenal team for many seasons. All the 63,000 spectators at Highbury will agree this was a match to remember for a long, long time.'

Bernard Lovewell sounded a similar note when talking to arsenal.com, 'I was a 12-year-old Arsenal supporter and watched this match from my normal vantage point on the North Bank. I have seen many great games at Highbury over the years but this one has always stood out in my memory.

'The fact that Arsenal lost was almost irrelevant because those of us who had the privilege of being there witnessed a great game played by fantastic players which we have remembered all our lives. The news of the lives lost in the crash was even more poignant for us all as the Manchester United players had given us so much pleasure just five days earlier.'

United and Arsenal players often ate and drank together after a match, but on this occasion Busby had decided that they needed to get home and get their rest before the arduous trip to Belgrade in the week, especially as he was destined to name the same 11 as had taken the field at Highbury.

Far from being deflated by their first European outing, United were inspired by it. They began their 1957/58 campaign as if determined to go one stage further than the previous year and cruised through their opening assignment against Shamrock Rovers by an aggregate score of 9-3. Dukla Prague were next up, but even their vaunted backline of Czechoslovakia internationals couldn't prevent goals from Colin Webster, Taylor and Pegg. By now United were getting used to two-legged ties and they didn't panic when Dukla Prague took the lead in the away leg; they simply made sure they didn't give the Czechs too many more sights of goal.

In the quarter-finals an accomplished Red Star Belgrade side had come to Old Trafford and taken a 1-0 lead before goals from Charlton and Colman, together with a powerful performance from Edwards, just gave United the edge.

At 2-1 though and with a long trip behind the Iron Curtain to come, United decided to charter a plane for that journey. It was a decision taken partly because of their experience in the previous round when fog in London had prevented the plane taking off from Prague airport. The club had to jump on a flight to Amsterdam followed by a boat to Harwich then a train and coach journey back to Manchester, which took a day longer than planned.

With the league still being set against United's participation in Europe, and looking for any excuse to penalise them for being late for a domestic fixture, suitable travel arrangements for any away trip had to be put into place.

The team, of course, had to concentrate on what was likely to be a tricky match, defending a smaller lead than they had done previously. They set about their task with relish, however, Viollet latching on to a lucky rebound with just 90 seconds played. A characteristic thunderbolt from Charlton made it two and when he also managed to get the final, decisive touch in a crowded penalty area, United were looking home and hosed at 3-0.

But shortly after half-time Red Star pulled one back and when a penalty gave them the chance to narrow United's lead still further, the game was well and truly back on. Although Red Star did equalise, it wasn't until two minutes from time and they had no chance to score the fourth which would have given them a replay (there was no away goals rule in those days so if the tie had finished 5-5 on aggregate there would have been a third game).

Despite their disappointment, Red Star laid on a post-match banquet at the Majestic Hotel in Belgrade, after which United set off for a routine flight home. Leaving Belgrade proved no problem at all; it was after a scheduled refuelling stop in Germany that the plane started to get into difficulties.

Munich.

A name forever linked with tragedy in the hearts and minds of not just Manchester United fans, but fans of football everywhere. Byrne, Edwards, Taylor, Colman, Jones, Whelan, Pegg and Bent all lost their lives. Blanchflower and Berry never played again. Viollet was never quite as good again. Wood and Morgans tried but their hearts weren't in it, as Morgans told the *Daily Mail* on the 50th anniversary of the crash: 'I stayed [at United] for two more years but I wasn't really interested. I missed the boys so much I just didn't seem to care.'

Blanchflower, who broke both arms, both legs and his pelvis, and suffered severe damage to his kidneys, said, 'It was the last match for so many. A long time ago now, but not so easy to forget. Some people may think about it every February, I have had to live with it every day since.'

In those terrible days after the plane crash, Jimmy Murphy, assistant manager and Busby's right-hand man, was charged with keeping the club going. Murphy hadn't gone on the Belgrade trip because in his capacity as manager of the Wales national side he had a World Cup qualifier at Ninian Park, Cardiff (in those days the national stadium), and Busby persuaded him that his place was there.

Poignantly it was a momentous night for Wales – victory over Israel meant that they had qualified for the 1958 World Cup finals, the only time in their history that they have done so. In Sweden the Welsh were to reach the quarter-finals before falling 1-0 to Brazil, the only goal scored by a 17-year-old called Pele.

Murphy had just returned to Old Trafford when Alma George, Busby's secretary, told his that the plane had crashed. 'She said many people had been killed,' Murphy recalled. 'She didn't know how many but some of the players had died. I couldn't believe it. I went into my office and started to cry.'

Although conditions in Belgrade had been good, a direct flight home was out of the range of the 'Elizabethan'-class Airspeed Ambassador plane, so a refuelling stop in Munich had always been planned. There the weather was much worse, with ice having to be cleared from the wings and slush on the runway (later blamed for the accident). The pilot had already attempted to take off twice, and had aborted due to boost surging – where the engines over-accelerate – a fault known to be quite common in that make of aeroplane.

A third attempt was made but just at the point when the plane reached velocity one (the point beyond which it isn't safe to abort a take-off), the air speed indicator dropped from 117 knots to 105 and the pilots knew that they couldn't make it. Edwards had already sent a telegram to his landlady saying 'All flights cancelled. Flying tomorrow' before that third attempt, but there seems to have been no serious objections to making it.

Possibly the thought of the Football League's attitude to European football was still at the back of people's minds – the knowledge that United would be penalised should they arrive home late for Saturday's meeting with league leaders Wolves, and a desire to prove that they could compete with the very best in Europe without compromising their form at home.

The Wolves match was postponed but on 22 February they faced Nottingham Forest at Old Trafford and chairman Harold Hardman wrote on the front page of *United Review*, 'Wherever football is played United is mourned … [but] we believe that great days are not done for us. The road back may be long and hard but with the memory of those who died at Munich, of their stirring achievements and wonderful sportsmanship ever with us, Manchester United will rise again.'

v Burnley 5-1

11

28 December 1963
Football League First Division
Old Trafford
Attendance: 47,834

MANCHESTER UNITED	BURNLEY
David Gaskell	Adam Blacklaw
Tony Dunne	John Angus
Noel Cantwell	John Talbut
Pat Crerand	Brian Miller
Bill Foulkes	Andy Lochhead
Maurice Setters	Jimmy Robson
William Anderson	Ray Pointer
Graham Moore	Willie Morgan
Bobby Charlton	Brian O'Neill
David Herd	Jackie Price
George Best	Alex Elder
Manager: **Matt Busby**	*Manager:* **Harry Potts**

'I THINK I've found you a genius.' So said Manchester United scout Bob Bishop in a telegram back to the club after seeing the 15-year-old George Best play for Cregagh Boys' Club in Northern Ireland. He was right, of course, but it was to be another two years before Best would make his United debut, against West Bromwich Albion on 14 September 1963.

West Brom defender Graham Williams did pretty well against Best that day, to the extent that Best switched wings in the second half to get away from him. Nevertheless rumour has it that when the two men met many years later, after both had retired, Williams requested that Best look him squarely in the face. When asked why, Williams replied, 'Because all I've ever seen of you is your arse disappearing down the touchline.'

It was an unremarkable 1-0 win for United, but Best immediately dropped back down to the reserves and didn't feature again until over two months later, in the game against Burnley. 'I was a little bit worried,' said Best, 'but I was sure I was good enough so I continued to work hard.'

The intervening period had not been a good one for United, with eight defeats in 17 matches, and Matt Busby had finally run out of patience. The catalyst was a 4-0 drubbing at Everton followed by an even worse 6-1 defeat by Burnley at Turf Moor.

The vagaries of the fixture list had thrown up a second meeting between the clubs just two days after that Boxing Day debacle, and Busby was determined not to let the same thing happen.

Best was back in Northern Ireland enjoying Christmas with his family when he received a telegram requesting that he report back to Manchester as soon as possible. He knew immediately that he must be starting (substitutes were still three seasons away in the Football League).

Burnley were a good side at the time, winning the league title in 1959/60 then finishing second, fourth and third in the three subsequent seasons. They boasted an experienced team with a number of players who appeared over 100 times for the club. Andy Lochhead was a prolific striker who scored 101 goals in 226 league appearances for Burnley; he had scored four of his team's six in the Boxing Day thrashing of United, and added the Clarets' only goal two days later.

Interestingly, Lochhead made his mark on United again some years later when he scored in both legs of the 1970/71 League Cup semi-final for Aston Villa – a 1-1 draw at Old Trafford followed by a 2-1 victory at Villa Park – which prevented United reaching the final and hastened the end for Wilf McGuinness as United manager.

On this second occasion, however, Lochhead's goal was no more than a consolation, coming as it did in the 87th minute, long after the game was won. David Herd had opened the scoring that day – Herd of course had played against United in their last game before travelling to Belgrade in 1958 but despite a successful career at Arsenal of 107 goals in 180 appearances he got frustrated at the lack of trophies.

In July 1961 he moved to United for £35,000 and a month later made his debut, on the first day of the 1961/62 season, against West Ham United. Four days later he scored in a 3-2 win over Chelsea and he went on to notch 145 goals in 265 appearances across all competitions. Herd is 16th in the list of all-time goalscorers for Arsenal and 13th on the United list – not many players in history have figured in the top 20 lists for two separate top clubs.

After Herd had given United an 11th-minute lead, Graham Moore put them 2-0 after 25 minutes, then came Best's moment – 38 minutes and his first United goal, it may not have born comparison with some of the great goals to come, but a legend had been born.

Bobby Charlton recalls, 'George came into the team with devastating effect. John Angus, who was in the England U23 team at the time and very highly rated, was playing for Burnley. He was a strong, solid right-back, but he was humiliated.

'The little lad from Belfast went up to him and beat him again and again. John was a pal of mine and I really felt for him. But George, even at the age of 17, was capable of destroying someone utterly. He would turn in the tightest of circles and was capable of getting out of any trap that was set for him.'

Team-mate Paddy Crerand added, 'George destroyed him. Absolutely murdered him. George ran him silly for the whole game, not just on the odd occasion. This was total annihilation. George was magnificent and from then on they couldn't leave him out.'

Further goals in the second half from Moore (68th minute) and Herd (70th minute) took the game even further away from Burnley, though Lochhead's late strike for them meant that United just failed to record a five-goal margin to equal Burnley's own of two days earlier. Best was back at home, in Belfast, that same night (he had asked to be flown back directly after the game) and was there when his local mates were reading about him scoring a goal in the report in the *Belfast Telegraph*.

How significant was Best's first goal? Probably not very in the sense that it had seemed inevitable from the day he first stepped on the Old Trafford stage. Harry Gregg remembered, 'My first recollection of George was at United's training headquarters when I was recovering from a back injury. We were working out when this little dark-haired kid went past me once, twice, three times. I immediately told Matt Busby there's a youngster up there who is something special.'

Best had always been confident in his own abilities; Busby remembered the scene before his debut, 'The atmosphere in the dressing room was a bit edgy, but the boy Best sat in the corner reading the match programme! He was completely unconcerned!'

Best was, in fact, quite a shy boy off the field as well as being slightly built, and there were doubts that he could survive the rough and tumble of First Division football. Just days after the ink had dried on his first professional contract, his father, Dickie, had taken Busby to one side and said, 'If George isn't going to make it, I'd be grateful if you'd let me know within six months because I have a position held open for him back home in the printing trade.'

Many years later, Dickie told *The Manchester United Opus*, 'We were worried sick about him living away from home. Fifteen-year-olds in those days weren't as worldly-wise as those of today. He really was still a child.'

Best became a fixture in the team for the rest of that season, playing 24 of the 26 games that remained and scoring a further four goals. He was also recalled to the youth team for United's first final since the heady years of the 1950s when they had won the competition five years in a row. After a 1-1 draw with Swindon Town in the first leg at the County Ground, they won 4-1 in front of nearly 25,000 at Old Trafford to claim the trophy 5-2 on aggregate. It was to be their last triumph in the competition until 1992.

It had been a long road back for United. Busby had said in the aftermath of the terrible events of 1958 that it would take five years for the club to recover, and not for the first time he was right.

While still in his hospital bed, Busby had whispered to his right-hand man Jimmy Murphy to 'keep the flag flying', but where to start? Not only had the club lost some great players, but so much of their structure too.

'Previously Old Trafford had worked like a well-oiled machine,' said Murphy. 'Matt at the top presiding over all our efforts, but now I had to try and keep the club in business without Matt's strength and guidance to fall back on, without Bert Whalley's unflagging energy and zeal, without Tom Curry, the team trainer and on the administrative side we had lost the club secretary,

Walter Crickmer, a man with a shrewd brain.' Murphy, however, proved himself more than capable, with the help of Bobby Charlton, a man Murphy described as 'doing extraordinary things. His talent was exploding in front of your eyes.'

An almost unbelievable runners-up spot in 1958/59 was followed by two successive seventh-placed finishes before a slip to 15th and then a flirtation with relegation in 1962/63 when United were 19th. But in that same season, United had once more reached the FA Cup Final. Kind draws had seen United face First Division opposition on only one occasion before the final – the fourth round tie in which Aston Villa were edged out 1-0.

In the final, however, United faced high-flying Leicester City (who finished fourth in the league and had taken three points out of four off United in their two league meetings). A 30th-minute goal from Denis Law gave United the half-time lead, which Herd increased shortly before the hour. Ken Keyworth pulled one back for Leicester with ten minutes remaining but Herd's second five minutes later ended all hopes of a comeback. Leicester captain Colin Appleton said, 'I can't understand how United finished where they did in the league.'

Eric Hobb in *The Guardian* wrote, 'This was too one-sided a game to merit any unqualified superlatives, but there was plenty of good football, especially from United. Above all, convincing proof was forthcoming that however a side may blunder its way through its league commitments, Wembley is as good a place as any whereat to make atonement in full. Nobody who has followed United closely in recent weeks could have believed that this was a team that had escaped relegation by a whisker.'

Busby felt that he had amassed a side of big-game players who were able to produce great quality on occasion, if not quite yet a whole season's worth. However, the FA Cup triumph had put United back into Europe for the first time since the 1958/59 season. The introduction of the European Cup Winners' Cup in 1960/61, for the winners of domestic cup competitions of the previous season, had given English clubs another route into Europe – and no obstacles were placed in the way of Wolverhampton Wanderers, Leicester City or Tottenham Hotspur entering the competition in its first three seasons. Not for the first time, Manchester United had blazed a path for others to follow, and to benefit from.

It wasn't to prove a glorious return for United, as in the quarter-finals eventual winners Sporting Lisbon overturned a 4-1 deficit from the first leg to win 5-0 in Portugal and put United out 6-4 on aggregate. But at least it was a return, and better was to come.

v Borussia Dortmund 6-1

11 November 1964
Inter-Cities Fairs Cup second round first leg
Stadio Rote Erde, Dortmund
Attendance: 25,000

MANCHESTER UNITED	BORUSSIA DORTMUND
Pat Dunne	Bernhard Wessel
Shay Brennan	Gerhard Cyliax
Tony Dunne	Theodor Redder
Paddy Crerand	Dieter Kurrat
Bill Foulkes	Wolfgang Paul
Nobby Stiles	Wilhelm Sturm
John Connelly	Reinhold Wosab
Bobby Charlton	Franz Brungs
David Herd	Harald Beyer
Denis Law	Friedhelm Konietzka
George Best	Lothar Emmerich
Manager: Matt Busby	*Manager:* Hermann Eppenhoff

BORUSSIA Dortmund were a typically strong German side, boasting plenty of experience (all but two of their team made over 100 appearances for the club, and three of them made well over 200), but in November 1964 in the second round of the Inter-Cities Fairs Cup United dismantled them.

Established in 1955, the competition was set up to promote international trade fairs – friendly games had long been held between cities hosting these fairs so a competition along the same lines seemed a logical progression. Initially open only to teams from cities which hosted such fairs, it was more of an invitational competition. In fact the first Inter-Cities Fairs Cup ended up being drawn out over three years (so as not to interfere with domestic leagues), with Barcelona defeating a London XI to take the first title.

By the 1964/65 season the competition was well-established and 48 teams entered, including United and Everton from England and other well-known clubs including Barcelona, Valencia and Atletico Madrid from Spain, Juventus, Roma and AC Milan from Italy, and Eintracht Frankfurt and Borussia Dortmund from Germany.

It looked a tough second-round draw for United but with their triumvirate of Bobby Charlton, Denis Law and George Best all getting on the scoresheet, it turned into a rout. The opening passages of play saw Law, of all people, clear a Harald Beyer shot off the line. On 12 minutes, Law was in action to devastating effect at the other end of the pitch, juggling the ball with head and foot before laying it off to David Herd to open the scoring. Charlton's first, crashing it home off the underside of the bar, increased the United lead to 2-0 at half-time.

Best scored the most exciting United goal shortly after the break after he slalomed through the defence and United weren't at all put out of their stride when Dieter Kurrat pulled one back from the spot after 51 minutes following a foul on him by Paddy Crerand. Although there was no more scoring for a 15-minute period, Law's goal re-established a three-goal margin and Charlton put the gloss on both the performance and the result when he scored in the 78th and 85th minutes, completing his hat-trick.

The *Daily Mail*'s Ronnie Crowther described it as a 'bombshell burst of brilliance', while Matt Busby called it 'Our greatest show in Europe for many years. I am delighted with such a team performance against a side that went to the European Cup semi-final last season and I am only sorry that more of our fans couldn't have seen it.'

At least they got to see United wrap up the tie three weeks later when a first-minute trademark thunderbolt from Charlton killed off any thoughts the German side may have had of mounting a comeback. A second from Charlton on 19 minutes and second-half goals from Law and John Connelly gave United a 10-1 aggregate win.

It is a further measure of United's dominance of Borussia Dortmund in these two matches that the German side won the domestic German Cup in 1965, which gave them entry into the European Cup Winners' Cup for the following year – which they duly won by beating Liverpool in the final at Hampden Park. It sounded a warning note to the rest of Europe that United were serious contenders once more.

United went on to beat Everton and Strasbourg before being defeated by Ferencvaros in the semi-finals. The Hungarian side were strong in that era, and indeed went on to beat Juventus in the final and win the cup, but United were disappointed by the manner of their defeat: in the first leg they had built up a 3-1 advantage but a late goal from Gyula Rakosi meant United only took a single-goal lead to Budapest.

This always left them open to a stroke of bad luck or a fluke, and the former duly arrived in the shape of a penalty just before half-time, for a Nobby Stiles handball, which was despatched by defender Deszo Novak. That was how the game stayed and with no away goals rule in those days, it meant a third, winner-takes-all match, ten days later. Ferencvaros won the coin toss to decide the venue, and so it was back to Budapest on 16 June. On that occasion goals either side of half-time put Ferencvaros in control, and they stayed there despite Connelly pulling one back late on.

It is worth noting that this was over a month after the completion of the English domestic season, which had finished at the end of April, so the United players did have some excuse for not being at their sharpest. Not that they made any, that isn't the United way.

'I thought the penalty [in the second match] was a harsh decision,' said Stiles, 'as I stopped it with my shoulder. In the third match we played well, indeed we paralysed them, but we lost because we simply couldn't put the ball into the net.'

Busby's words before that semi-final gave a clue as to his thinking, 'This series [against Ferencvaros] is not only a test of reputation and ability, but also of temperament and is an especially good test for us in view of our European Cup commitments next season.' While never one to turn down the chance of a trophy, Busby clearly felt he had bigger fish to fry in Europe the following season.

If the European campaign ended on a disappointing note, however, the domestic season did not. The runners-up spot of the previous year was converted, gloriously, into a first title triumph since the Busby Babes of 1956/57.

In one of the closest title races in league history, United pipped Leeds United on goal average. The teams had identical records of 26 wins, nine draws and seven defeats, but United's 89 goals for was equalled only by Chelsea (who finished third) while their total of just 39 goals conceded was 13 fewer than any other team.

Leeds player Johnny Giles recalls, 'We still had a long way to go and our success in our first season up was remarkable, but you could see that United had also covered a lot of ground from when I had left in 1963; there was a much greater solidity about their defence, where Nobby and Bill Foulkes displayed a great understanding, and of course with Charlton, Law and Best around they were always going to present a terrific threat to your goal.

'While United would inevitably always be seen as the cavaliers of the game, there was no doubt that some hard lessons had been learned at Old Trafford. They were developing more than a little iron, this was essential if they still wanted to compete at the very top of English football.'

If Charlton had a talent which was blossoming by the day, and Best had the impish ability to beat players, it was Law who completed the triumvirate. Has there ever been a better goalscorer than the Scotsman? Not at United. The statistics will show Law in second place in the all-time goalscorers list behind Charlton (and Wayne Rooney is likely to surpass both before his career is done), but Law's 237 goals for the club came from just 404 appearances – a strike rate which only Tommy Taylor might have threatened had fate permitted him a longer career.

Having moved from Manchester City to Torino for the huge sum of £110,000 in 1961, Law had found it difficult to settle in Italy. 'It was like a prison,' he was to say later. 'It wasn't long before I realised I had made a ghastly mistake. It all finally blew up when Torino refused me permission to play for Scotland. That was the end as far as I was concerned. I stormed out so quickly I left all my clothes behind!'

Torino threatened Law with legal action and told him that, under the terms of his contract, he could be sold to Juventus whether he wanted to go there or not. But Law was determined not to stay in Italy and eventually he was able to force through a move to United – the fee was £115,000, which enabled Torino to say they had made a profit on their transfer dealings concerning Law, but the club which really profited was United.

Law was the King of Old Trafford for a decade. His lightning reflexes and determination to score led to injuries galore, but also made him a huge fan favourite. In addition to being a great player, Law also had the bit of a devil about him, once declaring, 'When I get kicked I'm supposed to count to ten and then walk away. I can't. If a player deliberately kicks me, I'll kick him back. If they kick you and you don't do anything about it, they'll kick you again.' And the fans loved him for it.

'I think the word "electric" sums up Denis Law really,' said Charlton. 'He was so quick, sparks seemed to be flying everywhere when he was around and creating problems for defenders. If goalkeepers dropped the ball even six inches he was like greased lightning and had it in the back of the net.'

Law himself said, 'One of the nicest things was having so many great players around you; if you weren't playing so well, Bestie would be playing well. If he wasn't playing well, I might be having a good game. One of us would be having a decent game. Sir Matt's teams were always known to play football and the only instruction that he ever gave us really was, "Go out and play the type of football that you can play. No matter what the result is at the end of the game, if you've tried your best I can ask for no more." He made it as simple as that. We always felt that if the opposition scored one, we could score two, if they scored two we could get three. It didn't always work out that way, but that was the feeling, and it was all very special for me.'

In Graham McColl's comprehensive book *Manchester United in the Sixties*, he quotes Busby as being asked whether his teams played off the cuff and he replied, 'We hold tactical talks every week and before every match, but we do encourage individualism, especially that of Best, Charlton and Law. Unless you encourage individualism then you really have nothing. The players of course have to fit into the working pattern but use their basic skills as best they can. Many many times when they tried something that didn't come off I was quite happy because that's the right thing to do. I was always very happy that they were a creative side, building up creation rather than destruction.'

'There had been a sense that United were no longer a team of great players,' said Charlton, 'that some compromises had been made. But when Denis arrived, no one could dispute what it meant – United were back at the top of the game again, they had signed one of the most talented players in the game. As a statement of intent, you couldn't have beaten it. Denis was one of the few players who would have got into the pre-Munich side.'

Law for his part said, 'It was like turning a new page, and I knew in my bones it was going to be an exciting story.'

v Benfica 4-1 (aet)

13

29 May 1968
European Cup Final
Wembley
Attendance: 100,000

MANCHESTER UNITED	BENFICA
Alex Stepney	Jose Henrique
Shay Brennan	Adolfo Calisto
Tony Dunne	Humberto Fernandes
Paddy Crerand	Jacinto Santos
Bill Foulkes	Fernando Cruz
Nobby Stiles	Jaime Graca
George Best	Mario Coluna
Brian Kidd	Jose Augusto
Bobby Charlton	Jose Torres
David Sadler	Eusebio
John Aston	Antonio Simoes
Manager: Matt Busby	*Manager:* Otto Gloria

SALVATION can take a number of forms. For Manchester United, and for Matt Busby and Bobby Charlton in particular, it took place at Wembley on 29 May 1968.

More than ten years after Busby had assembled a team capable of taking on the best in Europe, he finally won the trophy that United had craved and which they had come so close to taking before the horrors of the Munich air disaster intervened. As the matchday programme editorial pointed out, 'United have been trying to win this tournament since 1956 and their previous attempts all ended at the semi-final stage.'

The most recent of those attempts was two years earlier when United had just been unable to overturn Partizan Belgrade's 2-0 win at home; a second-half Nobby Stiles strike was all they had to show for their efforts. Missing George Best, who had been injured in the first leg and had to have a cartilage operation, United got drawn into a scrappy affair in which Paddy Crerand and Ljubomir Mihajlovic were sent off for fighting. A distraught Crerand later told his manager that United would win the league next season and the European Cup the campaign after that.

There is little doubt, though, that Partizan were a good side and in the final they gave Real Madrid an almighty shock by taking the lead at the Heysel Stadium in Brussels before two quick goals in the 70th and 76th minutes narrowly turned it round for the Spanish champions.

But if the ending to United's 1965/66 European campaign proved a disappointment, there was cause for optimism in an astonishing semi-final display against Benfica.

The Portuguese champions had reached the final four times in the previous five seasons, winning the trophy twice, and were unbeaten in Europe on their home ground. Benfica had scored first, on the half-hour, but goals from David Herd (36), Denis Law (44) and Bill Foulkes (58) had built up what looked a comfortable lead. Then came Eusebio. Sending the United defence the wrong way with a quick shuffle of his feet, he delivered a perfect centre for Torres to head in.

'It was one of those nights when you could almost feel the crackle of the atmosphere,' said Best. A headline in the *The Times* declared, 'Precarious lead plucked from magnificent match'.

Tension was cranked up before the second leg kicked off when Eusebio was presented with his European Footballer of the Year award on the pitch, but when the game started it was another genius who took centre stage.

Best choose this match to show the world what he could do. Within six minutes he had headed home a Tony Dunne free kick, after 12 he slalomed past three Benfica defenders and two minutes after that he put John Connelly away for a third. Fifteen minutes gone and already United had scored more than any previous visiting team. 'Every time I looked up there seemed to be nothing but a United man to pass to,' said Best.

It was a glorious foretaste of what was to come, and after United had fulfilled the first part of Crerand's promise – taking the 1966/67 league title by four points from Nottingham Forest and Tottenham Hotspur – they were back in the European Cup.

The European campaign started in low-key fashion against the part-timers of Hibernians, Malta. A 4-0 home win, with two goals each from Law and David Sadler, made the return a formality and, perhaps mindful of the club's huge and enthusiastic following on the island, United were happy for the game to remain goalless.

A second consecutive scoreless draw in Sarajevo seemed like a good result, and so it proved when a 2-1 win in November 1967, courtesy of goals from John Aston and Best, took United through to the quarter-finals.

Next up were Gornik Zabrze, the Polish champions. A tough but fair game saw Gornik mostly keep a lid on Best until he escaped his marker Henryk Latocha on the hour and let fly a rocket of a shot which the goalkeeper could only palm into his own net. A last-minute Brian Kidd goal gave United the tiniest bit of breathing space – and they needed it as in the return leg Gornik's own wunderkind Wlodzimierz Lubanski (his country's all-time leading goalscorer with 48 from 75 international matches) scored with 20 minutes remaining to put his team in with a chance of forcing extra time in what was the first season in which UEFA applied the away goals rule. A disciplined defensive performance held them at bay, however, much to United's relief.

Another semi-final loomed, this one against the mighty Real Madrid. The first leg, at Old Trafford, saw Madrid curb their normal attacking play to restrict

United to a single-goal advantage, scored by Best after 36 minutes. Although Crerand hit the woodwork, chances were few and far between and the tie remained very much in the balance.

The Bernabeu Stadium witnessed a quite different Madrid team from the one that came to Manchester, all power and pace. Goals from Pirri, Francisco Gento and Amancio gave Madrid a 3-1 half-time lead, with United's only reply an own goal by Ignacio Zoco.

'Real had been running past us in that first half as if we didn't exist,' said Aston. 'In fact, if it hadn't been for Nobby Stiles they would have run up a rugby score.' But when United trooped back on to the pitch an incredible sight greeted them. 'Some of their players looked like it was an effort to drag one leg after the other. Compared with Real we were as fresh as daisies.'

United upped the pace and Sadler brought them level on aggregate after 73 minutes. Five minutes later Best embarked on a run down the right wing and turned the ball back, only for Bill Foulkes of all people to be steaming through in support. 'Goodness knows what he was doing so far upfield,' said Crerand. 'What the hell was he doing in their penalty area?' echoed Charlton.

Foulkes himself admitted, 'I still don't really know what possessed me to go forward. After so many games with no thought of scoring it seems unbelievable when I look back on it. All I had to do was side-foot it into the corner. There was complete silence in the crowd and then everyone jumped on me.'

Nine goals Foulkes scored for United. In 688 games. Two in Europe, in 52 games. 'When Bill scored, I knew it was meant to be,' said Busby.

In between the two legs against Madrid – a gap of 21 days – Busby had flown to Lisbon to watch Benfica take on Juventus in the other semi-final and had come away believing that if United could get through the tie with Real Madrid they would have a real chance of lifting the trophy. They still had to go out on to the pitch and do it, however, and a team featuring the magical Eusebio could never be discounted.

On 29 May 1968 at Wembley Stadium, it was time.

Benfica must have felt like they were playing not just 11 men from Manchester United but 92,000 fans and many millions all around the world desperate to see a happy ending to the story.

The first half passed more or less without incident as the two teams cancelled each other out, and tackling rather than goalscoring opportunities was the order of the day. Eusebio hit the crossbar with one effort, and a free kick which deflected off United's wall had Alex Stepney in goal scrambling to reach it.

Best was targeted by Cruz, and when the Northern Irishman escaped him, Humberto was there to forceful effect – too forceful on one occasion as he was booked after 20 minutes. Gradually, it dawned on United that if Benfica were putting two men on Best, and focusing all their efforts on not letting him reproduce the sort of performance he had two years earlier, then there must be a bit more space for someone else, somewhere.

That someone else was Aston, on the left wing, who began to have a growing influence on proceedings. After 53 minutes David Sadler, who had missed United's best chances in the first half, crossed from the left and Charlton rose higher than everyone to glance the ball into the net. Benfica switched into more attacking mode and with ten minutes left Torres headed down for Jaime Graca to equalise.

United then had to survive a nervy few minutes, and Eusebio had a great chance to win the cup for Benfica when through one-on-one with Stepney. The United goalkeeper pulled off a superb reflex save, and a few seconds later the whistle blew for full time. 'I had come out too far and I was trying to get back when he shot,' recalls Stepney. 'Fortunately he hit the ball straight at me.'

Busby strode out on to the pitch determined to rally his troops. 'I told them they were throwing the game away with careless passing instead of continuing with their confident football. I told them they must start to hold the ball and play again.' The coaches tried to keep everyone on their feet as Busby talked. 'Sometimes when you sit down on the field it's bloody hard to get up again,' said Charlton with feeling.

It was a much more direct route which provided a priceless early chance for United. Stepney kicked long downfield, Brian Kidd headed it on to Best, and he took off for goal. Away from his marker for once, Best went past Jacinto, sent Henrique the wrong way then took it round the keeper and popped the ball into an empty net.

Two minutes later Kidd, on his 19th birthday, saw his header miraculously saved at point-blank range but had the composure to nod in the rebound.

Benfica were beaten and before half-time in extra time Charlton had got his second of the game, flicking Kidd's cross high into the Benfica goal. 'I honestly felt it was something that was meant to be,' said Kidd later. 'We knew we had to do it, if only for Sir Matt.'

'I had come the whole way with the boss, trying to make Manchester United the champions of Europe,' said Foulkes. 'I thought the destruction of our team at Munich would have been the end of it, but he patiently put together another side. I'm proud to have been a part of it, and for those who lost our friends coming home from a European Cup tie in 1958, our victory seemed the right tribute to their memory.'

'Nothing could wipe away the nightmare of Munich, nothing could justify it,' said Wilf McGuinness, 'but still in all our different ways we had tried to make it good; we hadn't forgotten the lads, and here was the greatest possible tribute to the memory of them.'

For Busby it was the culmination of a dream that he had for over a decade, a dream which he had been convinced would have come true in 1958 but for the terrible events of that February. 'I have chased and chased this European Cup, with many disappointments, but here it is at last,' he said. 'I am the proudest man in England tonight.'

Charlton echoed those thoughts, saying, 'It had become like a mission for Manchester United and I think the older players felt as if we had been pursuing a sort of Golden Fleece of football. When the final whistle went I remember thinking that it was the ultimate achievement, not just for the players, but for the club and Sir Matt.'

Drained not just by the match and his efforts in it, but by all the emotion that went with his ten-year quest, Charlton missed most of the evening's celebrations, too exhausted to attend the party at the team's London hotel. The dream had come true.

v AC Milan 1-0

14

15 May 1969
European Cup semi-final second leg
Old Trafford
Attendance: 63,103

MANCHESTER UNITED	AC MILAN
Jimmy Rimmer	Fabio Cudicini
Shay Brennan	Angelo Anquilletti
Francis Burns	Saul Malatrasi
Bill Foulkes	Luigi Maldera
Nobby Stiles	Roberto Rosato
Bobby Charlton	Nello Santin
Paddy Crerand	Karl Heinz Schnellinger
Willie Morgan	Giovanni Lodetti
George Best	Gianni Rivera
Brian Kidd	Kurt Hamrin
Denis Law	Piero Prati
Manager: Sir Matt Busby	*Manager:* Nereo Rocco

'IT is the greatest moment of my life,' wrote Sir Matt Busby in the *Daily Express* the day after the triumph over Benfica. 'In 11 years since we first entered, the first English club to do so, we have tasted near-triumph, great disappointment, and disaster which nearly destroyed us. Now we are the first English club to have won this most coveted club trophy.'

Legend has it that United suffered a sharp decline in the aftermath of finally landing the one trophy they wanted above all others. The truth, as is so often the case, is rather more complicated than that. Yes, the league season did get off to a stuttering start, United winning just four of their first ten games. But nobody was hammering them – indeed all season only Chelsea and Arsenal administered a defeat by more than two goals – and in any case their focus was firmly on the two-legged Intercontinental Cup against Estudiantes de La Plata, winners of the previous season's Copa Libertadores, the South American equivalent of the European Cup.

The first leg was actually held at the Estadio Alberto J Armando, home of a much better known Argentine team, Boca Juniors, as Estudiantes's ground was deemed unsuitable. Marcos Conigliaro scored the only goal of the game in the 27th minute. It was a brutal match with Nobby Stiles cast in the role of villain-in-chief and finally getting sent off ten minutes from time after waving an arm in frustration at the latest of a number of dubious decisions by the Uruguayan linesman. Stiles and Bobby Charlton both needed stitches after the match, while George Best and Burns both floored in off-the-ball incidents. Even Sir Stanley Rous, the English president of FIFA, was moved to comment, 'The outstanding feature of it all was the tolerance of Manchester United.'

Well schooled by now in the art of two-legged ties, United were confident they could turn the match around but they were undone by a piece of slack defending early on which allowed Juan Ramon Veron to steal in with a header and put the Uruguayans in front on the night. Denis Law had to go off injured after a clash with the goalkeeper, then Best and Jose Hugo Medina squared up to each other and both received their marching orders.

Winger Willie Morgan, signed for £100,000 from Burnley in the summer, levelled the second leg late on, but United couldn't find the second goal which would have led to a third game (there was no away goals rule in the Intercontinental Cup, and a third match had been provisionally arranged to take place in Amsterdam three days after the second leg). Maybe that was just as well.

A postscript occurred the following year when AC Milan took on Estudiantes in a tie even more violent than that against United, so much so that three Estudiantes players were briefly jailed for assault and received long playing bans, and several European teams refused to take part in any further competitions.

With the Intercontinental Cup behind them, United's focus switched to defending their European crown. A gentle opener against Irish champions Waterford United resulted in a 10-2 aggregate scoreline. Then came Anderlecht, and while 4-3 looks quite close, United were in almost total control, winning the first leg 3-0 and going an early goal up in Brussels. Although Anderlecht ultimately won the second leg 3-1, they would have needed two more goals in the last ten minutes to progress.

And there was more good news when United found themselves facing Rapid Vienna in the quarter-finals rather than old foes Real Madrid. Rapid had put the Spanish champions out on away goals in the previous round but found United at Old Trafford much too strong.

Best, back after serving a suspension from the Anderlecht tie on account of his sending-off against Estudiantes, produced a masterclass of dribbling and shooting, scoring twice in the 3-0 win. A solid second-leg performance saw United keep their Austrian opponents goalless, and they were through to yet another semi-final.

Possibly United underestimated the Milan side, and goals in either half in the San Siro from Brazilian-born Angelo Sormani and Swedish star Kurt Hamrin gave Milan a comfortable lead to take to Old Trafford. One name that stands out from the Milan team-sheet in that first leg is a certain Giovanni Trapattoni, these days one of the most famous coaches having managed Milan, Juventus, Inter Milan, Bayern Munich, Italy and the Republic of Ireland.

United also made history in another way, by showing the match on giant screens on the Old Trafford pitch. Commonplace now, the idea was revolutionary back then and 23,000 spectators turned up to watch the black-and-white images beamed in from the famous San Siro Stadium.

'We are not beaten yet,' said Sir Matt after the first leg. 'We never give up while we have a chance. If we can score one at Old Trafford that will worry them and a second will earn us a replay.'

A three-week gap between the two legs allowed United's players a week's rest before getting back into full training then travelling to Ireland for warm-up matches in Waterford and Dublin.

Paddy Crerand had warned beforehand that being two down to a team like Milan was a tough task because they were so good at the back, and on the night, Milan displayed considerable skill in stifling United's best attacking moves while always looking dangerous on the break themselves.

With 20 minutes left on the clock, United did finally make the breakthrough: Best twisted and turned away from the close attentions of a couple of markers and made just enough space to thread it though to Charlton on the edge of the six-yard box. Charlton beat Fabio Cudicini with a smart, angled shot to notch United's 100th goal in European competition.

Now United poured forward looking to square the tie, and from one opportunity Denis Law was certain the ball had crossed the goal line. 'The ball was in,' he said. 'If that had been given we'd have gone on to beat Milan, and we would have gone on to win the European Cup.' The BBC, whose cameras were at the game, appeared to support Law's view.

Instead it was Milan who went through to the final, at Real Madrid's Bernabeu Stadium, where a Prati hat-trick and another from Sormani saw them easily beat the Ajax of Johan Cruyff 4-1.

United sportingly applauded their conquerors off the pitch as Sir Matt said, 'They gave everything they had to turn the game around. We had one or two chances we didn't take and you have to take them when playing a team with as good a defence as Milan.'

United fans at the Stretford End were a little less impressed than United's players, though. Irritated by the time-wasting and the Italians' propensity at the merest hint of physical contact to fling themselves to the ground as if hit by a ton of bricks, they decided to see what would happen if they were hit by a ton of bricks.

The victim was Milan's keeper Cudicini who needed prolonged treatment before being cleared to resume. After the tie, both clubs were warned over their future behaviour, and United were ordered to erect a screen behind each goal at Old Trafford to protect the players from missiles. Sadly, such measures were not to be needed for a further eight years.

The other big news of the 1968/69 season was, of course, the announcement that Sir Matt wanted to move aside from team affairs. The club issued a New Year statement saying, 'Sir Matt has informed the Board that he wishes to relinquish the position of team manager at the end of the present season. The Chairman and directors have tried to persuade him to carry on, and it was only with great reluctance that his request has been accepted. The Board fully appreciates the reason for his decision and it was unanimously agreed that Sir Matt be appointed general manager of the club, which he is very happy to accept.'

Sir Matt was approaching 60 that May and felt it was time for a younger man to take over. There was little pressure as United finished 11th in the league and a sixth round defeat in the FA Cup left them out of Europe and with no great expectations for an immediate return.

He also felt that he owed it to his wife, Jean, to spend a bit more time with her. He had always credited Jean with getting him through the darkest days after Munich; she had sat by his bedside while he slowly recovered, then picked the most opportune moment to say to him 'Matt, you know the lads would have wanted you to carry on.'

'Women are so much stronger than we are,' he recalled many years later. 'It was so dreadful facing up to it.' A second consecutive European Cup would have been the icing on the cake but in truth Sir Matt had already faced up to his demons. And conquered them.

v Orient 2-0

15

17 August 1974
Football League Second Division
Brisbane Road
Attendance: 17,772

MANCHESTER UNITED	ORIENT
Alex Stepney	John Jackson
Alex Forsyth	Bobby Fisher
Stewart Houston	Bill Roffey
Brian Greenhoff	Phil Hoadley
Jim Holton	Jeff Harris
Martin Buchan	Tom Walley
Willie Morgan	Barrie Fairbrother
Lou Macari	Ricky Heppolette
Stuart Pearson	Mickey Bullock
Jim McCalliog	Gerry Queen
Gerry Daly	Derek Posse
Manager: Tommy Docherty	*Manager:* George Petchey

HANDING over your baby is never an easy thing. Sir Matt Busby was the creator of the modern Manchester United and while on one level he was keen to hand over the reins, on another – understandably – he found it hard to let go.

The man appointed to replace him was Wilf McGuinness. Sir Matt had said they were looking for a younger man, which McGuinness obviously was, but also experienced as United were not in a position to experiment. 'He must have already proved himself as a leader who commands respect,' continued Sir Matt.

McGuinness appeared to be a great choice. Born in Manchester he had signed professional terms with United when just 17, but a badly broken leg in December 1959, when still only 22, ended his playing career. Keen to stay with United, McGuinness became youth team trainer (a role he also occupied for England from 1963 onwards).

McGuinness's appointment would lead to continuity but, as he was still only 31, he would have Sir Matt in the background to offer advice. It sounded like the ideal solution, and it was a structure favoured by many continental clubs, but the problem was two-fold.

Firstly, there was the question over McGuinness's age and experience: perhaps he didn't distance himself quite enough from the players. Some years later he admitted, 'There's no doubt that the fact that I was close to the players turned out to be a problem. I realised that I couldn't be as close to them as I once was, but that was so hard after all the years we were pals – going out together, going to family events, playing golf. These were lads I'd grown up with.'

The other problem was far more intractable, however. It was clear to all that United desperately needed strengthening, and McGuinness had some excellent ideas as to who they should be: Colin Todd, Sunderland's promising young defender who he was familiar with from England youth duty; Luton Town's free-scoring centre-forward Malcolm Macdonald; and Ipswich Town full-back Mick Mills.

Sir Matt stepped in with his own ideas, however, claiming that Todd was too pricey and signing Ian Ure from Arsenal instead. To be fair to Ure, who was a full international for Scotland, he did a decent job in shoring up the United defence in place of the ageing Bill Foulkes, but he was no Todd, who moved instead to Derby County for whom he made almost 300 league appearances, led to the league title in 1975, when he also won the Players' Player of the Year award, and won 27 caps for England.

Sir Matt also believed that Macdonald was destined to move to Liverpool, though in fact he went to Newcastle United where he became known as 'Supermac' and scored 95 goals in 187 league appearances.

It was clear that Sir Matt was still pulling the strings, and in stark contrast to when Busby had himself arrived at the club many years previously and demanded total control over all team matters, it was abundantly clear that the same privilege was not going to be afforded to McGuinness. Dropping Denis Law and Bobby Charlton was a brave step from the tyro manager, who has since said, 'I suppose the biggest lesson I learned was that if you're going to drop great players, you'd better have great players to put in their place.'

In the end, McGuinness was granted only one and a half years of his three-year contract. 'Maybe I was just too young,' says McGuinness, 'the signings I wanted would surely have made some difference, and it might have helped if we'd have won one of our three cup semi-finals, that might have given me a little breathing space. But none of it happened.'

So Johnny Carey's prophetic words in March 1967, when he had declared that it would be 'a very unenviable job for the man who takes Matt Busby's place' had come true, and Sir Matt was brought back in to manage team affairs.

The next man into the firing line was Frank O'Farrell, a softly-spoken Irishman who had had a solid playing career in the lower leagues with West Ham United and Preston North End. O'Farrell tried to insist on more control than McGuinness had been granted, requesting a bigger office than the one he was originally assigned and not being afraid to contradict Sir Matt.

In direct contrast to McGuinness, O'Farrell was also quite aloof with the players, insisting that they book appointments if they wanted to see him. Denis Law once said of him, 'Mr O'Farrell came as a stranger and went as a stranger.'

O'Farrell also felt he hadn't got much support from the club in his dealings with George Best, whose disappearances were becoming increasingly more commonplace. In the event, even his departure – which followed a 5-0 defeat by Crystal Palace on 16 December 1972 – was overshadowed by Best's announcement that he was retiring from football.

Although Best returned, his time was clearly drawing to a close, with even Sir Matt conceding that he had been given as much licence as he could expect. 'Every manager goes through life looking for one great player, praying he'll find one,' said Sir Matt. 'I was more lucky than most. I found two – big Duncan [Edwards] and George.'

Former England manager Graham Taylor summed it up when he said of Best, 'What George did was to show that tactics and formations are for the majority of us, while the genius plays the game in a way that is simply beyond mere mortals.'

The time had come for United to cast aside their shackles and rediscover the 'United way'. Cue Tommy Docherty, the larger-than-life character who instantly endeared himself to fans and the board by stating, 'This is the greatest club in the world, and I am so proud to be part of it.'

Things would get worse before they got better, though. The Doc had joked in his first season that if the club went any lower 'we'd fall off the pools coupons!' but in his second it was no laughing matter as United struggled throughout. The *coup de grace* was applied by, of all teams, Manchester City and, of all players, by United's former favourite son, Denis Law. At Old Trafford in the penultimate week of the season, Law back-heeled the winning goal and promptly walked away from English football.

Docherty expected to go the same way as McGuinness and Farrell before him, but his attitude convinced the United board that he was still the man for the job. 'It was disappointing to go down,' said Sir Matt, 'but towards the end of the season a pattern of play began to emerge again and this gives us confidence for the future.' Just as importantly Docherty had the support of the players.

'The Doc was a breath of fresh air,' remembers Willie Morgan. 'Very outgoing, very positive. I think his attitude alone saved us from relegation that year.' Lou Macari agreed, 'His strength as a manager was creating an atmosphere that was very, very positive.'

United started the season in the Second Division with a visit to the unfamiliar surroundings of Brisbane Road to face an Orient side who had only missed out on promotion to the First Division, and thereby passing United going in the other direction, by a single point the previous season.

Clearly, then, they couldn't be taken too lightly, and United didn't. Stuart Pearson, a £200,000 summer signing from Hull City, looked the real deal and although he didn't get on the scoresheet in the game against Orient, he led the line well and looked like becoming the perfect target man for United to play off. The *Daily Telegraph* report of the game said, 'Pearson lit up the United front line like a beacon: mobile, quick, dangerous, everything their forwards had not been last season.'

Pearson was an expert at holding the ball up with his back to goal and playing in the wingers, with first Morgan and later Steve Coppell being the main beneficiaries.

A sweeping movement brought the first United chance for Morgan which he struck narrowly wide from right to left past John Jackson's right-hand post. Then a beautiful chest trap by Brian Greenhoff in the centre circle allowed him the time to spread the play wide to Morgan again who cut in from the right and rifled home a cross-shot from left to right. Morgan continued to make hay down the right and drew a free kick from which Jackson made a good save of Pearson's looping flicked header at the near post which was heading for the far post.

Orient kicked off the second half but remained on the back foot because despite a fair bit of possession, their passing was not quite accurate enough to carve out any clear chances. Another free kick won by Morgan on the right-hand byline saw Alex Forsyth drive the ball across; any touch from Pearson in the six-yard box and it would have been a goal. Orient's best opportunity fell to Derek Posse when the ball went loose in the United penalty area but United were awarded a free kick, and then a driving run by Barrie Fairbrother ended with a right-to-left shot which could have gone in.

At the other end Pearson's barnstorming run and ball in would have found Morgan at the far post if it weren't for a vital deflection from Bill Roffey. Sammy McIlroy came on as a substitute for Lou Macari, but the second goal came from another Forsyth free kick on the right – he drove it across to the far post at pace where Houston got a powerful header back across the goal to beat Jackson all ends up. With 17 minutes left it looked unlikely Orient could recover, and so it proved.

United's first defeat in the league didn't come until their tenth game, when they lost 2-0 to Norwich City at Carrow Road. Another defeat by the same opposition put them out of the League Cup at the semi-final stage but they had already established their credentials by knocking out Burnley and Manchester City, both First Division teams at the time. Confounding the views of those who felt that United's slide might be inexorable, they topped the table from start to finish and by the time they came to their last game, against Blackpool, they were able to print a matchday programme announcing themselves as Second Division champions and even parade the trophy round before the match started in front of 58,769 spectators.

A 4-0 rout duly followed, with Pearson scoring twice to take his tally to 18 in his first season at the club, all celebrated with his trademark raised right fist.

Martin Buchan, already displaying the qualities which made him an obvious club captain, was not impressed. 'Lou Macari reckons the Second Division was a cakewalk,' he said later, 'but it was never as easy as he said it was. He might have had an easy time up front, but as a defender you still have forwards to mark. The good thing was that it got us used to winning which was important the next year But even so it was embarrassing to collect Second Division medals. We felt we and the club should never be in that position.'

Docherty himself had a more positive spin on the events of 1974/75. 'They always reckon that the Second Division trophy is the one that nobody really wants to win,' he said. 'It means that at some time you have to have failed to be competing for it – unless you have come up from the Fourth Division. I don't really take that view. We have won against tough opposition and now we are back at the top. And we haven't finished yet.'

v Liverpool **2-1**

16

21 May 1977
FA Cup Final
Wembley
Attendance: 100,000

MANCHESTER UNITED	LIVERPOOL
Alex Stepney	Ray Clemence
Jimmy Nicholl	Phil Neal
Arthur Albiston	Joey Jones
Brian Greenhoff	Tommy Smith
Martin Buchan	Emlyn Hughes
Sammy McIlroy	Ray Kennedy
Lou Macari	Jimmy Case
Steve Coppell	Terry McDermott
Stuart Pearson	Steve Heighway
Jimmy Greenhoff	David Johnson
Gordon Hill	Kevin Keegan
Manager: Tommy Docherty	*Manager:* Bob Paisley

THE 1976 FA Cup Final had been lost to Second Division Southampton when Bobby Stokes scored the only goal of the game. Martin Buchan had told the team in the Wembley dressing room straight after the game, 'We'll be back next year to win.'

United were true to his word but this time around they faced the dominant force in the English game at the time, Liverpool. Earlier in May Liverpool had beaten United at Anfield and despite drawing three and losing the other of their last four matches they had retained the First Division title by a single point from Manchester City. United, then, not only wanted to win the cup to ease their disappointment of 12 months before, but to prevent their most hated rivals from clinching a league and cup Double.

The day dawned bright and hot, and Liverpool's midfield triumvirate of Terry McDermott, Jimmy Case and Ray Kennedy quickly took control, although the only clear chance of the first half came when the last of these skimmed the outside of Alex Stepney's post with a header just before the half-time whistle.

United, however, started the second half in a more positive vein, with 19-year-old left-back Arthur Albiston – in in place of the injured Stewart Houston – making a charge upfield which seemed to inspire his team-mates. Albiston later offered his winner's medal to Houston, who had played in all the previous rounds in the cup, but Houston wouldn't take it.

In the 50th minute, a slightly loose header from Kevin Keegan on the halfway line gave Sammy McIlroy the opportunity to head on to Jimmy Greenhoff and he put in a beautiful headed flick on which gave Stuart Pearson a few inches of space for the first time. Pearson's speed off the mark took him clear and he kept cool to nod it on to his right foot then beat England goalkeeper Ray Clemence at his near post from the right of the penalty area. A quick trademark right-arm celebration then Pearson was engulfed by his team-mates. Greenhoff later described Pearson's finish as 'out of this world, it never got the recognition it should have done.' Certainly it was a great striker's goal, scored by a great striker.

Liverpool hit back almost straight away as they knocked it around in midfield before Joey Jones hit an inch-perfect cross to the edge of the United penalty area. Case killed the ball beautifully on his thigh, spun on it and in an instant planted it high to the left of Stepney, who did well to get his fingertips to it but couldn't prevent it going in.

The general feeling was that United hadn't held on to their lead for long enough to deflate Liverpool and the Merseysiders would go on to turn the match in their favour. And indeed if David Johnson had managed to control a ball while sitting on the shoulder of the last defender a minute later he would have been through one-on-one with Stepney. Johnson's reaction later was a bit churlish: he walked straight off the pitch without bothering with a lap of honour and said, 'We'd won the league with some lovely football but this game was so frenetic that precious little good stuff was actually played. There wasn't much service from the byline so I ran about all afternoon like a blue-arsed fly without ever having a serious effort on goal.'

Instead, after Johnson's near-breakthrough United tidied up and a few minutes later a seemingly aimless up and under ball was flicked on dangerously by the head of, of all people, little Lou Macari. Not only that but when Greenhoff and Tommy Smith tussled in the Liverpool penalty area, who was there to pick up the loose ball but Macari.

The 'shot' appeared to be going wide until it hit the chest of Greenhoff and changed direction, giving Clemence no chance as the ball looped slowly but unstoppably into the net. Smith and Emlyn Hughes insisted he had been fouled in the build-up, though John Motson's commentary at the time (his first FA Cup Final in that role) described it as a slip, saying Smith 'got in a bit of a tangle with Jimmy Greenhoff. He seemed to have got the ball away but he hadn't.' Greenhoff said later, 'I didn't think I impeded Tommy and neither did the referee.'

There was still half an hour for Liverpool to pull themselves back into the match for a second time, but the closest they got was when Kennedy clipped the top of the crossbar with his left foot just a couple of minutes before the end. And their last attack ended the way so many of their previous ones had done – with Martin Buchan, who had been nursing an injury all week and only passed a late fitness test, getting in front of Liverpool dangerman Kevin Keegan to head the ball to safety.

'I'd opened up my knee ligaments falling over Trevor Brooking,' Buchan recalled in his dry, sardonic manner. 'On the Tuesday morning I couldn't walk. By the Friday I could just about hobble. On Saturday morning I had a fitness test which consisted of standing there kicking balls to [coach] Tommy Cavanagh. There's no way I was fit.' Fit or not, Buchan hardly gave Keegan a kick, or a header, all match.

It was Tommy Docherty's eighth attempt to win as a player and a manager, a 'record' almost matched by Greenhoff, who had played in seven losing semi-finals, including replays, with Leeds United and Stoke City. 'My winner was a bit of luck and I knew it, but that didn't matter. This was an overdue experience,' he said.

It was United's first cup victory since the 1963 win over Leicester City.

At the start of the 1976/77 season, Docherty had almost completed his task of clearing out the older players in the United squad and fashioning the team in his own image. Only Stepney, who had joined from Chelsea for £50,000 in May 1966 and was 34 by the time of the 1977 FA Cup triumph, and Buchan were left from the players who had been brought to the club by previous managers.

Paddy Crerand had been appointed by Docherty as his assistant manager, as much because he thought it would go down well with Sir Matt as because he thought he would do a good job. But Crerand felt that Docherty was being a bit cavalier in his treatment of Busby's old warriors and he left to seek a manager's role for himself. 'He must have been very disappointed to have left United at his own request only to see us reach two successive cup finals,' remarked Docherty in a barbed tone.

Twenty-year-old Jimmy Nicholl had forced his way into the first team ahead of Alex Forsyth, Albiston and David McCreery were on the edges of the first team, and then there were the wingers. The arrival of Steve Coppell on 1 March 1975 had seen an upswing in United's fortunes and tempo. The young Merseysider was snatched from under the noses of Liverpool and, much to his surprise, was encouraged by Docherty to complete the economics degree he was studying at the time. In the 11 league matches between his signing and the end of the 1974/75 season, Coppell played a part in ten, and over the next eight years he made over 400 appearances for United in all competitions and 42 for England.

Those stats look even more impressive when you recall that Coppell was only 28 when he retired with a knee injury, the legacy of a horror challenge in a 1982 World Cup qualifier against Hungary which he described to BBC Radio Merseyside as feeling like 'someone had put a firework in my knee and it had gone off'.

Describing left-winger Gordon Hill as the last piece in the jigsaw is to conjure up images of the world's strangest puzzle, especially as he was on loan from Millwall to Chicago Sting in the summer of 1975 when United became aware of him. He was signed in November that year and over the next two and a half seasons made 133 appearances for United in all competitions, scoring 51 goals. There's no reason to think Hill wouldn't have continued in a similar vein for a few more years, but he was always more of a Docherty-type player than a Dave Sexton-type and to the fans' disgust he departed soon after Docherty did.

Hill was a quite different type of winger from the hard-working Coppell. He saw it as no part of his business to track back, or to cover his defence. Journalist Eamonn Dunphy's diary of the 1973/74 season at Millwall entitled *Only A Game?: Diary of a Professional Footballer* said of Hill, 'When you tell him to watch the full-back, he just watches him race away. He literally just watches him.'

Hill himself recalls, 'The years I was [at United] there was this sense of invincibility about Old Trafford; you just thought no one could touch us and anything you did would come off. It was a lovely feeling.'

It is a sentiment echoed by his then manager, who once said, 'Old Trafford is the only stadium in the world that's absolutely buzzing with atmosphere when it's empty. It's almost like a cathedral.'

Whatever his defensive shortcomings, Hill was a fans' favourite and played a full part in Docherty's mantra of attacking football. The Doc had also led United back into Europe, their third-place finish in 1975/76 – although a slight anti-climax after they had promised more – being sufficient for a place in the UEFA Cup, which had replaced the Inter-Cities Fairs Cup for the 1971/72 season.

In the first round they overturned a 1-0 deficit from the away leg against Ajax to win 2-0 with Macari and McIlroy getting the goals. In the second round Hill produced a sumptuous performance at home to Juventus, lauded by opposition manager Giovanni Trapattoni as 'a very clever player indeed', but his 31st-minute strike was all United had to show for it. The streetwise Italians overturned that on the half-hour, went in front on the hour and sealed the deal five minutes from the end.

'We were babes in Europe that season,' admitted Docherty. 'We were short of experience at that level and in Turin it was a case of men against boys.'

Sadly for Docherty – and quite possibly for United – he wasn't to get the benefit of another season in Europe. Parading around the Wembley turf with the FA Cup lid doubling as a hat was his last act in anger for the club he loved.

There is little doubt that these days having an affair with a married woman, even if she was married to a colleague, would not result in dismissal. The 1970s was a different time but more to the point, Docherty's ruthlessness in clearing out both playing staff and management he considered surplus to requirements had left him with few friends in high places. Sir Matt Busby in particular found the whole matter rather sordid, and without his support Docherty had little chance of surviving.

Chairman Louis Edwards and his son, Martin, were disposed towards standing by their manager but other board members seemed to feel that they could hardly add to physiotherapist Laurie Brown's anguish at his wife leaving him by also dismissing him from his job. Instead they asked for Docherty's resignation and when he refused, they fired him.

Docherty could scarcely believe it. 'People don't lose their jobs because they fall in love with someone,' he said. 'I have been punished for falling in love. This has nothing to do with my track record as a manager.' Docherty was undoubtedly being naive if he thought things would just carry on the same although he had a point when he said, 'There's a hell of a lot of politics in football. I don't think Henry Kissinger would have lasted 48 hours at Old Trafford.'

v Liverpool 2-1

5 April 1980
Football League First Division
Old Trafford
Attendance: 57,342

MANCHESTER UNITED	LIVERPOOL
Gary Bailey	Ray Clemence
Jimmy Nicholl	Phil Neal
Arthur Albiston	Phil Thompson
Gordon McQueen	Alan Hansen
Martin Buchan	Alan Kennedy
Ray Wilkins	Ray Kennedy
Lou Macari	Jimmy Case
Steve Coppell	Terry McDermott
Joe Jordan	Graeme Souness
Brian Greenhoff	David Johnson
Mickey Thomas	Kenny Dalglish
Manager: Dave Sexton	*Manager:* Bob Paisley

THE worst thing about the way Tommy Docherty's managerial career came to an end at Manchester United, for the club at least, is that it left Sir Matt Busby and the board deciding on a safe pair of hands for their next appointment. Dave Sexton was a perfectly competent manager at both club level for Chelsea (where he won the FA Cup in 1970 and the European Cup Winners' Cup the following season) and Queens Park Rangers and as England U21 coach. He was not, however, a Manchester United manager.

It was not so much that he failed to bring any silverware to Old Trafford – although that was disappointing after expectations had again risen in the wake of two successive FA Cup finals – as that the football that team played under him was dour.

On 14 July 1977, barely a fortnight after Docherty had departed, Sexton was in, and it quickly became clear that he was more of a thinker and a planner, in stark contrast to his predecessor's off-the-cuff style.

In some ways Sexton was a man ahead of his time. 'Football is a family game and I would like to see stadiums providing areas for family seating,' was one of his pronouncements. Another was, 'Sponsorship is another aspect of the game which can be developed and I wouldn't be surprised to see players wearing shirts bearing a sponsor's name before long.'

Sexton also signed a number of players who became firm favourites at Old Trafford, not least when he raided Leeds United twice in quick succession. He signed fearsome striker Joe Jordan on 6 January 1978, and added his equally fearsome fellow Scotsman, central defender Gordon McQueen, on 9 February. McQueen immediately endeared himself to the fans by declaring, 'Ask all the players in the country which club they would like to join and 99 per cent would say "Manchester United". The other one per cent would be liars.'

United's other new arrival was rather more fortuitous. Alex Stepney, who had won everything with the club but was by now in his mid-30s, had been eased out of the first team in favour of Paddy Roche. But Sexton felt that Roche's confidence was shattered by the 5-1 defeat at Birmingham City on 11 October 1978, and he moved for Coventry City's highly rated Jim Blyth. Then disaster. Blyth failed the medical on account of a back problem (though he carried on at Coventry until 1982). Rather than eat humble pie and turn back to Roche, Sexton decided to promote 20-year-old Gary Bailey. Bailey went on to make over 350 appearances for United in all competitions.

United did reach another FA Cup Final under Sexton in 1979 when a dull game that Arsenal had largely controlled sprung into life in the last five minutes as first McQueen pulled a goal back for United, than Sammy McIlroy danced through the Gunners' defence to level the scores. United elation turned to despair when a minute later, Alan Sunderland got on the end of a Graham Rix cross to win it for Arsenal.

A week later Sexton signed Ray Wilkins from Chelsea for a then-massive fee of £777,777 and the side which began the 1979/80 season contained five players bought or introduced by Sexton.

United stayed on Liverpool's coat-tails throughout that season and on 5 April a 2-1 victory over the defending champions gave them genuine hope that they could still bridge the six-point gap which existed at the start of the match.

The game didn't start that way. Kenny Dalglish, so often a thorn in United's side as player and manager, benefited from a slip by big Gordon on a muddy and rutted pitch and slotted past Bailey from a narrow angle after just 14 minutes had gone. It was his 20th goal of the season.

But the picture changed completely just five minutes later. Steve Coppell and Alan Kennedy were chasing after a loose ball when Kennedy's hamstring went. Unable to pursue Coppell, he could only watch as the United winger crossed for Mickey Thomas to equalise in a goalmouth scramble. Clemence looked to have done enough but the ball squirmed out of his grasp and Thomas stayed aware enough to prod it home. Kennedy obviously couldn't continue either and came off to be replaced by Sammy Lee.

The atmosphere of doom and gloom around Old Trafford had changed significantly; now United had renewed hope and began to crank up the pressure. Liverpool were kings of England, and of Europe, and hardly prone to panic even though United were chucking the proverbial kitchen sink at them.

The champions survived comfortably enough until half-time; Alan Hansen, of all people, made a charge up the pitch, lobbing the ball over the United defence as they tried to play offside and going through one-on-one with Bailey. If Hansen had slotted it home himself, the goal probably would have stood, but he chose to tap it across for Dalglish, who was offside from earlier in the move.

With just over an hour gone, Thomas almost scored an even scrappier goal than his first as Jordan headed on a Wilkins crossfield pass but Thomas's touch was not quite firm enough and gave David Johnson the chance to clear it off the line. From the ensuing corner, Jordan got up above the Liverpool defence and Jimmy Greenhoff, by now a 33-year-old veteran, got the final touch into the net. Jordan's header might have been going in anyway, but few would deny Greenhoff the goal.

Lou Macari had a chance to put United further ahead from a flowing United move, but was foiled by an excellent save from Clemence, and then Wilkins crashed one against the bar with Clemence well beaten. Liverpool's best chance to equalise came from a Jimmy Case free kick on the edge of the penalty area which took a deflection off the wall and only just cleared the bar.

In Ivan Ponting's *Red And Raw*, which covers United's clashes with Liverpool between 1946 and 1999, Greenhoff recalls, 'I had been out for nearly a year with a succession of pelvic injuries. Two men had told me I shouldn't play again, but a third held out some hope so here I was. Still I'd not had a full game for the first team, only one for the reserves and not much training when Dave Sexton asked me to face Liverpool. I told him I was nowhere near fit but he needed me so I gave it a go.

'I felt shattered during the game but then this corner came over from the right, Joe Jordan nodded it towards goal and I got a little deflection with my head to send it past Ray Clemence. It was enough to win the game and it just about kept our faint title hopes alive. In the end we hung on until the final Saturday of the season, though I must be honest and say that Liverpool always had a bit in hand.'

United did all they could to get back into the title race, winning five matches on the trot. Going into the last weekend, though, United had to win at Leeds and hope that Liverpool couldn't beat Aston Villa at Anfield. Neither happened as United lost 2-0 and Liverpool pulled away to win 4-1 over Villa.

Liverpool actually lost their game in hand, at Middlesbrough, but by then the title was won – by two points and a goal difference 21 goals better than United's.

It was as close as Sexton was ever to get to a trophy with United (unless you count the shared Charity Shield, which had finished in a dull 0-0 draw with Liverpool). Two hopelessly unsuccessful European campaigns didn't help, as United lost to Porto in the 1977/78 European Cup Winners' Cup and to Widzew Lodz in the 1980/81 UEFA Cup, though in fact it was events which transpired off the field which ultimately cost him his job.

The first of these was the death of chairman Louis Edwards, from a heart attack possibly brought on by allegations of improper payments to young players, a charge which Edwards always strongly denied. His son, Martin, took over and made it clear he wanted a more expansive, exciting brand of football to be played. Sexton occasionally seemed to suffer from paralysis by analysis, an example of which could be found in his over-complicated corner routines which left many of the players confused.

After one session had been going for some 45 minutes, McQueen said, 'Dave, do you fancy one of my corner kicks?' Sexton inquired what it was and McQueen said, 'Someone takes the f***ing thing and I put my big head on it and put it in the back of the net.'

Everyone liked Sexton. Macari describes him as 'a good man' while Buchan, for so long the captain and heartbeat of the side, said he was 'the nicest man in football', but perhaps the job was a little too big for him.

'I've got to be honest and say the image of Manchester United overawed me, to a certain extent, but the job has got to be the peak of ambition for any manager. There is something awesome about Old Trafford,' Sexton said. He added that he felt awkward saying things like 'we'll murder 'em' and those sorts of things. 'I want to see the team winning and playing attractively. Which comes first? It must be winning.'

As a sentiment it is perfectly reasonable, but unfortunately Sexton was able to deliver neither. A succession of draws – 18 in all, 11 of which were at home and eight of which which scoreless was not the sort of football Martin Edwards wanted to see.

Devastated by injuries, he also bought badly – or unluckily. Garry Birtles was United's record signing when he joined the club for £1.25m in October 1980. Despite the enormous price tag, if Birtles had been able to replicate the kind of form he had shown when scoring 32 goals in 87 games for Brian Clough's Nottingham Forest side, money would not have been an issue. He couldn't. He couldn't even come close. Not least because Birtles and Jordan were both extremely left-footed and therefore tended to want to occupy the same space rather than make runs off each other. United drifted into a kind of malaise and Sexton did not appear to have the wherewithal to pull his team out of it.

Eventually an exasperated Edwards summoned Sexton to a board meeting at which he showed him some of the letters he had received from fans despondent at the football they were seeing. Edwards was an astute businessman and could not allow the club to keep haemorrhaging fans – the crowds were an average of 7,000 down on the previous season, and 10,000 down on what they had got under Tommy Docherty. Edwards later said that he felt the team 'had gone backwards' and it was 'having an effect on gates'.

The last of these was unacceptable to Edwards, the first man to see the possibilities of United as a 'brand'; if it was to be a brand, United were in the business of entertainment – and that meant a more entertaining style of football which would bring the crowds flocking back in. It meant Ron Atkinson.

v Brighton & Hove Albion 4-0

18

26 May 1983
FA Cup Final replay
Wembley
Attendance: 92,000

MANCHESTER UNITED	BRIGHTON & HOVE ALBION
Gary Bailey	Graham Moseley
Mike Duxbury	Steve Gatting
Arthur Albiston	Graham Pearce
Gordon McQueen	Tony Grealish
Kevin Moran	Steve Foster
Ray Wilkins	Gary Stevens
Bryan Robson	Jimmy Case
Arnold Muhren	Gary Howlett
Frank Stapleton	Michael Robinson
Norman Whiteside	Gordon Smith
Alan Davies	Neil Smillie
Manager: Ron Atkinson	*Manager:* Jimmy Melia

I F Dave Sexton was appointed Manchester United manager as a reaction against the larger-than-life Tommy Docherty, then Ron Atkinson was most certainly a reaction against the quiet, studious approach of Sexton. New chairman Martin Edwards wanted razzmatazz, he wanted entertainment and he got it.

It is worth bearing in mind that at the time Atkinson was in charge at West Bromwich Albion, who had actually finished higher in the table than United, but Atkinson liked what he saw and heard from Edwards. 'His knowledge was good, his interest was high, I thought he knew the game. And he told me I'd only see him when I wanted to see him.'

Atkinson swept through the United roster of playing and coaching staff, bringing in Mick Brown – his right-hand man at West Bromwich Albion – to be his assistant manager. Brian Whitehouse, another from the Hawthorns, became chief coach and, perhaps most significantly of all, Eric Harrison was lured from Everton to be youth team coach. A decade on, Harrison would be credited with discovering the Class of 92.

Atkinson then turned his attention to the playing side. An out-of-contract Joe Jordan had departed for Italy and AC Milan so a striker was needed urgently. Frank Stapleton was bought from Arsenal for a tribunal-set fee of £900,000 (closer to United's valuation of £750,000 than Arsenal's of £2m), John Gidman arrived from Everton in a swap deal with Mickey Thomas going in the other direction, and then came Atkinson's coup.

In 1981 few people had heard of perm-haired Bryan Robson, but Atkinson knew all about him from his days at West Brom. 'I was a big gamble for Ron to pay that much money for me. I think a number of people in the Old Trafford boardroom must have said "Bryan who?"' Atkinson was having none of it. 'I told Martin [Edwards], "This one ain't a gamble, he's solid gold."'

For around £2m, United acquired not just Robson but his West Brom team-mate Remi Moses; in one fell swoop he had rebuilt the United midfield with what he described as a sure-fire, copper-bottomed investment.

Towards the end of Atkinson's first season in charge Norman Whiteside was thrown into the fray, making his debut on 24 April in a league win over Brighton & Hove Albion. Only just 17, Whiteside nevertheless looked and played like a man. 'I knew Norman was going to be something special,' recalls Sammy McIlroy. 'He was a man well before his time. We used to joke that he was nine when he was born. He was big and strong and difficult to knock off the ball, but he had a lot of control for a big fella.'

Whiteside went back to the youth team for a few games but Atkinson fielded him again in the last match of the season, against Stoke City, and he scored the second goal in United's 2-0 victory. It made Whiteside the youngest United goalscorer in history.

Atkinson always maintained that if he had had a yard more pace, Whiteside would have been one of the greatest ever, but the man himself is more modest. 'I've no left foot, I'm not too good in the air and I'm not that fast. A lot of fouls awarded against me were intended to be tackles, I was just too slow getting there,' he said.

A man who undoubtedly was one of the greatest was the other goalscorer on that May day against Stoke in 1982: Bryan Robson. A legend as a player and as a captain, Robson was, for my money, the greatest box-to-box midfielder in United's history.

It is often forgotten that Robson had suffered three separate leg breaks early on in his career, at West Brom, but had still managed 39 goals in almost 200 appearances. At United his tally was to end on 99 goals in 461 appearances, but Robson was never one for facts and figures. 'Money was never my main motivation,' he said. 'I simply wanted to be a winner.'

It took just one more season for that to happen, and once again it was the FA Cup which proved to be United's natural habitat.

Robson, as was his wont, had torn his ankle ligaments during the League Cup semi-final win over Arsenal, which had led to his missing the final, lost 2-1 to Liverpool. Arsenal can't have been happy to see him regain his fitness just in time for the FA Cup semi-final where, inevitably, he scored one of the goals in another 2-1 win.

Brighton were a First Division team that year but had already been relegated by the time of the FA Cup Final. United had finished third, an improvement on the previous year but still some way off Liverpool. However Liverpool had lost 2-1 to Brighton at Anfield in that season's biggest FA Cup shock and United went into the final as firm favourites. The status improved still further with the news that Brighton's inspirational skipper Steve Foster would miss the match through suspension. Foster even tried appealing to the courts, but the case was dismissed.

Brighton started the final brightly with Gordon Smith opening the scoring on 14 minutes, but gradually United took control and second-half goals from Stapleton and Ray Wilkins looked to have turned the game in their favour. Then Gary Stevens equalised from a corner by Jimmy Case (formerly of Liverpool), out of the blue with three minutes remaining and the match went into extra time.

In the last minute of the extra time period, Smith found himself one-on-one with Gary Bailey but failed to beat him, meaning the FA Cup Final would go to a replay. A radio commentary by Peter Jones became famous for his 'and Smith must score' comment – a quote which was later used as a title for a Brighton fanzine in a fine example of football fans' black humour.

Bailey though always felt that Smith was hard done by. 'It wasn't a miss,' he said, 'it was a save. Gordon's shot was on target.' And he's right. The shot might have been scuffed a bit and not hit as cleanly as Smith would have wanted, but it wasn't as if he had blasted it miles wide or blazed it over the bar.

Five days later the two teams reassembled at Wembley for the replay and Foster was eligible to play again, though Moses was still suspended as his red card in a league match against Arsenal meant a two-game ban. Foster took the place of young Chris Ramsey in the only change made by either manager.

Brighton had the first chance of the replay as a good interchange between Smith and Michael Robinson required a timely penalty area challenge from Kevin Moran, who did just enough to put the striker off. In the 25th minute a move developed down United's left, started by the cultured left foot of Dutchman Arnold Muhren, carried on by Wilkins, Arthur Albiston and Whiteside. A beautiful layoff from Alan Davies to Robson on the edge of the box saw the skipper drove home the first goal with his favoured left foot.

'That's the goal Manchester United wanted from their captain,' said John Motson.

United grew in confidence and only five minutes later Davies won a corner down the right. The corner was overhit but there was Davies – now on the left-hand side – to retrieve the ball and knock a beautiful cross in for Whiteside, making a powerful run across the box, to head home.

Brighton fought back gamely, forcing Bailey into one superb save when he stretched up to tip over a ball which appeared to be going over his head. First Case won the ball with a crunching tackle deep in his own half, then he picked up a return pass and his piledriver cannoned off the shoulder of Moran and almost sent Bailey the wrong way, but he twisted to knock it over the bar.

A minute before half-time, a Muhren free kick found Stapleton at the far post and he headed back across goal where Robson dashed in to apply the finishing touch. The ball was probably going in anyway, but Robson was leaving nothing to chance.

The game was over by half-time and as United took their foot off the pedal Brighton did have more of the ball without carving out another clear-cut chance. Shortly after the hour mark, Robson was through on goal from a Stapleton pass down the right when he was pulled back by a despairing Gary Stevens. Contact didn't appear to be too strong, but the linesman immediately flagged for a penalty.

Robson was on a hat-trick, but he waved away calls for him to take the penalty, insisting that Muhren, who had volunteered to take them in the absence of regular penalty-taker Steve Coppell, do so. The technically gifted Dutchman made no mistake, placing it low to Graham Moseley's left and accurately enough to hit the inside-netting first.

United were the FA Cup winners again. All that remained was to play out the last half-hour, then collect the trophy, though there was still time for Whiteside to hit the underside of the bar with Moseley beaten, and for Gary Bailey to pull off a good double save from Steve Gatting (brother of England cricketer Mike) and Robinson to keep a clean sheet. In one lovely touch the United fans cheered for Sir Matt Busby, who duly acknowledged them by removing his hat and smiling.

A sad footnote to a successful season for United was the leg injuries to both Steve Coppell and Alan Davies, who had been one of the stars of the FA Cup triumph. Coppell had missed the final as his knee had broken down yet again, and another operation over that summer was to prove to no avail. Coppell was forced to retire in October 1983, still aged only 28.

Davies's story was even sadder: a serious leg break just as the next season was about to kick off saw him out of the game for eight months and robbed him of the chance to establish himself in the first team. Tragically Davies was to take his own life when he was just 30; he will always be remembered at Old Trafford for his part in the 1983 FA Cup win.

The replay had been classic Atkinson, a one-off display of pace and power which would have swept aside teams much stronger than Brighton. Stuart Jones in *The Times* wrote, 'United, with an utterly convincing triumph, had at last fulfilled their expensive promise and confirmed their individual potential. Robson has few rivals as Europe's most complete all-round player, nor Stapleton as a target man. The 18-year-old Whiteside continued to take his achievements beyond the realm of fantasy.'

It was United's first trophy since the 1977 FA Cup win over Liverpool and it had been won with exactly the kind of buccaneering football for which Atkinson had been brought to the club.

v Everton 1-0

19

18 May 1985
FA Cup Final
Wembley
Attendance: 100,000

MANCHESTER UNITED	EVERTON
Gary Bailey	Neville Southall
John Gidman	Gary Stevens
Arthur Albiston	Pat Van Den Hauwe
Paul McGrath	Kevin Ratcliffe
Kevin Moran	Derek Mountfield
Gordon Strachan	Peter Reid
Bryan Robson	Trevor Steven
Mark Hughes	Graeme Sharp
Frank Stapleton	Andy Gray
Norman Whiteside	Paul Bracewell
Jesper Olsen	Kevin Sheedy
Manager: Ron Atkinson	*Manager:* Howard Kendall

THE 1983/84 season saw United finish closer in points to Liverpool but one place further away in fourth. Early round defeats in the League Cup and FA Cup by lower league opposition – Oxford United and Bournemouth respectively – hardly helped but a decent run in the European Cup Winners' Cup at least kept the fans happy.

A Captain Marvel performance from Bryan Robson had almost single-handedly enabled United to turn around a 2-0 deficit against a Barcelona side that included Diego Maradona. Robson not only scored two goals but inspired the whole team into a performance that is rated by many as the finest of the Ron Atkinson era. 'I have never heard a noise like it,' said Robson. 'That magical night when we did what everyone thought was impossible will stay with me forever.' Sadly United narrowly failed to do the same in the semi-finals, losing 2-1 to Juventus in Turin after drawing the home leg 1-1.

Shorn of his entire first-choice midfield of Ray Wilkins (through suspension), Arnold Muhren and Robson (through injury), Atkinson was forced into fielding a makeshift collection of Paul McGrath and Mike Duxbury, both defenders, alongside Remi Moses. As well as boasting half of Italy's 1982 World Cup-winning side, Juve boasted Michel Platini and legendary Polish striker Zbigniew Boniek. World Cup hero Paolo Rossi got the 89th-minute winner.

After that United's league form collapsed too, and two draws and three defeats in their last five matches enabled Liverpool to increase the final points margin to six, and also let Southampton and Nottingham Forest edge ahead of them.

The 1984/85 season kicked off with United, as usual, aiming to close the gap on their arch-rivals. But there was a new force in the land in the shape of the blue half of Merseyside. Draws in their first four league games wasn't quite the start United were looking for, then a certain amount of momentum was established through five wins out of their next seven, plus a hard-fought 1-1 draw with Liverpool at Old Trafford.

It all came to a shuddering halt at Goodison Park towards the end of October when United were thrashed 5-0 by a rampaging Everton, and three days later Howard Kendall's excellent side came to Old Trafford and knocked United out of the League Cup, though at least on that occasion the scoreline was a more respectable 2-1.

With Everton displaying such tremendous form in the league, the FA Cup once more looked like being United's best opportunity for silverware, but to do that they were going to have to get past the holders – Everton.

With both teams playing their 60th games of the season it is little wonder that the players appeared a little jaded and clear-cut chances were somewhat sparse. Norman Whiteside clattered Neville Southall early on with a foot that was sufficiently high to bring at least a yellow card these days, but luckily no lasting damage was done.

Then Peter Reid of all people had a long-range shot, a volley from the edge of the penalty area which he caught sweetly enough to have brought him his fifth goal of the season but for the post which it glanced off. And that was pretty much all the action of note in the first half.

In the second, United had the first glimmer of an opening, but the ball didn't come down quite quickly enough for Robson, then Reid got the byline and beat Arthur Albiston to set Andy Gray up inside the penalty area. It was the sort of chance Gray had been taking all season but on this occasion he got under it and scooped it over and wide of Gary Bailey's goal.

The game remained level, with the defences mostly on top. Whiteside was put through one on one with Southall but the goalkeeper did a fine job of rushing out to stifle the threat. Disaster struck for United when in the 78th minute McGrath gave the ball away to Reid in the centre circle and Kevin Moran chopped Reid down before he could make the most of the break.

It was a bad challenge, but referee Peter Willis was possibly a little harsh in issuing a red card; Moran appeared to be going for the ball and Reid surely didn't have the pace to claim he would have been through on goal from that position. Certainly the commentary team didn't feel it should be a red card at the time (though it would be these days), and Reid himself went over to have an apologetic word with Moran on the touchline. It was the first red card in an FA Cup Final.

United went all out for a winning goal, in an attempt to avoid having to play half an hour of extra time with ten men, and a neat one-two between Gidman and Whiteside was hurriedly cleared by Pat Van Den Hauwe over his own bar.

Duxbury came on for Arthur Albiston in the left-back position and United got the game back underway. Chances remained hard to come by, with a highlights reel showing only a long-range effort from Paul Bracewell, comfortably held by Bailey, and a decent United move down the left which ended with a good ball across the six-yard box from Duxbury which was missed by Southall. No damage was done, however, as there were no United players there to take advantage.

As the players changed ends for the third time, it was pointed out that there had never been a 0-0 draw in a Wembley FA Cup Final, and only three in history, the last of which had been in 1912. There has been one more since, of course, the famous one between United and Arsenal in 2005.

But there wasn't to be one this year. Five minutes into the second period of extra time came a beautiful flowing move from United, began by Jesper Olsen knocking a short ball into Hughes who beat Bracewell in the middle of the United half and set Whiteside away down the right with a lovely pass delivered with the outside of his right foot. Whiteside took it down the wing, then dipped inside and with his left foot curled a shot around the outside of Van Den Hauwe and beyond the outstretched arms of Southall to nestle in the far corner of the Everton goal.

It was a wonder goal, and Everton were beaten. The Merseysiders had nothing left and were denied a treble of league, FA Cup and European Cup Winners' Cup by one of the all-time great cup final goals. 'I had been substituted by then,' recalls Albiston, 'so I was sat on the bench directly behind where Norman shot from and as soon as he took it inside on to his left foot, I could see the goal coming.' Atkinson, with his usual penchant for understatement, described it as 'arguably the greatest cup win any side will ever have at Wembley.'

A couple of interesting postscripts to the 1985 FA Cup Final: much was made of United being the first club to field a side consisting entirely of players who had represented their countries, including substitute Duxbury. As all but one of Everton's players had, or would, also play international football (the sole exception being Derek Mountfield who won an under-21 cap for England but never a full cap), the final could lay claim to boasting the highest quality of player of any final to date. Moran rather churlishly had his winner's medal withheld on the day, but at least he got it later.

On the open-top bus ride to Manchester Town Hall the next day, Moran declared, 'We won the cup for the supporters of Manchester United because they are the best. The greatest in the world.' Later he would say that people are afraid to ask him about his sending off, but 'it never really bothered me because we won the game. If we had lost, I think that I would feel a little bit sick even now.'

The European campaign had ended disappointingly in 1985 with quarter-final defeat at the hands of Hungarian side Videoton who got the penalty shoot-out they seemed to be playing for, and then won it. Both United and

Everton were denied deserved places in European competition the following season because of the Heysel Stadium disaster when rioting Liverpool supporters caused the deaths of 39 fans and led to English clubs being banned from competing in Europe for five years.

The 1985/86 season opened with United recording ten straight victories and a first title in 17 years looked on, but as the season wore on, inconsistency – and injuries – took their toll. 'We didn't have the same strength in depth that later United teams had,' said Albiston recently. 'If we had two or three influential players out, we couldn't cope.'

Even Atkinson lost his usual cool after a section of the Old Trafford crowd booed following United's first home defeat of the season, which didn't come until 21 December, against Arsenal. 'They seem to forget I've brought them the FA Cup twice, and Bryan Robson wouldn't be playing here if it wasn't for me! They have very short memories,' he complained.

The season drifted, though, with United ultimately finishing in fourth yet again, on 76 points – 12 behind Liverpool, who recaptured their crown from Everton by two with West Ham United third on 84. It was beginning to look like fourth was the limit of where Ron Atkinson could take United. And Atkinson tendered his resignation, but chairman Martin Edwards persuaded him to stay on.

Then disaster. The 1986/87 season started in a completely opposite vein to the one before it – United lost their first three games, and six of the first ten, beating only mid-table sides Southampton and Sheffield Wednesday in that period.

Two months after Atkinson's offer to step aside had been rejected, he was out. 'Nobody wants to leave United,' he said, 'whether they are the boss or the tea boy. But I've no axe to grind. I've worked for a chairman who I consider to be as good as any in the game.

'When people ask me, "Why didn't you win the league?" I always say, "Two words: Ian Rush." Every year he'd weigh in with 40 goals a season. We were always in the frame though, which we hadn't been before. And remember the five years I was at United in four of them the English champions were also champions of Europe.'

It is a reasonable defence of his time in charge of United, and there's no disputing the fact that Atkinson brought back exactly the sort of football both the board and fans had been craving. He said, 'When I was offered the Manchester United job I was both thrilled and flattered. I couldn't help feeling that we were made for each other – I have always said the biggest stage is the best place to entertain. That means Frank Sinatra at Carnegie Hall, Richard Burton at the Old Vic and Manchester United at Old Trafford.'

On the day of his dismissal, Atkinson threw a party for the players. That summed up his whole approach – to football and to life. 'Ron's the only man I know who could throw a party the day he is sacked,' said Whiteside, while

Robson added, 'He may not be the greatest manager in the game, but I haven't met a finer bloke.'

The last word should go to Atkinson himself. 'Managing Manchester United? Hey, that will do for me.'

v Oxford United 0-2

20

8 November 1986
Football League First Division
Manor Ground, Oxford
Attendance: 13,545

MANCHESTER UNITED	OXFORD UNITED
Chris Turner	Tony Parks
Mike Duxbury	Neil Slatter
Arthur Albiston	David Langan
Graeme Hogg	Les Phillips
Kevin Moran	Gary Briggs
Paul McGrath	Ray Houghton
Remi Moses	Kevin Brock
Clayton Blackmore	Malcolm Shotton
Peter Barnes	John Trewick
Peter Davenport	David Leworthy
Frank Stapleton	John Aldridge
Manager: Alex Ferguson	*Manager:* Maurice Evans

RON Atkinson had got closer than most to the promised land of a league title, but who could United turn to in order to take them that extra step? The answer did not seem to be the rather dour, uncommunicative 44-year-old Aberdeen manager with a reputation as a strict disciplinarian.

How wrong we all were.

Alex Ferguson was appointed Manchester United manager on 6 November 1986. It might have been a day late for Bonfire Night, but there were going to be plenty of fireworks.

As Ferguson sat nervously in the dugout, chewing gum in the way we all were to become accustomed to seeing, it was John Aldridge who stole the show. Driving into the penalty area he was tripped by Kevin Moran and got up to convert the spot kick himself. That was in the 16th minute, and shortly after he had another chance which was only just smuggled away by the United defence.

United were toothless in attack with a half-chance for Peter Barnes about all they had to show for their first-half work. The boss's first half-time team talk at least saw United get into the Oxford penalty area where Frank Stapleton crashed a shot against the angle of the bar and post. But it was still largely Oxford in charge and although striker David Leworthy missed a golden opportunity to put them two up when he scuffed a shot, ten minutes from the end a corner from the right was only half-cleared.

Ray Houghton, later to have a successful five years at Liverpool, hooked it back in and even though his cross was slightly overhit Kevin Brock knocked it back across the face of goal and full-back Neil Slatter was on hand to turn it in.

Clayton Blackmore struck a fine shot just a few feet wide before the end, but afterwards all the talk was of Aldridge, and his transfer request. Apart from a few autograph hunters, little attention was paid to Ferguson.

How wrong we all were.

What were Ferguson's first impressions at United? Arthur Albiston, for one, was surprised. Having worked with Ferguson for the Scotland team, his experience was that Ferguson was quite easy-going, but on that first matchday he looked round the changing room and wondered how a team packed with internationals and experienced First Division players could have lost to Oxford United. 'You know you've got to impress a new manager but none of us did that at Oxford, we played badly,' said Kevin Moran. 'It was probably an eye-opener for him, and not a nice one.'

Ferguson didn't like the fact that at half-time the players had ambled across the pitch towards the dressing room – he wanted them to jog off, and jog on again, as he felt it reflected a desire to be out there, playing. Perhaps some of these players didn't have that hunger, that desire any more; if that was the case they were going to get a rude awakening as Ferguson most certainly did. His changes quickly took on an air of revolution rather than the evolution he had anticipated.

His first 'signing' wasn't a player at all, it was his assistant at Aberdeen, Archie Knox. Knox needed no second bidding to join Ferguson at United and together they set about reforming the culture.

'There was a discipline problem at the club,' recalls Knox. 'And there were leaks about it from the dressing room. We stopped that dead. Players were doing similar things at other clubs, but you never heard about it. Anfield in particular. Alex became a little bit obsessed with Liverpool, nothing ever came out of there.'

The club's relationship with the outside world, and the media in particular, changed. The Cliff, then United's training ground, was open and accessible to all and journalists would wander round, picking up quotes, chatting to players both on and off the record, watching training. Ferguson thought there should be a bit more distance so he insisted that reporters make appointments to speak to players or staff, and if they didn't have one they couldn't just hang around. It was a bold move. Before he was himself firmly established, Ferguson had laid out a new set of ground rules which might just give the media cause to lambast him given half the chance.

The other aspect that changed fast was training. Atkinson had famously taken a slightly *laissez-faire* approach to training – although he claims that it wasn't quite as relaxed as was supposed at the time – and Knox did not. Bryan Robson said after a few weeks of the new regime, 'There's no doubt that things have changed and the players seem to like the way things are being done. I've got to say that I've never felt stronger in my legs than I do now.' Clayton Blackmore takes up the theme.

'The main thing I remember is the "boxes". The boss brought in this drill where you make boxes of ten by ten, put eight players inside the box and try to retain possession. It sounds simple, but in a space like that everything has to be on the floor – short passes, quick feet and a real feel for the ball.'

'Changing training to start at 9.30am was clever,' recalls Stapleton. 'It gave us the sense that we were going to work.' Ferguson himself was at work by 7am every day. 'His car was always there,' says Blackmore. 'I've never seen anybody so committed.'

Players were shaken out of their comfort zone. Albiston says Ferguson didn't make big speeches but he would quietly challenge players as to whether they wanted to win things or not. Ferguson couldn't make immediate changes to personnel – chairman Martin Edwards had made it clear that he would have to sell before he could buy, even announcing the fact at the press conference to unveil Ferguson as the next manager, and the astute Ferguson wanted a good long look anyway before he made any decisions.

So for six months, Ferguson watched and waited. 'I felt that I had to give myself time to look at the players I had taken over,' he said. 'I knew that I would eventually make changes, and I have gone on record as saying that I think I need to strengthen as many as five positions. It may turn out that I have the players for those positions already here [at the club], but it's up to them to show me that. If not, I will find them elsewhere.'

United's season continued to be a turbulent one, though they did haul themselves out of the relegation positions into the relative comfort of mid-table, ending in 11th place. The new manager quickly endeared himself to the fans by masterminding a double over Liverpool – a 1-0 Boxing Day win at Anfield courtesy of Norman Whiteside, who latched on to a free kick by Robson (playing an unfamiliar role in defence) and despatched a vicious 20-yard strike past Bruce Grobbelaar in the 78th minute.

At Old Trafford in April the scoreline was repeated when Liverpool-born Peter Davenport scored just two minutes from the end, after a mistake by Alan Hansen of all people, to decide a scrappy match which left Liverpool six points adrift of leaders Everton and finally put to bed any chance they had of retaining their league title.

That, plus the marked improvement in their league position, gave Ferguson a bit of breathing space and in the summer of 1987 he began his long-term fashioning of a side in his own image.

Stapleton moved to Ajax where former team-mate Arnold Muhren was extending his career in a more gently-paced league than the English one, while John Sivebaek went to St Etienne and Terry Gibson to Wimbledon. In their places came England full-back Viv Anderson – a snip at £250,000 from Arsenal – and the free-scoring Brian McClair from Celtic for £850,000.

It was a lot of money, although Celtic had wanted £2m, but McClair wasted no time in paying it back. Signed on 1 July, McClair made his debut on the first day of the 1987/88 season in the 2-2 draw at Southampton and scored his first goal for United in the third match of the season, a 2-0 home win over Watford. By the end of the season McClair had scored 31 goals in 48 appearances across all competitions – the previous season the top scorer had been Davenport with 16.

In December, Ferguson was forced into the transfer market again when an injury to Paul McGrath left him short of central defenders, and Steve Bruce joined the club from Norwich City for £825,000. Alex Ferguson's first building blocks were in place.

v Nottingham Forest 1-0

21

7 January 1990
FA Cup third round
City Ground, Nottingham
Attendance: 13,545

Manchester United	Nottingham Forest
Jim Leighton	Steve Sutton
Viv Anderson	Stuart Pearce
Gary Pallister	Des Walker
Steve Bruce	Brian Laws
Clayton Blackmore	Terry Wilson
Lee Martin	Garry Parker
Russell Beardsmore	Gary Crosby
Mike Phelan	Toddy Orlygsson
Brian McClair	Steve Hodge
Mark Hughes	Nigel Clough
Mark Robins	Nigel Jemson
Manager: Alex Ferguson	*Manager:* Brian Clough

'THE new manager will need time,' said chairman Martin Edwards presciently. 'He has to assess his players as well as the opposition in the English League, which is new to him. He's got a lot to do and a lot to learn. I don't think we can expect miracles overnight.'

Not overnight, no, but by the start of the 1989.90 season fans were starting to mutter. Alex Ferguson had had time to ship out a few more players who he deemed too old or just not quite good enough, including most of his backline with central defenders Paul McGrath, Kevin Moran and Graeme Hogg shipped on to Aston Villa, Sporting Gijon and Portsmouth respectively, while Arthur Albiston was allowed to move on a free transfer to West Bromwich Albion. Albiston said it was probably fair enough as he was in his 30s, and of the others probably only McGrath was a mistake.

But with McGrath it wasn't all about his performance – even with two shot knees which required eight operations over the years and often prevented him from training, he was a wonderful reader of the game – so much as his lifestyle. Ron Atkinson had once joked that he didn't know whether to pay the big Irishman appearance money or disappearance money, and McGrath himself admitted that whereas life under Big Ron was relaxing 'the new boss will steam in first time you step out of line and hit you with everything he's got'.

In later years McGrath came to realise that Ferguson had had the best interests of the club at heart, even telling the BBC in 2006 that he wished he had listened to the new United manager and changed his lifestyle. 'He has been nothing but kind to me since I left the club,' said McGrath, 'and has shown himself to be a really decent human being.' McGrath had a measure of payback in his playing days, defeating United in the 1994 League Cup Final, adding another two years later and in total playing another seven years for Villa and winning the PFA Player of the Year award in 1993.

McGrath said after the defeat by Oxford United in Ferguson's first game in charge that he 'came to the immediate conclusion [Ferguson] didn't rate me'. McGrath was wrong, however. Ferguson thought he was a brilliant player, 'He was an exceptionally skilful and stylish defender, with marvellous innate athleticism, a man whose abilities stood comparison with any central defender in the game. Ian Rush never scored against United when McGrath was playing.' High praise indeed from a man who didn't give it out unnecessarily.

But McGrath was part of the drinking culture which Ferguson was determined to end at United, and for that reason Norman Whiteside also departed despite Ferguson saying of him that 'his eyes were as cold as steel and he had a temperament to match. As a player he was close to the genius category.'

The pity of having to let McGrath and Whiteside go was that in other circumstances they would both have been very much Ferguson-type players. If he had got to the club five years earlier and put a stop to their off-field activities they could have both become all-time greats. The same claim could probably not have been made of Peter Davenport, Jesper Olsen or Gordon Strachan, all of whom seemed a little bit lightweight for Ferguson's ideal, looking at who he brought in in their stead: Mal Donaghy, Mike Phelan, Neil Webb, Paul Ince, Gary Pallister and, of course, a returning Mark Hughes.

Hughes had never wanted to leave United in the first place. 'Not really. It was one of those things that snowballed. United kept breaking up teams to try and find the next big thing, and I was a victim of that, I suppose. Right up until the moment I stepped on the plane I was hoping that something would happen to keep me at United.'

Hughes's move to Barcelona had not been a huge success and he was on loan at Bayern Munich – where ironically he had recaptured a semblance of form, scoring six goals in 18 appearances. Ferguson wanted Hughes back at Old Trafford; so much so that he flew to Germany and hit the Welshman with an irresistible sales pitch. 'He told me I should never have been sold in the first place. He wanted a signing to get the fans going and he felt I was the man to do it. I felt a real emotional tie to United and I think the fans tuned in to that.'

Hughes rewarded Ferguson for his tenacity by taking his United goal tally up to 163 in 467 matches, placing him ninth in the club's all-time scoring charts.

Other signings, however, were struggling to make the same impact. Pallister in particular did not settle in at all, despite having Steve Bruce alongside him, Ince was still only 22 and did not yet have the experience to dominate games, while Webb and winger Danny Wallace (acquired from Southampton soon after the start of the 1989/90 season for £1.3m) picked up injuries.

The other factor was the terrible state of the Old Trafford pitch. The undersoil heating system was not working properly and couldn't cope with a hard frost in some areas of the pitch. Clayton Blackmore says, 'It's not just an excuse, believe me. The pitch was a major problem, you couldn't pass the ball smoothly and it was difficult to put in the killer ball. When you think of how United like to play, that was really important.'

So in spite of the financial outlay on both players and pitch, United continued to be consistent only in their inconsistency – able to beat Millwall 5-1 one week and lose 5-1 to Manchester City the following week (this in a season in which City finished one place below United, in 14th). December brought four defeats and two draws and New Year's Day saw a dull 0-0 home game against Queens Park Rangers, who were also to finish in mid-table. Fans unfurled a banner which read 'Three years of excuses and it's still crap… Ta-ra Fergie'.

An FA Cup third round draw against Nottingham Forest hardly held out the promise of salvation, United having lost to the same opponents in the sixth round the previous year, and with Bryan Robson, Paul Ince and Neil Webb all missing through injury. Ferguson started with 21-year-olds Lee Martin at left-back and Russell Beardsmore in midfield in a makeshift side which was also without both the experienced Wallace and promising teenage newcomer Lee Sharpe to offer any width down the left.

Although Forest's league form wasn't much better than United's, they had won the League Cup the previous season and would go on to retain it in 1990; furthermore the FA Cup had become something of a Holy Grail as it was the only trophy that Brian Clough, one of the most acclaimed managers in the game, had not won.

On a bare mudbath of a pitch it was a rather disjointed game at first though Martin did a good job down the left, laying on one half-chance for 20-year-old striker Mark Robins who fashioned an opening with a neat turn and shot that Forest keeper Steve Sutton did well to palm away to safety. That was more or less the only chance of note in the first half, and United continued to take the game to their opponents at the start of the second half.

In the 56th minute Martin, again looking sharp, nicked the ball off a dawdling Toddy Orlygsson down United's left and played it to Hughes. Hughes had time and space and hit a beautiful pass with the outside of his right foot which curved perfectly in behind the Forest defence. If the defenders were a little slow to react, Robins most definitely was not, nipping in ahead of Stuart Pearce to direct a careful header back across Sutton and beyond the reach of his outstretched right hand.

Forest were woken from their slumbers, though their first real chance came from nothing more than a big punt upfield from Sutton, well controlled by Nigel Clough and taken on by Steve Hodge. Gary Crosby sprung the offside trap and Jim Leighton had to rush a long way out of his goal to narrow the angle and make if difficult for Crosby. Even then the ball was still in play and

United's first championship winning team, in the 1907/08 season. Back row (left to right): Ernest Mangall (manager), Fred Bacon (trainer), Jack Picken, Hugh Edmonds, Mr Murray (director), Harry Moger, John Henry Davies (chairman), Tom Homer, Mr Lawton (director), Alex Bell, Mr Deakin (director). Middle row: Billy Meredith, Richard Duckworth, Charlie Roberts, Sandy Turnbull, Enoch West, George Stacey. Front row: Arthur Whalley, Leslie Horton, Harold Halse, George Wall.

Johnny Carey proudly holds the 1948 FA Cup, a trophy with which United has always had a special affinity.

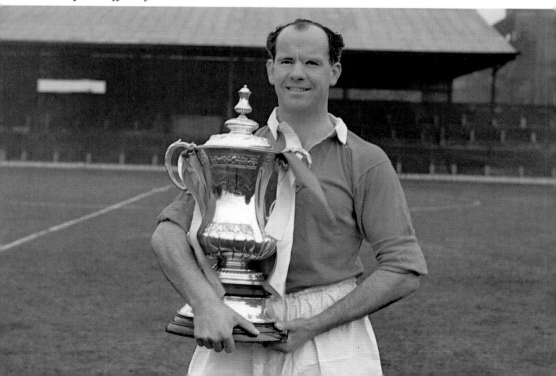

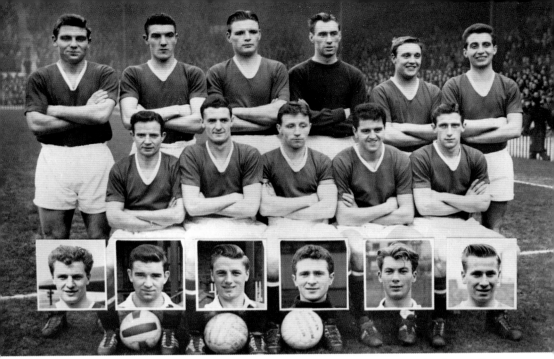

The 1957/58 squad which was torn apart by the Munich air disaster. Back row (left to right): Duncan Edwards, Bill Foulkes, Mark Jones, Ray Wood, Eddie Colman, David Pegg. Front row: Johnny Berry, Billy Whelan, Roger Byrne, Tommy Taylor, Dennis Viollet. Inset: Geoff Bent, Jackie Blanchflower, Albert Scanlon, Harry Gregg, Kenny Morgans, Bobby Charlton.

The late, great George Best, in familiar pose, advancing down the wing.

Goalscorers in the 1977 FA Cup Final Stuart Pearson (left) and Lou Macari (right) on either side of manager Tommy Docherty, with Gordon Hill on the far right.

Eric Cantona salutes the fans after making his United debut as a half-time substitute for Ryan Giggs in the 2–1 win over City, 6 December 1992.

United fans display a 'You can't win anything with kids' banner during the 1996 FA Cup Final win over Liverpool.

A shirtless Ryan Giggs celebrates scoring the greatest goal in FA Cup history.

Teddy Sheringham has just got the flick-on from which Ole Gunnar Solskjaer is going to score the winner in the 1999 Champions League Final against Bayern Munich.

Wayne Rooney (and team) with the League Cup after the 2010 win over Aston Villa.

Cristiano Ronaldo was a worthy successor to the likes of George Best, Bryan Robson and Eric Cantona in the iconic No. 7 shirt.

Some used to take the mickey out of so-called 'Fergie time' but the club scored so many crucial late goals under Sir Alex it was no wonder he kept a close eye on the time.

a not terribly good cross from Orlygsson was almost turned into more than it deserved by Nigel Jemson, who screwed it wide. Jemson did the same a few minutes later when a great pass from Pearce gave him an opening he should have made more of but his shot only went across the goal.

With three minutes left on the clock, a poor punch by Leighton sent the ball straight up in the air rather than out of the danger zone, and Jemson got up highest to nod into an unguarded net for 1-1. Except it wasn't. A linesman's flag saved United and denied Forest a fully deserved equaliser. United were through, and on their way.

'FA Cup games are always a bit different,' said Robins, 'especially the third round. The players knew there was pressure on the manager because it was in all the newspapers, the knives were being sharpened.'

The knives were sheathed once more, at least temporarily. United had mixed fortunes in the rest of their cup run – they faced lower league opposition in every round until the final, but they were drawn away from home on every occasion. The fourth round saw a 1-0 win at Hereford United with Blackmore the scorer of the game's only goal; the fifth round a 3-2 win at Newcastle United as Brian McClair, Wallace and Robins got the goals. McClair was on the scoresheet again in the sixth round win at Sheffield United, and in the semi-final United avoided Liverpool to draw Oldham Athletic.

The match took place at Maine Road and for once United were firm favourites but it was Oldham who opened the scoring through their brilliant defender Earl Barrett after just three minutes. Robson equalised on the half-hour, Webb put United in front but Ian Marshall's volley sent the match into extra time. Wallace thought he had won it for United, only for Roger Palmer to equalise yet again. The replay also went to extra time as Andy Ritchie cancelled out McClair's opener, but Robins put United into the final. Oldham would go on to lose the League Cup Final to Forest.

In the final United faced not Liverpool but Crystal Palace, managed by one of United's favourite sons, Steve Coppell. Palace had defeated the Merseysiders 4-3 after extra time in a clash every bit as epic as United's against Oldham – Alan Pardew notching the 109th-minute winner at Villa Park.

Palace went ahead in the final thanks to an 18th-minute goal from Gary O'Reilly. Robson, inevitably, levelled the game up after 35 minutes and Hughes put United in front shortly after the hour-mark. But Palace were far from finished. A certain Ian Wright, on as a substitute, made it 2-2 and then two minutes into extra time put Palace 3-2 up before Hughes completed a double of his own in the 109th minute. The main story in the build-up to the replay, five days later, was the omission of goalkeeper Jim Leighton. 'It was an instinct, nothing else,' explained Ferguson. 'I smelled danger after the first Wembley game and I knew Jim had to be dropped.'

The match was a more mundane affair than the first meeting, decided by Martin's 59th-minute strike – Martin only scored three goals in his United career, and two of those were in the 1990 FA Cup-winning run which eased the pressure on Ferguson. It was a great goal, too, with Martin making a 50-metre run down the left and smashing the ball into the roof of the net with his right foot. 'I just saw this space and ran into it, and it paid off,' Martin said after.

Stuart Jones in *The Times* wrote, 'Lee Martin, who cost Manchester United nothing, last night became the most precious jewel in their £13m crown. Alex Ferguson's decision to replace Leighton with Les Sealey almost defied belief but ultimately proved to be justified.'

Blackmore, however, summed it up best when he said, 'The difference between winning and disaster that season was nothing at all.'

Or perhaps it was the performances of those two 21-year-old, Mark Robins and Lee Martin, who will forever be enshrined in United folklore as the vital goalscorers en route to United's first trophy under Ferguson.

v Manchester City 1-0

22

4 May 1991
Football League First Division
Old Trafford
Attendance: 45,286

MANCHESTER UNITED	MANCHESTER CITY
Nicky Walsh	Martyn Margetson
Denis Irwin	Andy Hill
Gary Pallister	Neil Pointon
Steve Bruce	Adrian Heath
Clayton Blackmore	Colin Hendry
Mike Phelan	Steve Redmond
Bryan Robson	David White
Neil Webb	Mark Brennan
Brian McClair	Niall Quinn
Mark Hughes	Alan Harper
Ryan Giggs	Ashley Ward
Manager: Alex Ferguson	*Manager:* Peter Reid

ONE happy side effect of United's epic matches against Oldham Athletic in the 1990 FA Cup semi-finals was the acquisition of Denis Irwin. The 25-year-old Irishman had already made over 150 appearances for Oldham when he signed for United for £625,000 in the summer of 1990. Irwin, described as a 'little diamond' and an 'unbelievable player' by Alex Ferguson, can lay claim to being the best pound-for-pound buy the United manager ever made, going on to make 529 appearances for the club in all competitions.

Irwin not only took care of business at the back with his incisiveness in the tackle, two good feet (it's easy to forget that he played on the right when at Oldham but switched to the left at United to accommodate Paul Parker), a good distributor of the ball once he had won it and solid enough in the air given his lack of inches. But what Ferguson really loved him for was his charges forward. A superb crosser of the ball, from both dead-ball situations and on the run, Irwin's pace made him hard to catch, in attack and defence.

But if Irwin was solid gold, a players' player, there was another figure about to burst on to the scene who would become a fans' favourite, the sort of player who excites everyone in football, not just his own team's supporters.

Ryan Giggs had signed as a trainee at United in the summer of 1990 and, on 29 November, his 17th birthday, he was offered his first professional contract.

Ryan Wilson, as he was then named, was first spotted by Dennis Schofield, a milkman and part-time scout who was watching a group of eight-year-olds play at Grosvenor Road Primary School. 'They had this boy who ran like a gazelle and was dynamite on the ball. I asked if his parents were at the game and was pointed in the direction of his mother. Even at that age I knew he was an absolute gem. His dad was a class act as a rugby league winger and young Ryan had his speed and balance to swerve past people as though they weren't there. I've been a coach and part-time scout for over half a century and he was the best prospect I'd ever seen,' said Schofield.

Ironically Schofield was a Manchester City fan and was desperate to get Giggs to sign for his team but while City waited, Ferguson pounced. 'He and Joe Brown, United's chief scout, were after Ryan. Sir Alex went straight to his house and got him.'

'Having the manager come round to your house – it tells you there's no messing, it's not casual, he really wants you,' recalls Giggs. 'It's very flattering when you're 14 and Alex Ferguson comes in for you. You tend to think "yeah".'

'I remember the first time I saw him,' says Ferguson. 'He was 13 and he floated across the ground like a cocker spaniel chasing a piece of silver paper in the wind.'

Although he was young, and quiet in the dressing room, Giggs remembers his early days with fondness. 'There was a winning mentality in that dressing room, I loved listening to the banter. You don't really get involved at 17, 18, but it was great. And when you were playing they'd look after you – especially if some defender tried to kick you.'

Not that Giggs was ever fazed by the physical stuff, he would just bounce back up and carry on tormenting whichever unlucky defender he was up against. Gary Pallister put it best when he said, 'When Ryan runs at players he gives them twisted blood. They don't want to be a defender any more.'

Giggs bypassed the reserves and made his first-team debut in March 1991 as a substitute in the league match against Everton, a 2-0 home defeat. Martin Keown, better known as an Arsenal defender but in those days with Everton, had heard from Bryan Robson how good Giggs was 'and when someone like Robson says someone is going to be outstanding, you take notice' emphasises Keown.

'We were 1-0 up thanks to a Mike Newell goal when Giggs came on for the injured Denis Irwin. He was wearing a number 14 shirt that was too baggy for him, his pace stood out straight away and although we won 2-0 with a goal from Dave Watson, we got a glimpse of why United would become so successful.'

Giggs came on earlier than expected that day, as Irwin had to go off after just 35 minutes. 'I can't remember too much of the game,' he said, 'but obviously it was a great opportunity for me. I'd been in the squad the week before but it was totally unexpected really.'

'His time had come,' said Ferguson, 'it was inevitable it was going to happen, it was just picking the moment to do that.'

Giggs's first start was the Manchester derby on 4 May 1991 at Old Trafford. It was a scrappy affair between teams destined to finish fifth and sixth in the table but a long, long way behind champions Arsenal. In keeping with the nature of the game, the only goal was a scrappy affair too. A good lay-off from

Mark Hughes midway inside the City half, a run and cross down the right from Brian McClair, a faint touch from Giggs, a huge deflection from City defender Colin Hendry and a United win.

'I didn't really score it,' protested Giggs. 'It was a goalmouth scramble. The ball hit me, then hit Colin Hendry and went in. It was an own goal but no defender wants to take responsibility for that and as it was my debut the boss told the press that I'd got it. I was 17, I wasn't going to argue.'

There would be more important and more spectacular goals in Giggs's United career, but as he says, at 17 he would take any that were on offer. And of course it was against Manchester City. What better way to endear yourself to the Stretford End?

v Barcelona 2-1

23

15 May 1991
European Cup Winners' Cup Final
Feijenoord Stadion, Rotterdam
Attendance: 45,000

MANCHESTER UNITED	BARCELONA
Les Sealey	Carles Busquets
Denis Irwin	Nando
Gary Pallister	Jose Ramon Alexanko
Steve Bruce	Ronald Koeman
Clayton Blackmore	Albert Ferrer
Mike Phelan	Jose Mari Bakero
Bryan Robson	Andoni Goikoetxea
Paul Ince	Eusebio
Brian McClair	Julio Salinas
Mark Hughes	Michael Laudrup
Lee Sharpe	Txiki Begiristain
Manager: Alex Ferguson	*Manager:* Johan Cruyff

FIVE years English clubs had been away from European competition, following the Heysel Stadium disaster, and there was a fear that they would have been left behind. Fortunately that proved not to be the case – although Aston Villa, the sole representatives in the UEFA Cup, lost in the second round it was only by 3-2 on aggregate to an Inter Milan side who went on to lift the trophy.

There was no representation in the European Cup as league champions Liverpool had to serve a one-year extra ban, so it was left to United to fly the flag in the European Cup Winners' Cup. And fly it they did, all the way to the final.

In truth United were blessed with a kind draw, facing first Hungarian club Pecsi Mecsek, who they beat 2-0 at home and 1-0 away, then Wrexham, beaten 3-0 at home and 2-0 away.

The quarter-finals looked like being a stumbling block when United could only draw 1-1 at home with Montpellier despite a first-minute goal from Brian McClair. But in the away leg they scored either side of half-time – the first in stoppage time at the end of the first half by Clayton Blackmore, the second a Steve Bruce penalty four minutes into the second – which knocked the stuffing out of the French side.

United again got lucky with their semi-final draw, taking on Legia Warsaw while Barcelona and Juventus were left to contest the other semi. Warsaw took the lead in the first leg in Poland but goals from McClair (who scored in every round up to the final) in the 38th minute, Mark Hughes (54) and Bruce (67) gave United a comfortable margin to take back to Manchester.

At Old Trafford a 28th-minute goal from Lee Sharpe put United even further ahead on aggregate and although Warsaw grabbed a 1-1 draw on the night, the United lead was never in real danger.

So to the Feijenoord Stadion in Rotterdam, and if the Dutch could be excused for wanting to make sure there were no incidents, the build-up to the final saw a party mood among the 15,000 Manchester United fans who had made the trip and refused to let repeated downpours dampen their spirits.

Alex Ferguson's carefully constructed gameplan was for United to take the game to Barcelona and put them under continual pressure, in particular their 24-year-old debutant goalkeeper Carles Busquets who was deputising for the suspended Andoni Zubizarreta. United had goalkeeping problems of their own as Les Sealey had cut his knee badly during the League Cup Final defeat by Sheffield Wednesday and his movement was restricted by the bandage he was forced to wear as a result.

The first half of the final produced little of note from either side in terms of clear-cut chances though a good interchange of passes between Gary Pallister and Bryan Robson created some space for McClair whose pass split the Spanish defence but before Sharpe could latch on to the ball the impressive Busquets had rushed out to gather it. The next chance fell to McClair himself but an awkward bounce led to him lifting it over the bar.

United had a half shout for a penalty when Hughes was sandwiched between two defenders and appeared to be nudged over by Nando, but Swedish referee Bo Karlsson wasn't interested. Barcelona were largely restricted to long-range shots and Sealey was well protected by his defence, though it must have been obvious that he was in a degree of discomfort.

The second half continued in the same vein, though Hughes chested down a McClair pass and tried to chip Busquets but couldn't keep his shot down. Then Busquets punched away a disappointing Bruce free kick, so when United got another one a few minutes later, Robson took over and floated a ball to the edge of the penalty area where Bruce got in a firm header. Busquets came for it before realising the trajectory of Robson's free kick was going to beat him, and he tried to get back in the goal, but too late. Bruce thought it was his goal all the way, but just before it crossed the line, Hughes ran in, and applied an unnecessary finishing touch – and then claimed the goal, like all good strikers. They had played 67 minutes.

Barcelona manager Johan Cruyff quickly made a change, replacing Jose Alexanco – who had conceded the free kick from which United had opened the scoring, albeit hardly in a threatening position – with Antonia Pinilla. Barcelona started to pressure a bit more but in the 74th minute a clearance by Robson of a Barca corner ended up in the path of Hughes. The Welshman had a little bit of space into which to run, but still a heck of a lot of work to do too.

But didn't he just do it well. Perfect control with his first touch, a Hughes trademark, even though it was with his weaker left foot, he then took it round the onrushing goalkeeper – who had come way out of his penalty area – but in doing so he was forced quite wide. 'A chance for another one here,' said the TV commentary, followed by 'maybe not now', but Hughes stayed in control and although at full stretch he rifled home a fierce drive.

Hughes ran to the United fans, spread his arms wide and waited to be engulfed by his team-mates. There was only a quarter of an hour left – surely the cup was won? Forced to attack, Barcelona started to show what a good team they really were. A couple of dangerous corners were cleared, then a lunging, two-footed challenge by Robson (which these days would almost certainly result in a red card) led to a Barcelona free kick. It was too far out for even the famed dead ball deadliness of Dutchman Ronald Koeman, though, surely. Sadly for United, it was not. From all of 30 yards, Koeman struck a curling right-footed shot which dipped just in front of Sealey's outstretched hand, and in.

There were still ten minutes to play, a period which Ferguson was later to describe as 'the worst ten minutes of my life'. Barcelona flew at United from all sides and when Michael Laudrup charged down the left wing and crossed for Pinilla to force the ball home they were back on level terms. And then it was ruled out for offside. The offence looked marginal, at best, but United didn't care, they had had a reprieve.

To make matters worse for a frustrated Barcelona, in the 84th minute Nando was sent off for a tackle on Hughes which would have won him a place in any self-respecting rugby side as he wrapped an arm round Hughes's neck and hung on, determined not the let the striker, who was on a hat-trick, get away. It was a perfect illustration of one of Hughes's biggest virtues, the ability to give his team-mates an 'out' ball and to hold play up either to kill some time or until someone else was in a better position.

If going down to ten men ended Barcelona's hopes, they had a funny way of showing it. Instead they mounted attack after attack, winning a corner which Sealey failed to punch properly clear and then he twice had to dive at the feet of onrushing attackers to keep his team in front.

Barcelona's best chance to get back on level terms came when Bruce was a little hesitant in clearing a long ball and as he slipped Pinilla took it to the byline. Sealey came out and did enough to slow the attack, but Pinilla retained possession, checked back on to his right foot and looked to lay off a pass to someone making a late run into the box. That someone was Laudrup, an attacking midfielder from Denmark with a knack for getting crucial goals for club and country. Luckily for United the ball just slightly stuck under Laudrup's feet and in digging it out he couldn't get quite as much pace on it as he would have wanted. Clayton Blackmore, well positioned on the goal line (Sealey's dash out to the feet of Pinilla had given the United defenders time to get back) was able to clear.

It was to be Barcelona's last chance, and a glorious night for United and for goalscorer Hughes who had spent a fruitless season with the Spanish club. 'I had no axe to grind with Barcelona,' he said. 'I had a chance when I was at the club and I didn't take it. That's history now. I said before the game that my ideal would be to score a special goal against them and it meant a lot to me. Some of the lads thought I had taken it too wide and were expecting me to have to cross but I could still see a lot of the goal and I was confident in what I was trying to do. I made good contact and in it went. It was a special night and the beginning of some great times at Old Trafford.'

Ferguson agreed with that point. 'It was a major step forward for the club, there's no doubt about that. The way Barcelona set up tactically made things very difficult for us in the first half – they played two wide players and no centre-forward and crowded the midfield. Once we got organised at half-time we were the better team. It was a fantastic night for us. With the support we have, we have got to win things. The supporters who were in Rotterdam were out of this world and the ones back home who have supported us all season will know that this win is for them.'

It was also a win for English clubs, to show that they could still compete at the highest level, a win for United, who otherwise would not have been in Europe again the following season, and a win for attacking football. Barcelona were perfectly capable of playing free-flowing football but for whatever reason Cruyff had not set them up to play that way from the start and they only began to show what they were capable of after the game was all but gone.

Not that United cared. 'It was a superb performance,' said chairman Martin Edwards. 'Barcelona crept back into the game towards the end but I felt on the night we were by far the better side. We played in the tradition of Manchester United.'

'Now we have to have more success,' concluded Ferguson. 'We have to use this as a platform to get more.'

v Notts County 2-0

24

17 August 1991
Football League First Division
Old Trafford
Attendance: 46,278

MANCHESTER UNITED	NOTTS COUNTY
Peter Schmeichel	Steve Cherry
Denis Irwin	Charlie Palmer
Steve Bruce	Alan Parris
Clayton Blackmore	Craig Short
Paul Parker	Dean Yates
Darren Ferguson	Don O'Riordan
Bryan Robson	Dean Thomas
Paul Ince	Phil Turner
Brian McClair	Dave Regis
Mark Hughes	Mark Draper
Andrei Kanchelskis	Tommy Johnson
Manager: Alex Ferguson	*Manager:* Neil Warnock

THE opening day of the 1991/92 season, and on the back of their European triumph three months earlier United had high hopes of mounting a serious and sustained challenge for the title. Certainly their fans expected it as there was a capacity crowd and thousands more of them locked outside the ground on a day which had started wet but turned into glorious sunshine.

Their visitors were newly-promoted Notts County, back in the top flight after a seven-year absence. County had benefited the previous season from the decision to increase the First Division to 22 teams, though having finished fourth they still had to fight their way through the play-offs, beating Middlesbrough over two legs in the semi-final then Brighton & Hove Albion 3-1 at Wembley.

Led by the feisty Neil Warnock, County were a decent side who fought hard to retain their place in the division that year, only to fall short by four points and go back down (alongside West Ham United and Luton Town). They comprised mostly journeymen in their 20s plus a goalscorer par excellence in 19-year-old Tommy Johnson.

They battled well and for much of the first half hour gave as good as they got. Then six minutes before half-time a United free kick was misheaded by Dave Regis and fell to Mark Hughes. Hughes stuck out a leg, 1-0.

Just approaching the hour mark a corner was not properly cleared and Bryan Robson volleyed home spectacularly from 20 yards. From then on, United had a measure of control, dealing comfortably with Steve Cherry's long clearances and mounting several more dangerous-looking attacks of their own.

It finished 2-0 which was probably a fair reflection of the way the match had gone, though it might have been different had Johnson been able to make more of an early second-half chance when he was through on goal. He was unlucky that the ball bobbled at the crucial moment allowing the United goalkeeper to clear, and United debutant Peter Schmeichel had an otherwise largely untroubled first afternoon.

The giant Dane had come to the attention of United for his performances for Brondby, with whom he had won the domestic league in 1987/88, and for Denmark at Euro 88. United were in the market for a goalkeeper as Les Sealey was in his mid-30s and having only been offered a one-year deal he turned it down in favour of a transfer to Aston Villa. He did later return for another spell at United as Schmeichel's understudy but only played twice.

Meanwhile, youth team keeper Mark Bosnich was deemed surplus to requirements – he did return to United as first-choice keeper when Schmeichel left, after a successful career with Aston Villa, but it was not a happy move for player or club. Schmeichel, however, was the real deal and at £505,000 quite possibly the best pound-for-pound buy that Alex Ferguson ever made.

A giant of a man, Schmeichel stood 6ft 4in and seemed to fill the goal not just physically but with his very presence. He would stride out on to the pitch, kick each goal post as part of his warm-up routine then stand there and dare opposing strikers to try to beat him. His hands were like shovels, once memorably described by that excellent journalist Jim White as looking like 'he was permanently wearing a pair of foam pointy-finger hands'.

'I was lucky in that I was always a little bigger than everyone else,' confessed Schmeichel, 'and I could always develop that physical side of the game, the one that involves coming for crosses and intimidating opposition players.'

One of the biggest weapons in a substantial armoury was his famous star jump – Schmeichel would spread himself and spread his arms and legs wide and challenge the opposing forward to get the ball past him. Schmeichel says the technique developed from his days playing handball when he was younger, where the goalkeeper has to try anything and everything to get some part of his body to block the ball from going in the goal.

'Everyone talks about Peter's size but he was so quick,' said goalkeeping coach Eric Steele. 'People didn't realise that but all of a sudden, bang, he'd be out of the goal, and on top of you with that huge frame of his.'

'Being a goalkeeper is a completely different sport from being an outfield player,' says Schmeichel. 'It's not about skills, it's not about how you move your feet with the ball. it's about agility, balance, being brave, being strong. There are lots of things you have to do as a goalkeeper, but above all you've got to have control of your body. Every movement has to be measured. You have to be spot on all the time. It you're not, it's a goal.'

And of course being a United goalkeeper brings special pressures all of its own – everyone wants to score against United, every team wants to beat United so any mistakes you make are magnified ten-fold, and covered ad nauseam. Just ask Jim Leighton whose game never recovered from being dropped for the 1990 FA Cup Final replay.

'I always saw the penalty box as my territory,' Schmeichel grins. 'Nobody would get anything easy in there. It was a pride thing. Every time I conceded a goal I was angry. I would always take it very personally and that's the attitude which made me so focused when I was playing. I was always seen as aggressive but I was just focused. I always felt, even if the ball was in the other box for 20 minutes that I was somehow right in the middle of the action. That was my way of dealing with the game. Goalkeeping is a lonely job and mentally you have to be strong.'

Along with his technical ability and his forceful personality, Schmeichel had one other quality which was a crucial element in the way United liked to play – he could throw the ball about half the length of the pitch. In this way he was not only United's last line of defence but often their first line of attack. In my mind's eye I can still see him dominating his area, snuffing out a goal threat then in almost the same motion setting an attack going by throwing the ball out for one of United's famed wingers to go haring down the touchline.

'I don't believe a better goalkeeper has played the game,' said Ferguson of Schmeichel. 'He is a giant figure in the history of Manchester United.'

One of those wingers at that time was Andrei Kanchelskis, a £650,000 buy from Shakhtar Donetsk at the end of March 1991. The Ukrainian made only one league appearance before the end of the 1990/91 season, in the 3-0 defeat by Crystal Palace on 11 May, but for the next four seasons he was to be a regular part of the United team, and he too started the first match of 1991/92. Kanchelskis was dynamite: quick, skilful and powerful, he profited more than most from Schmeichel's style of goalkeeping.

Neither Kanchelskis nor Ryan Giggs had been part of the 1991 European Cup Winners' Cup Final squad, one signing and one breaking through just too late for serious consideration. By the start of the 1991/92 season, however, they were ready – together with Lee Sharpe – to offer Ferguson the width and pace for which he had long been looking.

Kanchelskis played 148 games for United, scoring 48 goals, and many fans were disappointed that he didn't stay longer, but he fell out with his manager and declared that he had to leave.

Like many before, and after, him, Kanchelskis later admitted he had made a mistake, 'I regret the day I left United. I must have been a fool. They are a truly great club. The players were marvellous to me and the fans treated me and my family with love and respect.'

There was a third new man in the United line-up for the game against Notts County, and that was Paul Parker. A right-back who had made his name first at Fulham and then at Queens Park Rangers, Parker joined in the nick of time for that start of the season, signing on 8 August for £1.7m.

The worthy Viv Anderson had been allowed to leave for Sheffield Wednesday on a free transfer in January 1991 and Parker's arrival meant a switch to left-back for Denis Irwin. Ferguson now had the pace on both flanks in defence as well as in attack. 'Paul wasn't the footballer that Lee Martin was,' recalls Eric Harrison, 'but he was lightning quick, and a tough little so-and-so to boot.'

Ferguson said of Parker's time at United, 'He was one of those players you never really noticed because he was so efficient and good at his job. We didn't lose too many matches when Paul was playing.'

Schmeichel himself, who was never averse to shouting at his defenders and even swearing at them in his strange mixture of Danish and Mancunian accents, had praise for Parker's role in securing the right flank. 'Just nothing is getting through from his side of the field,' the keeper said.

The team was beginning to take shape, but United's defence of their Cup Winners' Cup was hamstrung by the introduction of a new rule regarding the number of foreigners a team could field in European competition. It was a rule made with the best of intentions, but with no concession to 'Britishness' it meant that Irish, Scottish and Welsh players were considered foreigners. United's squad of 23 included only 14 Englishmen, of which two were reserve goalkeepers, but seven more were Scottish, Welsh, Northern Irish and the Republic of Ireland's Irwin. The immediate upshot of the ruling was that Alex Ferguson instructed his scouts to concentrate on finding him English players. In the meantime Ferguson was faced with an almost impossible balancing act and while he could put out a team that despatched the Greek side Athinaikos handily enough, it was a different matter facing the accomplished Spanish side Atletico Madrid who boasted Paulo Futre and Bernd Schuster among their ranks. Two late goals in the Vicente Calderon Stadium made life very difficult for United.

For the second leg, Ferguson took the pragmatic view that since his team needed to go on all-out attack to try to recover a three-goal deficit, he would put Gary Walsh in goal in place of Peter Schmeichel and free up an additional outfield spot, allowing Giggs to play. Although Mark Hughes's fourth-minute strike at Old Trafford a fortnight later did give them brief hope of overturning the 3-0 deficit, they could make no further headway. When Schuster equalised on the night, midway through the second half, the game really was up.

United did pick up another piece of European silverware, however. The European Super Cup, traditionally played between the winners of the previous season's European Cup and Cup Winners' Cup, featured United against Red Star Belgrade. Normally played over two legs, the outbreak of civil unrest in Yugoslavia made such a prospect unthinkable so United gained the unexpected bonus of a single match, played at Old Trafford. That only 22,110 bothered to turn out to see it is perhaps a fair indication of the perceived value of the trophy, but those who were there saw a 1-0 win for United which was just about deserved.

A first-half penalty from Steve Bruce was well saved but after Clayton Blackmore had cleared a shot off the line United gradually took control and when a Neil Webb effort crashed back off the post, Brian McClair was the first there to turn the loose ball in. It was Ferguson's second triumph in the 'competition' as his Aberdeen side had won it in 1983, but in the Ferguson and United trophy cabinet it was destined to become of minor interest only.

v Nottingham Forest 1-0

25

12 April 1992
League Cup Final
Wembley
Attendance: 76,810

MANCHESTER UNITED	NOTTINGHAM FOREST
Peter Schmeichel	Andy Marriott
Denis Irwin	Gary Charles
Steve Bruce	Brett Williams
Gary Pallister	Des Walker
Paul Parker	Darren Wassall
Mike Phelan	Roy Keane
Andrei Kanchelskis	Gary Crosby
Paul Ince	Scott Gemmill
Brian McClair	Nigel Clough
Mark Hughes	Teddy Sheringham
Ryan Giggs	Kingsley Black
Manager: Alex Ferguson	*Manager:* Brian Clough

I N their long and illustrious history, United have never given that much consideration to the League Cup. By the time they won it for the first time they already had seven league titles, seven FA Cups and three European trophies to their name.

But in 1991 they had got agonisingly close to winning the League Cup as well as the European Cup Winners' Cup. They tore through the competition, beating three of the five sides who finished above them in the league. Having beaten Halifax Town 5-2 on aggregate in the second round they had comfortably got past Liverpool at Old Trafford in the third, a Steve Bruce penalty in the 37th minute being followed just a minute later by a Mark Hughes strike. When Lee Sharpe extended the lead to 3-0 in the 81st minute, United had won and the 83rd-minute goal from Ray Houghton was little more than a consolation.

The fourth round witnessed one of the most remarkable matches of the season as United, who had already lost a fractious league game at home to Arsenal, travelled to Highbury and won 6-2. Clayton Blackmore gave United a dream start, striking a low shot home. Next Hughes was given the freedom of the penalty area to put United 2-0 up with virtually the last kick of the first half. But not quite, there was still time for Lee Sharpe to charge through and hit a wonder goal with his right foot, high into the top corner of the net.

Arsenal did pull two goals back in the second half but rather than panicking United just went back on the attack. Denis Irwin and Hughes combined well down the right and Sharpe headed United 4-2 in front. Sharpe completed his hat-trick from a great through-ball by Danny Wallace and slotted another right-footed goal. Wallace got the last goal, and fully deserved it was for his all-round performance.

The quarter-finals pitched United against Southampton and a hard-fought 1-1 draw in the first match meant a replay, which United won by 3-1 thanks to a Hughes hat-trick. In the semi-finals against Leeds United, a 2-1 victory in the first leg at Old Trafford – thanks to goals from Brian McClair and Sharpe – left the tie still in the balance. But a great performance at Elland Road where Sharpe, again, got the only goal of the game, saw them safely through to Wembley.

Possibly United took it too easily after so many fine victories, but in the final against a Ron Atkinson-managed Sheffield Wednesday, then in the Second Division (although they won promotion in the league also), they couldn't quite find their 'A' game. Wednesday won the trophy through a 37th-minute goal from their Republic of Ireland international midfielder John Sheridan.

United began the 1992 League Cup campaign looking determined to right that wrong, despatching Cambridge United 4-1 on aggregate in the second round, Portsmouth 3-1 in the third and Oldham Athletic 2-0 in the fourth. Then came the crunch tie, away to Leeds. United produced one of their best performances of the season, winning 3-1 with goals from Blackmore, Ryan Giggs and Andrei Kanchelskis.

Another two-legged semi-final, against Middlesbrough, was a taut affair especially after a 0-0 draw in the first leg. At Old Trafford on a pitch that looked particularly boggy in the central areas, United sensibly made use of the flanks and some quick passing on the half-hour set Sharpe up for the opening goal. Middlesbrough's own winger, Stuart Ripley, tried his hardest to bring his team back into things, and from one of his runs down the left he created just enough room for himself to get the ball in to Middlesbrough's top goalscorer Bernie Slaven who tied things up at 1-1.

Gary Pallister than had to clear off the line before the game went into extra time. Middlesbrough had a great chance to take the lead but a fine Peter Schmeichel save denied Willie Falconer. Giggs finally settled the tie in the second period of extra time when a Bryan Robson header found him at the right-hand post and he slammed into the far side of the goal with his trusty left foot.

So to the final and a match against a Nottingham Forest side who finished eighth in the league but recorded a home and away double over United. At least that ruled out any possibility of complacency and United set about their task with some relish.

Forest won the toss to choose their home strip so United kicked off wearing their change kit of the day – white shorts with a blue pattern, blue shorts and blue socks. A strange choice on the part of Adidas (and possibly a factor in the club switching their shirt deal to Umbro the following year), more in keeping with the other lot down the road. For that reason it was never one of the club's more popular away designs, though the Pride of Manchester website says it did spawn a wonderful bootleg version with the wallpaper design pattern rearranged to read 'F*** off Leeds'.

An early cup final bonus for United was the absence of Forest's England defender Stuart Pearce, who missed several weeks because of a knee injury. He was replaced by his understudy, Brett Williams. Roy Keane and Teddy Sheringham, however, did play – for Forest.

United created the first half-chance through a neat interchange between Phelan and Giggs. No disrespect for Phelan's admirable midfield qualities is intended when I say that United fans might have preferred Giggs to be on the end of the move – it ended in a comfortable save for Forest keeper Andy Marriott (greeted by Forest fans with a rendition of 'Swing Low, Sweet Marriott').

Giggs and Irwin continued to work the left flank before switching play for Kanchelskis to win the first corner of the game on the other side of the pitch. Giggs hit it just too long for Hughes to get his head on it.

United continued to play most of the football in the opening period, and by double-teaming on the Forest dangermen – a favourite tactic of Ferguson's, made possible by having so many players with pace in the United squad – ensured that any hint of a threat would be snuffed out before it materialised. The only opening they had was when Keane burst through the middle and hit a low shot which Schmeichel gathered comfortably enough.

Then Hughes got to the byline and pulled it back for Brian McClair to slot the opening goal, but it was disallowed for a Hughes tug on the covering defender. Forest had a period of possession, which included a couple of corners, but without creating a genuine opportunity.

On 14 minutes a patient passing move in midfield sent a ball in to McClair, who had his back to goal. A swift lay-off to Giggs and a quick turn and McClair was in position to take the return pass. Giggs shaped as if to shoot but instead delivered a perfectly weighted pass into McClair's feet. The Scotsman took it in his stride and slotted it left-footed past Marriott, to the keeper's left.

The goal settled United and they started to knock the ball around confidently. Des Walker, such a good defender who made over 600 appearances in the Football League and Premier League (not to mention a season in Serie A with Sampdoria and 59 England caps), kept United at bay defensively but his side was unable to create much going forward. Walker was harshly penalised for a foul on the edge of the area, but United failed to test Marriott from the ensuing free kick.

Forest were further disrupted when they lost their other first-choice full-back; Gary Charles was only just back from a hamstring injury and was struggling, particularly to keep pace with Giggs wide on the left. He was replaced by Brian Laws, himself an accomplished defender who made over 100 league appearances for three different clubs (Burnley, Middlesbrough and Forest).

Although Forest didn't suffer in defence, and Williams did a fine job in ensuring that they didn't miss Pearce, they were still failing to carve out much in the way of scoring chances. United seemed happy to let Forest have the ball in midfield, relying on the pace of Irwin and Paul Parker to stop Forest making progress down the flanks. One quick break involving first McClair down the right then Kanchelskis cutting in and laying it off to Hughes was broken up only by a good block on the edge of the Forest area.

Getting frustrated, Forest started to give away a lot of fouls in the middle of the pitch, but United were unable to make anything of them and when they did get a decent ball into the Forest area there was Walker to make a crucial challenge or block.

United kicked off the second half, playing left to right, and hoping to make use of the big Wembley pitch because Forest had played three league matches in the ten days before their Wembley date (in fact they were destined to play a total of nine matches, including the League Cup Final, in April). United had only played one in that same period so were relying on having fresher legs as the game wore on.

Both teams got the ball into the opposition's penalty area early in the second half, with a bit of pinball resulting but nothing which could accurately be called a chance. Hughes and McClair almost conjured something between them on the right-hand side but the eventual corner from Giggs came to nothing.

Next McClair made a sharp break, but Kanchelskis, not having one of his best games, lost the ball for a Forest throw. Nor could he make anything of a delightful McClair flick into space, though from the resulting corner Paul Ince had a snap shot which was turned behind for another corner. Then a jinking run from Giggs took him past two defenders and Ince got in a goalbound shot which was blocked by Darren Wassall for another corner.

Into the last half hour and the game continued to be played out mostly in the middle of the pitch, with the occasional foray by either side down the flanks. Keane and Walker were doing a good job in breaking up United moves, but Forest had few genuine chances to get back into the match. Brian Clough and Pearce looked on anxiously from the dugout as their team, despite plenty of possession, produced little of note in the final third.

A real chance came United's way as the match moved into its final quarter, as Marriott came a long way for a high ball and lost it in a challenge with Hughes. Hughes brought it down and set McClair up for a shot which Laws blocked on the goal line. It was a superb effort from Laws to keep his side in the match, but still they couldn't produce anything to threaten Schmeichel's goal.

Sharpe came on for Kanchelskis for the last 15 minutes – hardly a respite for Forest's busy full-backs. Long throws, quickly taken, seemed to be Forest's most dangerous weapon, and they rarely disconcerted Schmeichel. A ball in along the ground from Sheringham at least obliged Schmeichel to come off his line to make a save, but for all their huffing and puffing Forest had little to show for it. A Nigel Clough curler again made Schmeichel move sharply to his left but he had it covered as it hit the side netting.

Not then, a cup final to live long in the memory, but United didn't care – they had won the first League Cup in their history.

26

v Crystal Palace 3-2

15 May 1992
FA Youth Cup Final second leg
Old Trafford
Attendance: 14,681

MANCHESTER UNITED	CRYSTAL PALACE
Kevin Pilkington	Jimmy Glass
John O'Kane	Paul Sparrow
George Switzer	Scott Cutler
Chris Casper	Mark Holman
Gary Neville	Russell Edwards
David Beckham	Andy McPherson
Nicky Butt	Mark Hawthorne
Simon Davies	Simon Rollison
Colin McKee	Stuart McCall
Ryan Giggs	George Ndah
Ben Thornley	Tim Clark
Manager: Eric Harrison	*Manager:* Stuart Scott

IT isn't often that an FA Youth Cup Final impacts on to the public consciousness. But then again it isn't often that an FA Youth Cup Final features five players on one team who who go on to represent their countries at full international level (plus two more who came on as substitutes). Nor is it often that they go on to form the nucleus of a league championship-winning side at the same club where they grew up. But such was the case with the 1992 Manchester United FA Youth Cup winners, who have become so legendary that they have even had a documentary dedicated to them – *The Class of 92*.

United of course had always been great believers in a youth policy, from Sir Matt Busby's Babes onwards. Alex Ferguson took up that mantle from the day he walked into Old Trafford, instructing Eric Harrison – the youth team coach appointed by Ron Atkinson – to bring more promising youngsters through the youth system. Harrison pointed to a few successes he had had, not least Norman Whiteside, but Ferguson argued that it was not enough. 'Right, we'll do a deal,' said Harrison. 'You get me better-quality players and I'll get you more youngsters in the first team.' 'Done!' replied Ferguson. And the seeds of United's future were sown right there and then.

Ferguson kept his end of the bargain, revamping the club's scouting network and increasing it in number and holding regular meetings with scouts to motivate them. Les Kershaw was brought in to head up the scouting system, while former players Nobby Stiles and Brian Kidd were employed as youth team coaches. Harrison, though, did much more than simply hold up his end of the bargain. He established a veritable production line of gilded youth which continues to this day.

As a young professional, Harrison had been at Hartlepool when Brian Clough was first cutting his managerial teeth and learnt from the master of player psychology. 'If I have had an influence, it's a mental one,' says Harrison in his autobiography, *The View From The Dugout.* 'I used to sit young players down and have one-to-ones with them. Probably the biggest impact I've had is by telling them individually how good they are, but I'd have to be right because it is soul-destroying for kids if I was wrong. I don't think you had to be too clever to know that the likes of David Beckham was going to play in the first team but it was a massive, massive motivating factor for them and I think it's a role that should not be underestimated.'

In the two-legged final against Crystal Palace, the first leg was held at Selhurst Park on 14 April in front of 7,825 and United were quickly into their stride. Nicky Butt scored the first goal after 17 minutes and David Beckham made it 2-0 on the half-hour. That was it on the scoring front until a flurry of activity towards the end of the match. First substitute Stuart McCall reduced the arrears in the 86th minute, only to see Butt restore United's two-goal advantage three minutes later.

McCall started the second leg – which took place a month later – in place of Canadian international-to-be Niall Thompson (who he had replaced in the first game). McCall became the only player to score in both legs of the final when he scored in the 62nd minute to level the second leg at 2-2. Earlier Andrew McPherson's first-minute header from a Scott Cutler corner had given Palace a sniff of overturning the two-goal deficit from the first leg but on the half-hour Ben Thornley ran down the left and cut in; just as everyone was looking for the cross, Thornley decided to go it alone and slotted home a fine right-footed strike.

In the 50th minute the lesser-known George Switzer, a left-back, made a fine run down the left and a one-two with Simon Davies took him into the penalty area for a left-footed strike. Jimmy Glass got down to make an excellent save but the ball rebounded kindly to Davies who knocked it home. Palace still weren't done and McCall got the aforementioned equaliser after George Ndah had made a nuisance of himself on the edge of the United box.

Butt almost put United back in front with a spectacular overhead kick. Yes, that's right, Nicky Butt, with a perfectly executed overhead which produced an excellent tip over from Glass. But before the end, United made sure of victory on the night when a beautiful reverse pass from Thornley put Ryan Giggs away down the left and he put over a cross which had 'goal' written all over it. Colin McKee duly obliged with a simple glanced header that gave Glass no chance.

Glass, incidentally, who had a good game that night, many years later carved out his own little bit of footballing history. He was on loan to Carlisle United in 1999 (from Swindon Town) and on 8 May Carlisle had to beat Plymouth Argyle to retain their place in the Football League. With just ten seconds remaining and the scoreline locked at 1-1, Glass came up for a corner and when

Scott Dobie's goalbound header was parried out, there was Glass to volley the ball home. It was literally the last kick of the game.

As for United's youngsters, they celebrated with the cup, but the thoughts of most of their players that day were already on higher things. 'They were so gifted technically and they had so much desire and determination,' says Harrison. 'I had to teach them quite a lot about team play… they've got to be prepared properly if it's not to be a shock to them when they play in the first team.'

There are a few legends around that United youth team of 1992 – as you can see from the teams neither Paul Scholes nor Phil Neville appeared, though they did play the following year when United lost to Leeds United in the final.

Robbie Savage started the first leg but was dropped to the bench for the second, in favour of Giggs, though he did come on later in place of Davies. Savage signed a professional contract with United but never made a first-team appearance for the club, though he had a successful career elsewhere with Leicester City and Derby County in particular, making well over 500 Football League and Premier League appearances, and also won 39 caps for Wales.

The other substitute for United was Keith Gillespie who couldn't quite force his way past Andrei Kanchelskis into the first team. Gillespie played nine times, even scoring on his debut in an FA Cup third round tie against Bury on 5 January 1993, and two years later was the makeweight in the deal which brought Andrew Cole to United from Newcastle United. Gillespie later admitted to being addicted to gambling and was declared bankrupt in 2010, though he did manage an impressive 86 international caps for Northern Ireland.

Of the players who didn't manage to kick on to a successful career with United, the reasons were many and varied. Switzer, the speedy and skilful left-back, was offered a professional contract but Ferguson changed his mind, feeling Switzer was a little too small for top-flight football. Davies played 20 first-team games for United but could never quite force his way past Giggs or Lee Sharpe – no disgrace in that. The only goal Davies scored for the United first team was a memorable one – it was the opener in a 4-0 rout of Galatasaray on 7 December 1994. McKee, who scored the final goal of the match, which enabled United to win both legs, was another who was offered a contract in the wake of the win, but after making a solitary appearance for the first team he decamped to his native Scotland where he played for Kilmarnock.

The other two names which stand out from that team were Chris Casper and Ben Thornley. Casper was the organiser at the back and though he took some time to break through into the senior ranks, his illustrious junior career took in captaining the England youth team with which he won the European Championship in 1993 and playing for the England under-21 side in the Toulon tournament in 1996. Casper moved to Reading in 1998 but the following season – still aged just 24 – he suffered from a double leg fracture during a game against Cardiff. Casper later received undisclosed damages in an out-of-court settlement, but he never played professional football again.

Thornley was also to suffer serious injury. Always prone to problems, Thornley played nine times for the United first team but never got a lengthy run. Then in the spring of 1994 he suffered a severe knee ligament injury during a reserve match against Blackburn Rovers. It kept him out for over a year and he never really re-established himself.

At the launch of *The Class Of 92*, Gary Neville said of Thornley, 'He was a very quick winger, two-footed, scored goals and was an intelligent player. In fact, he was probably our best player. If you think about David Beckham or Paul Scholes at that age, Ben was above them in terms of the level he was playing at between the ages of 16 and 18. But he got that terrible injury. It was a real shame, it's something I think about even when I see him now.'

'It was a long time to miss,' agrees Thornley, who does hospitality work at Old Trafford and is on MUTV radio. 'Not that there's ever a right time for such an injury but that one really did come at the wrong time because the manager was starting to integrate us all into the first team. It would have been nice to know if I'd been able to hold my own in the Premier League on a more sustained basis.'

Thornley did make a comeback of sorts but his searing pace had gone. And so had his change of pace. 'The injury was a killer, I still have a letter from [Alex Ferguson] saying how sorry he was that the injury had happened. Such is life.'

In more recent times the youth academy flourished under the guidance of Rene Meulensteen, who Kershaw once described as 'the best coach in the world for kids'. 'We want players who can do the unpredictable,' the Dutchman said.

The United way accepts that children are going to be competitive and want to win, that is taken as read. What needs developing are their skills, so United abandoned the traditional eight-a-side matches in favour of smaller, four-a-side games which allow the youngsters to concentrate on improving their technique. It is also about getting the youngsters ready for first-team football, and United have always believed the best way to do that is to have the same system throughout the club. It is thought that David Moyes' lack of interest in youth team development may have counted against him when first-team results weren't going his way.

Whatever the truth of that, McClair, Butt, Scholes and Casper are all involved in some capacity at youth team level, as is Paul McGuinness, son of Wilf. And United continue to prioritise youth development – they have won the FA Youth Cup on three occasions since the boys of 1992 (in 1995, 2003 and 2011), and are the most successful team in the history of the competition by some margin having won ten titles to second-placed Arsenal's seven. But until a group of players comes along who all break into – and stay – in the first team, the Class of 92 will have a special place in our hearts.

v Manchester City **2-1**

27

6 December 1992
Premier League
Old Trafford
Attendance: 35,408

MANCHESTER UNITED	MANCHESTER CITY
Peter Schmeichel	Tony Coton
Denis Irwin	Ian Brightwell
Steve Bruce	Terry Phelan
Gary Pallister	Steve McMahon
Paul Parker	Keith Curle
Bryan Robson	Andy Hill
Lee Sharpe	David White
Paul Ince	Mike Sheron
Brian McClair	Niall Quinn
Mark Hughes	Fitzroy Simpson
Ryan Giggs	Rick Holden
Manager: Alex Ferguson	*Manager:* Peter Reid

ALTHOUGH United were delighted to win the 1992 League Cup and take their trophy tally to three in three years, the whole club knew that the Holy Grail was the league title. That made the 1991/92 campaign all the harder to take. Under previous managers a runners-up spot would have been acceptable, even praiseworthy, but not under Alex Ferguson. And if the fans were happy enough with another trophy, the players themselves felt it had been an opportunity wasted.

'They say the best team always wins the league, but we gave the title to Leeds,' said Paul Parker. 'We played fantastic football for most of the season, but dropped off in the last few weeks. Players and managers never like admitting it, but it was due to nerves. Everyone was getting anxious because it was so long since United had won the title and it got to us.'

Out of nowhere, goalscoring became a problem – having scored 40 in their first 20 matches, United managed only 17 from the next 17. 'Even before Easter we felt it slipping away from us,' confessed Clayton Blackmore. 'We weren't getting enough goals.' Leeds, of all teams, were the beneficiaries of United's wobble.

That autumn, Leeds manager Howard Wilkinson asked his chairman, Bill Fotherby, to enquire of United whether Denis Irwin might be for sale as their regular right-back in the championship-winning season, Mel Sterland, had picked up a serious-looking injury. Martin Edwards said there was no chance that they would sell Irwin to their biggest rivals, but made a casual enquiry about the possible availability of Eric Cantona. Cantona had been recommended to Leeds by no less a figure than Michel Platini, but had never quite worked out.

'Eric liked to play to the crowd,' said Fotherby. 'That wasn't Howard's way at all, he wanted his players to be disciplined and adhere to a certain pattern whereas Alex gave him a free role and probably wasn't quite as strict with him.'

With an additional payment to Nimes about to be triggered, Leeds were happy to let Cantona go. The £1.2m fee represented a profit of £300,000 for Leeds, who were surprisingly hard-up considering they had just won the league title. United were happy to have him. 'Our football had become stereotyped,' says Parker. 'Sides doubled up on Sparky [Mark Hughes], Giggsy and Lee Sharpe and we didn't have another dimension to our game. Until Eric came.'

Ferguson had looked into, and enquired about, other forwards including Mick Harford, David Hirst and, most famously, Alan Shearer. Cantona was a quite different player from any of those, not being in any way a traditional centre-forward, but he had other qualities which Ferguson saw would mesh well with his team. 'He was terrific for the likes of me, Sharpey and Andrei Kanchelskis,' recalls Giggs, 'because one of his best skills was being in that central position and being able to hit the angled pass to play the winger in. You could make runs knowing he'd find you.'

Cantona joined at the perfect moment – United were off to Portugal for a week for a warm-weather break which included a friendly against Benfica to celebrate Eusebio's 50th birthday. It meant that Cantona could get to know his team-mates on and off the pitch away from the hullabaloo that accompanies United whenever they sign a new player. When they returned, Cantona was omitted from the first game back – an excellent 1-0 win at Highbury over Arsenal – and then named as substitute for the next match, an Old Trafford derby against City.

Cantona made his first appearance for United as a second-half substitute for Giggs against City. The Manchester derby didn't have quite the importance in the 1990s as it does today because City were rarely in contention; although United started the day just two points ahead, City were in tenth position and had risen only to ninth by the end of the season. They were also knocked out of both the League and FA Cups by Spurs, who also did the league double over them, and their squad was one of honest grafters rather than any real quality.

That said, they did have Steve McMahon and, sometimes, player-manager Peter Reid in midfield, while established players such as Garry Flitcroft and Paul Lake also notched up over 100 appearances for the club and Niall Quinn's goalscoring tally of around one in three was on the mark that distinguishes top strikers from the also-rans.

When Cantona ran on, to be greeted, inevitably, by a strong challenge from McMahon, United were already one up. Mark Hughes had nodded a Robson free kick into the area and when Steve Bruce laid it off for Paul Ince, the midfielder struck an unstoppable shot just inside the post. On a cold and wet day, United continued to weave pretty patterns and one Irwin cross required the fingertips of City keeper Tony Coton to edge it out of the danger area, while Giggs tormented the City defence with every twist and turn.

Cantona actually had a quiet 45 minutes – and there weren't to be too many occasions in his United career when we could say that. A few neat touches, a couple of good crosses (one of which Hughes probably should have done better with) and he was gone. 'He'll be glad to get that one over with,' was Ferguson's succinct appraisal afterwards.

That is not to say the game itself was quiet, however. Far from it. In the 73rd minute Hughes, who had looked energised by the signing of Cantona, looked to have settled the 117th Manchester derby when he controlled the ball on his chest about 25 yards out, bounced it off City defender Keith Curle and hammered a dipping, swerving shot past Coton then stood, arms spread wide as the rain bucketed down, milking the applause of the Stretford End.

Almost from the kick-off though, Rick Holden got clear and crossed for Quinn to stab the ball home. Suddenly City, who had been largely outplayed and out fought, believed they could get something out of the game and poured forward only for Schmeichel to make a fine double save from Andy Hill and David White to keep United in front and give them the three points.

Cantona was by no means certain to be a hit at Old Trafford, but almost immediately his impact could be felt. Yes, he was talented, that much was known already. What wasn't was his prodigious workrate and his willingness to train. By a happy coincidence Eric arrived at Old Trafford at a time when a crop of extremely talented young players were on the verge of breaking through into the first team, and they watched him and learnt from him.

The Class of 92 were the first to admit that they took their cue from Cantona, so when he stayed behind to do some extra shooting practice, or returned in the afternoon to do some drills, so did they. It became part of the culture at United, and the club was to feel the benefit as much as the players themselves.

David Meek, a former United correspondent for the *Manchester Evening News* and knowledgeable about all things Red Devils, said, 'Anyone watching a youth team game before and after the arrival of Cantona could see the change. The young players had talent but Cantona helped to bring out vision and style.' Ferguson was later to utter very similar sentiments, 'He was the perfect professional, he came at the right time and he gave us vision that we maybe lacked in terms of winning the championship. He was the final piece in the jigsaw who gave us composure at important times.'

Parker said simply that United were a good side that didn't have experience of winning 'until Eric'.

Cantona was also a scorer of important goals, and Clayton Blackmore says that he brought the best out of Hughes. Far from being anxious that he would lose his first-team place, Hughes was inspired by Cantona and even started developing aspects of his game due to the fact he was now playing alongside a fellow striker who could read what he was going to do. 'Mark's crossfield passes sometimes lacked control, so unless they went to feet they would go out of play. When Eric hit those balls, the weight of his pass was perfect and Mark started learning this from Eric.'

'Eric changed the way we viewed the game,' agrees Hughes. 'You saw Eric do things and you thought to yourself, "Oh I'll try that." You can't expect to be as good at it as Eric is, but I think he just freed us all up a little.'

'He's the player to light up our stadium,' said Ferguson on completing the signing. It was neither the first nor last time that Ferguson took what others might have thought was a gamble, but his willingness to take risks and to trust his instincts has always been one of his greatest gifts as a manager. Ferguson described Cantona as the 'can opener', but many thought it might be no more than a can of worms, and even Ferguson had a few second thoughts.

But he knew something had to be done to shake United out of the lethargy which seemed to have inflicted them in the wake of their surrendering the title the previous season, and he believed Cantona was it. 'Has there ever been a player more made for Manchester United?' he once asked rhetorically. 'Some players, even those with established reputations are cowed and broken by the size of expectations here. Not Eric. He swaggered in, stuck his chest out and surveyed everything as if to say, "I'm Cantona. Are you big enough for me?" He was born to play for United.'

The training aspect is one that is often overlooked. Wilkinson, the Leeds manager who had been happy to let Cantona go to his team's greatest rivals, admitted, 'The true, happy Eric Cantona was terrific, a fantastic technician and a wonderful trainer. And what an athlete he was. In the pre-season in 1992/93 we did all the fitness tests and my coaches were coming back to me with Eric's readings saying "f***ing hell. His standing jump… all the power tests… incredible".' But despite having this knowledge, Wilkinson mis-read Cantona – he was not some sort of arrogant, aloof, dilettante but a determined, self-disciplined worker. The disciplinary problems which he had had previously – and which, infamously, he was to have again – were never those of an I-can't-be-bothered type.

'Eric would start his extra session by running the length of the pitch while keeping the ball up in the air,' recalls Blackmore. 'Then he'd do finishing. I'll always remember one day when he got Brian Kidd to put crosses into the penalty area and the idea was to try to score a volley from about ten yards out. Everyone was hit and miss except Eric, he scored every time.'

Cantona himself, despite giving the appearance of being aloof and slightly superior to it all, was a team player through and through. 'People draw attention to me,' he said. 'But it is the personality of the team that is important. I came to United to make the difference but they have marvellous players here and the most important thing is the collective for this is a team game.' And Eric Cantona was about to make United the best team in the land.

v Sheffield Wednesday 2-1

28

10 April 1993
Premier League
Old Trafford
Attendance: 40,102

MANCHESTER UNITED	SHEFFIELD WEDNESDAY
Peter Schmeichel	Chris Woods
Denis Irwin	Roland Nilsson
Steve Bruce	Viv Anderson
Gary Pallister	Carlton Palmer
Paul Parker	Phil King
Ryan Giggs	Chris Waddle
Brian McClair	Danny Wilson
Paul Ince	John Sheridan
Lee Sharpe	Nigel Worthington
Mark Hughes	Gordon Watson
Eric Cantona	Nigel Jemson
Manager: Alex Ferguson	*Manager:* Trevor Francis

A SUPERB 3-1 win away at Norwich City, completing a double over the East Anglians, had kept United in second place, just one point behind Aston Villa. It was early April and goals from Ryan Giggs, Andrei Kanchelskis and Eric Cantona in the first 21 minutes had put United in a comfortable position despite the semblance of a second-half fightback from the Canaries which included a goal from Old Trafford old boy Mark Robins.

The next round of matches saw both United and Villa at home, to Sheffield Wednesday and Coventry City respectively. United's was much the trickier of the two tasks as Wednesday had been enjoying a cracking season – in eight days' time they were to lose in the League Cup Final to Arsenal and the following month to lose the FA Cup Final to the same opponents, after a replay.

The first league meeting between the sides, on Boxing Day 1992, had been a corker, with Wednesday taking a three-goal lead and United contriving to miss from seemingly unmissable opportunities.

David Hirst, the subject of a £3.5m bid from United, scored the first after just two minutes then proceeded to lay on goals for fellow striker Mark Bright and Irish midfielder John Sheridan. Brian McClair finally beat Chris Woods on 67 minutes, then did they same again on 80 with Lee Sharpe putting on a masterclass of power and pace on the left wing. A scruffy 84th-minute equaliser from Cantona gave United a share of the points which was the least their performance deserved.

United, then, were not particularly looking forward to the return match at precisely that stage of the season when their title hopes faded the previous year. 'Our record against them is bloody awful,' said Ferguson. 'It there was one team we didn't want it was them, going into two cup finals and confident as well.'

Many thought Wednesday might be focused solely on the cups and certainly they began in slightly distracted mode, and if others had been on the same wavelength as Cantona, United could have been out of sight before the interval.

Inside ten minutes the Frenchman, playing a little deeper than usual, ran on to a pass from Ince and crossed for Giggs, only to see the ball taken off the Welshman's toes by the charging Ince who could only hit it straight into the huge hands of a grateful Woods. Almost immediately after that McClair was foiled by another United old boy, Viv Anderson, and then brought a diving save from Woods after a Cantona ball had opened up the defence.

United kept pressing, but his forwards over-elaborated on occasion, and when they didn't there was still Woods to beat. 'They were being far too clever,' said Ferguson later. 'But when you have creative players, sometimes you have to live with them. When they are precise, when they keep the passes simple, they are good enough to play like that and it we had got the early goal our efforts probably deserved then we could have gone on to score a few.'

Having ridden out the initial United storm, Wednesday started to create a few opportunities of their own, with Denis Irwin forced to head a Chris Waddle cross out from under his own crossbar. And then, disaster. Wednesday hadn't had a lot of chances, but they were a dangerous team and when they suddenly got forward shortly after the hour mark, the alarm bells started ringing. With Waddle growing in influence by the minute, a Phil King ball into him on the left of the penalty area drew a rash challenge from Ince and Sheridan slotted home the resulting penalty, calmly along the ground to Peter Schmeichel's right while the great Dane went the other way. United had 25 minutes left to salvage the match, arguably to salvage their season.

Bryan Robson, who had been patrolling the touchline, was brought on for Paul Parker. 'I was thinking about that change anyway,' said Ferguson, 'even before the goal went in. So when it did I brought him on straight away and it worked for us.'

Did it ever. The 36-year-old Robson made only six starting appearances all season, with a further 11 as a substitute, but when he was fit he would still be tearing around like the box-to-box midfielder he was ten years earlier. 'He brought us a sense of purpose and nerve, too,' said Ferguson. 'He wanted to have the ball and get involved all the time and his passing improved the team.'

But still United couldn't score. Then with four minutes of regular time left on the clock, Hughes robbed Carlton Palmer about 35 yards out, slalomed his way into the penalty area past three defenders and toe-poked it with the outside of his right boot. Woods saved. Steve Bruce went up for the resulting Irwin corner and directed a venomous header which even Woods couldn't keep out. Gasps of relief all round – United had matched the draw which Villa had recorded with Coventry and not ceded any ground.

The drama was far from finished, however. There was plenty of injury time to be played as referee Michael Peck had earlier sustained an injury which had forced him to be replaced by linesman John Hilditch. Hilditch's first toot of his whistle had been to award Wednesday their penalty. There had been numerous other stoppages too so the boss waved his men forward in search of a winner.

'From the moment we equalised, I stood on the touchline directing operations, cajoling the lads, praising them,' recalled Ferguson in *Managing My Life*. 'Trevor Francis, the Wednesday manager, was signalling to the referee that time was up when we won a corner. Ryan Giggs took it, it ended up on the other side of the pitch where Gary Pallister raced out to regain possession and, without looking, he hit a really good cross in that landed in Brucie's path.

'I was right in the line of the ball as it arrowed its way into the corner of the net. Reminding us how brave he was, Bruce stuck his head in front of one of their defenders and glanced the ball high into the far corner.'

Ironically, Bruce himself had been bemoaning the lack of goals the night before on local television and wondering whether it could cost United in the run-in.

'Nothing frightened Brucey,' said fellow defender Paul Parker. 'Nothing was impossible. He had more determination than anyone. He won more headers at 6ft than the average centre-half of 6ft 4in, and it wasn't always easy – you could tell the cost by looking at his nose!'

The result seemed to drain all the tension out of United's play during the rest of the season. 'We sensed from the start of the game that the pressure was on them to go and win the league,' said Francis, who claimed that he clocked Bruce's winner at 'seven minutes and 14 seconds into injury time' even joking with Ferguson that his team had scored their winning goal 'in the second leg'.

It gave rise to the famous phrase 'Fergie time', marked by the man himself stalking the touchline staring pointedly at his watch and, frequently, tapping it too. On this first occasion of Fergie time, however, the Scot remained quite unmoved. 'The truth is that the extra minutes were totally legitimate. That night I watched the video of the second half and used my stopwatch to time all the stoppages for injuries and substitutions,' he wrote in *Managing My Life*. 'There should in fact have been an additional 12 minutes.' No doubt he would have pointed that out to replacement referee Hilditch, but seven were all his team needed.

Two days later United managed what Villa could not and beat a fading Coventry team through a 40th-minute Irwin goal. Then on 17 April they despatched Chelsea 3-0 at Old Trafford with goals from Hughes (23) and Cantona (48), plus an own goal from Steve Clarke (44). Villa's victory over Manchester City a day later kept the gap at one point, but the picture changed significantly during the next round of matches, on 21 April.

United were at Crystal Palace, who were fighting against relegation, a battle they were destined to lose on goal difference. Palace scrapped for everything and gave United a few scares from set pieces but a 64th-minute volley from Mark Hughes – his 18th of the season and 100th league goal for the club – put United in charge. Ince's last-minute goal clinched it. At the same time Villa were losing 3-0 at Blackburn Rovers, so United went in to May with a four-point lead.

'The criticism last year was that at the end we ran out of goals,' Hughes had said after the victory over Chelsea. 'That won't happen this time. He added after the Palace win, 'This was probably the most significant goal I've scored and I can't see anybody stopping us now.'

Prophetic words. On Sunday 2 May, Villa stumbled again, losing at home to Oldham Athletic (a result which went a long way to ensure Oldham's survival in the top flight for another season). With a four-point gap but Villa having only one match remaining, the title was United's after a 26-year wait.

Ferguson, famously, was on the golf course. Never one for sitting around, he had decided activity was the best course of action and took to the greens with son Mark. At the 14th hole, they were waiting for the group ahead when Mark turned to his dad. 'I think Villa must have won,' he said. 'Someone would have told us if they'd lost.' And just at that minute, a car pulled up, someone leapt out and told father and son that United had won the league. They hugged and celebrated and for once the United players were allowed to party before a match.

The last rites to the season still had to be administered and the day after United had clinched the title without playing, they did have to play: at Old Trafford against Blackburn Rovers. With 'We Are The Champions' booming through the speakers and Ferguson admitting, 'The atmosphere beneath the main stand was one of relaxed enjoyment of a job well done', it came as a shock when Blackburn had the audacity to score first, through Kevin Gallacher on eight minutes. Nothing was going to douse the United fires, however. Giggs equalised after 21 minutes, Ince put United ahead on the hour and Gary Pallister rounded it off with the last goal right at the death. Then the party began.

'It was a long time coming,' said a relieved Robson. 'It's great for the fans, and great for the younger players. The 26-year thing has gone from around their neck now and they can get on and win championships to come.'

A glance at the final table shows United winning the league by ten points in 1992/93; it looks comfortable because Villa lost 2-1 at Queens Park Rangers on the last day while United won 2-1 at Wimbledon, Ince and Robson the scorers. United fans will know that does not begin to tell the story of their team's season, a season in which two matches against Sheffield Wednesday went a long way towards deciding the destiny of that long-awaited title triumph.

v Chelsea 4-0

14 May 1994
FA Cup Final
Wembley
Attendance: 79,634

MANCHESTER UNITED	CHELSEA
Peter Schmeichel	Dmitri Kharine
Denis Irwin	Steve Clarke
Steve Bruce	Eddie Newton
Gary Pallister	Jakob Kjeldbjerg
Paul Parker	Erland Johnsen
Andrei Kanchelskis	Frank Sinclair
Eric Cantona	John Spencer
Paul Ince	Craig Burley
Roy Keane	Mark Stein
Mark Hughes	Gavin Peacock
Ryan Giggs	Dennis Wise
Manager: Alex Ferguson	*Manager:* Glenn Hoddle

THE 1993/94 league season was, for the most part, a celebratory stroll. The burden of winning the title having been lifted, United looked free to play the sort of football they had, at times, been too nervous to play the previous season.

'When we came back for pre-season, the boss made a speech about not resting on our laurels,' recalls Paul Parker. 'But there was no need. We wanted to win again as much as he did. When we stepped on the pitch we felt unbeatable. More than anything, it was enjoyable.'

United only lost four matches in the league all season, and only one at home, but two of those four defeats had been by a determined Chelsea side. So it was with some trepidation that United emerged on to the Wembley turf in the middle of May to face Chelsea for the third time in the season, only now the FA Cup was at stake, and the tantalising possibility of a league and cup Double.

'Going into the final we were hurt by the fact that they had done the league double over us and we did not want to lose all three,' said Gary Pallister. 'They went into the cup final with no fear.'

And Chelsea duly took the game to United in the first half – their best chance being a Gavin Peacock shot which thumped back off the bar after a wonderful piece of skill had seen him chest down Pallister's clearance. 'Gavin got the winner in both games in the league [they both finished 1-0 in favour of Chelsea],' said Pallister, 'and when I saw the ball leaving his boot I thought he'd done it again.'

Peacock was a thorn in United's side for the whole of the first half, playing in that 'hole' just in front of the United back four which had proved so successful in both league meetings between the two teams. In the very first minute, a quick exchange of passes had put Eddie Newton clear but his shot was blocked. Later in the half Pallister had been obliged to clear from off the line after John Spencer's touch had beaten Peter Schmeichel but not carried enough weight to prevent Pallister getting back in time to clear.

If there is one thing you have to to do against Alex Ferguson's United, it's to score when you are dictating the play. United have too much talent in their ranks to be quiet for a whole 90 minutes and we have proved time and again that we will find a way to score a goal, particularly after the manager's 'hairdryer' treatment at half-time.

And so it came to pass. United had already started to knock the ball around in their traditional fashion and if Chelsea were not yet chasing shadows they were at least starting to see the danger. Erland Johnsen had been booked early on for taking out the flying Ryan Giggs so had to be circumspect about where and how he made his tackles. On the hour, Giggs knocked the ball around Steve Clarke, and got a toe to it just ahead of Craig Burley and knocked the ball in to Denis Irwin, who was standing just inside the Chelsea box. Newton lunged in, possibly unnecessarily, and upended Irwin for a clear penalty. Eric Cantona, shirt collar up as always, stepped up and put the ball firmly to Dmitri Kharine's left – while the goalkeeper went right – ignoring Dennis Wise's rather pathetic attempts to put him off.

Six minutes later Mark Hughes sent a defence-splitting pass from the centre-circle into the path of Andrei Kanchelskis. Frank Sinclair used his own pace to keep up with the Ukrainian winger but nudged him slightly as the two contested the ball. Contact was slight – and probably outside the penalty area in any case – but referee David Elleray was struggling to keep up with the pace of play and Kanchelskis's sprawl was enough to convince him to award another penalty. It looked soft in real time, and even softer on the replays, but given the pace at which Kanchelskis was travelling, you could see why it was given.

Elleray later wrote in his autobiography *The Man in The Middle* that he had blown his whistle without thinking and realised he had made a poor decision almost immediately. Too late for Chelsea.

Cantona did exactly the same as he had the first time and calmly slotted it to Kharine's left while the Russian goalkeeper moved to his right.

Glenn Hoddle brought himself off the substitutes' bench straight after the second goal in an attempt to turn the tide, but it was already too late: his team were demoralised and three minutes after Cantona's second successful penalty, Hughes put the game beyond them.

Sinclair was unfortunate that the ball seemed to squirt away from him off the pitch made slicker by the rain, and even more unfortunate that it ran right into the path of Hughes who hardly had to break stride before shooting home from right to left, easily beating Kharine. Three goals in under ten minutes, and the game was over.

Brian McClair added gloss to the scoreline in injury time when he was the beneficiary of Ince getting round Kharine and squaring the ball into an unguarded goalmouth.

'We played some good stuff in the first half,' said Peacock. 'But the second penalty killed us. Four-nil was a very poor reflection of the game but Cantona was the best player I ever played against. He had presence, class and was a real entertainer.'

Interviewed directly after the game, Irwin admitted that United hadn't played all that well 'but never mind', while Roy Keane and Ince both admitted they were flattered by the scoreline and that they didn't believe they had played all that well. Hughes added that they could see Chelsea were very down after the second goal and his third just ensured that there would be no comeback.

United had cruised through the earlier rounds of the FA Cup, despatching one Premier League opponent after another. Sheffield United, Norwich City and Wimbledon were all beaten away from home with varying degrees of difficulty but with nary a goal conceded. Charlton Athletic, United's only opposition from outside the top flight, at least managed to score a goal at Old Trafford in the sixth round but only after United had scored three of their own and had Schmeichel sent off.

In the semi-final doughty cup fighters Oldham Athletic almost put paid to the Double dream when Neil Pointon put them ahead in the second half of extra time. Hughes somehow found an equaliser in the dying seconds with a trademark volley which Oldham manager Joe Royle described as a 'stroke of genius'.

The Maine Road replay saw United in cruise control. They won 4-1 with goals from Irwin (nine minutes), Kanchelskis (15), Robson (62) and Giggs (68), though Pointon did produce one for the personal scrapbook by scoring in the replay to add to his goal in the first game.

United very nearly landed a domestic Treble as they also reached the final of the League Cup, but there an Aston Villa desperate for revenge for the previous season's title battle played too well on the day. Villa had actually had a surprisingly poor season in the league, dropping from their runners-up spot to tenth and losing in the FA Cup to Bolton Wanderers, who had only just climbed their way back into the First Division – the new second tier – where they were to finish 14th.

But motivated by who they were facing and marshalled by Ron Atkinson, Villa tore into United and after surviving an early scare which could have seen keeper Mark Bosnich sent off, they scored a smart opening goal. Andy Townsend played the ball in to Dean Saunders who flicked it over the top for Dalian Atkinson.

A rather fortuitous Saunders touch made it two after 75 minutes; Hughes pulled one back with a poacher's strike but United could not find an equaliser. The penalty and red card for Kanchelskis gave Villa the chance to seal the match 3-1.

The other minor disappointment was in Europe, where a lack of experience in the European Cup led to a degree of naivety in their second round match against Turkish champions Galatasaray. Having won both home and away against the modest Honved, United were drawn to play the first leg against the Turks at home but after establishing a 2-0 lead United adopted a swashbuckling approach which played into their opponents' hands rather than shutting up shop defensively. Three goals from the Turks actually put them in front before Cantona equalised in the 80th minute; the damage was done, Galatasaray put ten men behind the ball in Istanbul and United lacked the know-how to break them down.

The match was played out against a backdrop of political unrest and United players and fans were continually targeted in a manner which in more enlightened times would most likely have led to a sizeable fine and even a stadium closure for the Turkish side. Lee Sharpe 'scored' a perfectly good goal which should have stood, and at the end of the game United players were assaulted by Turkish fans which the police not only allowed but appeared to join in. Bryan Robson, not known to be a shrinking violet, said that both he and Cantona were hit by Turkish police, 'If that had happened to the Turks in Manchester, we would have been kicked out of Europe and banned for years!'

Of course those were the days when regulation of 'foreign' players was in place, forcing Ferguson to tinker with his team selection every match.

And one of the players who fell foul of the rule was new signing Roy Keane, from the Republic of Ireland. Legend has it that Keane and Blackburn Rovers agreed a £4m deal but it was held up as Kenny Dalglish, the then Blackburn manager, didn't have all the right paperwork and as it was a Friday afternoon the formalities would have to wait until Monday.

Ferguson saw an opportunity not only to sign the hottest property in English football at the time, but to get one over on Dalglish. It is difficult to say which of those two possibilities was the more appealing.

United being much more efficient than Blackburn they got the correct paperwork ready then and there and Ferguson went and met Keane on the Saturday and persuaded him to join United instead. The coup was made even more perfect when United got him for £3.75m, £250,000 less than Blackburn had been about to pay albeit still a British transfer record at the time.

Keane wrote in his autobiography that Dalglish was insisting he honour a deal that he hadn't signed, 'The same Kenny Dalglish who'd spent months "tapping" me up behind [Forest manager] Brian Clough's back. The more he swore at me, the less my conscience bothered me.'

If Keane's post-playing career has sullied his reputation among some fans, there is no denying the on-field impact he had in his time at the club. For my money he was no Bryan Robson but he filled the great man's shoes better than almost any other player could have, and gave United a decade of sterling service which saw them win every trophy possible.

On a sadder note, Sir Matt Busby passed away in mid-season, on 20 January 1994. He was buried alongside his beloved wife, Jean, who he had credited with getting him through the darkest days after the Munich air disaster, in Southern Cemetery, Manchester. Sir Matt had lived long enough to see United rebuilt and crowned once more as champions of England and rediscover the legacy which he had played the biggest part in establishing.

v Port Vale 2-1

30

21 September 1994
League Cup second round first leg
Vale Park
Attendance: 18,605

MANCHESTER UNITED	PORT VALE
Gary Walsh	Paul Musselwhite
Gary Neville	Bradley Sandeman
David May	Allen Tankard
Roy Keane	Andy Porter
Denis Irwin	Gareth Griffiths
Keith Gillespie	Dean Glover
Brian McClair	Kevin Kent
Nicky Butt	Robin van der Laan
David Beckham	Martin Foyle
Simon Davies	Lee Glover
Paul Scholes	Tony Naylor
Manager: Alex Ferguson	*Manager:* John Rudge

PORT Vale's matchday programme on 21 September listed the United side their team would be playing in the Coca-Cola Cup (as it then was) second round match that evening: Schmeichel, May, Irwin, Ince, Bruce, Pallister, Kanchelskis, Cantona, McClair, Hughes, Giggs.

Imagine the fans' disappointment, then, when of that line-up only May and McClair were actually starting. In fact, so disappointed was local MP Joan Whalley – in whose constituency the club is located – that she complained in the House of Commons and even briefly threatened to take action against United under the Trade Descriptions Act.

Hindsight is always a wonderful thing of course, but in fact that MP should consider herself lucky to have witnessed an early outing of a bunch of teenagers who would go on to become the most successful English team of all time.

'I smile when I think back to the days when I perhaps startled people by ringing the changes,' said Alex Ferguson. 'In particular I remember the fuss my selection for that League Cup tie at Port Vale provoked. We had Roy Keane in the [unfamiliar] role at centre-half and Brian McClair in midfield, but that was really the extent of our experienced players. Vale supporters took their complaints to the press and John Rudge, who was the Port Vale manager, told me that even his wife had complained! What they didn't know of course was that they would be witnessing the launch of the David Beckham era, and we know how successful they went on to become.'

Letters poured into *The Sentinel*, the local newspaper, saying that United should refund the fans they had short-changed, not just for their tickets but for their travel too. One pithily put it, 'If I pay to see Frank Sinatra, I don't expect to see Rolf Harris!' A Football League spokesman confirmed that they too had received complaints.

'I like to think that I never took my policy to extremes and that I always sincerely felt every team I selected for the League Cup was good enough to win,' said Ferguson. 'I don't think we've ever been off the mark and given a boy his chance too early. That can be very damaging. If he's not up to the standards we require at United, then we don't venture there – the last thing we'd want is to humiliate a player.'

The truth is, those teenagers were ready for first-team action. 'Nothing beats the thrill of watching a young unknown, bred by United and filled with the Red ideology, coming into the team and staking his claim,' wrote Richard Kurt in *United We Stood*. 'Their appearance fulfilled the desire that lies within every red, a longing instilled in the fans since the 1950s and that is still there.' So while the Port Vale fans might have been disappointed not to see United's biggest stars, it should be noted that the team which United did field was still good enough to beat them on the night, 2-1.

Vale opened the scoring when a corner from United's left wasn't properly cleared and defender Bradley Sandeman hit a fine right-footed strike from the edge of the area. It might have been going in anyway, or at least would have made life difficult for Gary Walsh in the United goal, but Lee Glover got his head on it and just slightly re-directed the ball.

United struck back on 37 minutes when a mix-up in the Port Vale defence between Allen Tankard and Dean Glover allowed Paul Scholes to nip in and steal possession. Scholes, wearing a number ten shirt which looked like it could comfortably accommodate two of him, did what he did best. He took it on a few strides then calmly hit the shot from right to left, past Paul Musselwhite's outstretched right hand to the far post, where it glanced off the inside of the woodwork and nestled in the side netting. It was Scholes's first goal for the first team.

Into the second half and McClair headed the ball out to Simon Davies on the left wing. Davies twisted and turned, first dummying to cut back inside then using the couple of feet of space that gave him to go wide and cross in with his left foot. It was a good cross and one which Scholes met perfectly to head back across the keeper and into the right of the goal. 'What a night for young Paul Scholes, his debut, the 19-year-old' said commentator Hugh Johns. 'Didn't he head that well?'

Although Scholes's second came in the 53rd minute, that was the way the score stayed until the end. In the return leg a fortnight later goals from McClair (35 minutes) and May (61) gave United safe passage into the third round, where they lost to Newcastle United.

As for the youngsters, they slowly began to make their mark: Nicky Butt with 22 starts and a further 13 as a sub, and Gary Neville with 23 starts and four substitute appearances established themselves as first choices, or close to it, joining Ryan Giggs. Scholes made ten starts and 15 substitute appearances, David Beckham seven and three respectively. Phil Neville, Gary's younger brother who captained United to the 1995 FA Youth Cup triumph, appeared twice, with two further appearances from the bench.

If the youngsters weren't quite ready to explode yet, then one man certainly was. A routine league match at Crystal Palace on 25 January 1995, 'a nothing game' as the website The Republik Of Mancunia accurately described it, saw Palace's Player of the Year Richard Shaw continually niggle at Eric Cantona, sometimes legally, mostly not. 'Some of the tackles were disgraceful,' remembered Ferguson. 'The referee Alan Wilkie's inability to stamp them out made subsequent trouble unavoidable.' Cantona finally took exception and kicked back, was spotted by a linesman and red-carded for the first time in several months.

A Palace fan called Matthew Simmons ran down from where he was sitting to hurl abuse at Cantona, who was being escorted off the field by kit man Norman Davies. Simmons hilariously told *The Sun* newspaper that he said, 'Off you go, Cantona – it's an early bath for you'; witnesses suggest that 'f*** off, you motherf***ing French b******' was closer to the mark. Davies certainly recalled the abuse being 'pretty nasty'. Whatever the provocation, Cantona launched himself into the crowd and kung-fu kicked Simmons.

'When Eric got to the dressing room he said nothing, but you could sense he knew how serious it was,' said Ferguson

It made the front pages of nearly every newspaper. *The Sun* seemed to adopt a particularly venomous and over-the-top stance, publishing a 13-page feature on 'The Shame of Cantona', detailing all the player's misdemeanours and past brushes with authority. Of Simmons's past there was little mention but the 20-year-old already had a conviction for assault (as a 17-year-old he attacked a petrol station attendant with a spanner) and went on to pick up further public order offences before being convicted for assaulting the coach of his son's football team in 2010.

Simmons clearly was no angel, but Ferguson's ire was directed at the press who continued to run stories about Cantona's temper. *The Sun* paid Simmons for his story and did all they could to keep it at the forefront of the daily news, to get their money's worth. John Sadler wrote, 'We have seen the best of him [Cantona], now we have got to see the back of him.' Richard Williams of *The Independent* was one of the few to urge a sense of perspective, 'You didn't have to look very hard and long at Mr Matthew Simmons of Thornton Heath to conclude that Eric Cantona's only mistake was to stop hitting him. The more we discovered about Mr Simmons, the more Cantona's assault looked like the instinctive expression of a flawless moral judgment.'

United suspended Cantona until the end of the season and fined him two weeks' wages (the maximum permissible). However, the FA's disciplinary commission took it upon themselves to extend that ban for a further four months. Worse, Cantona had to attend Croydon Magistrates' Court where a two-week jail sentence was imposed. The club now felt things had got out of hand and decided to step in, launching an immediate appeal which resulted in the sentence being reduced to community service.

Even so, the disillusioned Cantona fled to France over the summer. In the wake of the FA declaring that his taking part in a behind-closed-doors training session constituted a breach of his ban, staying overseas seemed a very real possibility for Cantona, who was linked with a move to Inter Milan. Then Ferguson – not for the first time – took that hands-on approach for which so many players down the years had cause to thank him. The United boss took time out to fly over to Paris and persuaded Cantona to return.

Whether the Cantona ban – both in terms of depriving the club of its most influential player and in terms of the effect it had on morale – was the deciding factor or not, United ended the season losing their league title by one point to Blackburn Rovers. A 1-1 draw with West Ham United on the final weekend was not quite sufficient to overhaul Blackburn, who lost, ironically, at Liverpool. Any sort of scrambled goal in the dying minutes would have been sufficient for United to retain their title.

They also lost the FA Cup in the final match of the season, beaten by a Paul Rideout goal for Everton on the half-hour, a lead which the Merseysiders defended thanks to a superb performance from Welsh international goalkeeper Neville Southall.

It may have been United's first season in six that they did not win a major trophy, but Ferguson decided that radical surgery was called for as he started fashioning his next great team from the embers of the first.

As for Cantona, he performed his community service with relish. Ordered to coach schoolchildren for his 120 hours of 'punishment', Cantona found he enjoyed it so much that he carried on with it long after the court-imposed sanction had passed. Typical of the man, he had taken a negative and made a positive out of it.

31 v Middlesbrough 3-0

5 May 1996
Premier League
Riverside Stadium
Attendance: 29,922

MANCHESTER UNITED	MIDDLESBROUGH
Peter Schmeichel	Gary Walsh
David May	Nigel Pearson
Gary Pallister	Steve Vickers
Denis Irwin	Branco
Phil Neville	Derek Whyte
Nicky Butt	Neil Cox
Paul Scholes	Juninho
Ryan Giggs	Robbie Mustoe
Roy Keane	Jamie Pollock
David Beckham	Nick Barmby
Eric Cantona	Jan-Aage Fjortoft
Manager: Alex Ferguson	*Manager:* Bryan Robson

'YOU can't win anything with kids.' So spoke former Liverpool defender turned TV pundit Alan Hansen.

It was the first day of the 1995/96 season and Manchester United had just lost 3-1 at Aston Villa. Des Lynam, the doyen of sports presenters, declared that United were scarcely recognisable from the team of the past couple of seasons and asked Hansen what he felt was going on.

He replied, 'I think they've got problems, I wouldn't say they'd got major problems. Obviously three players have departed – the trick is always to buy when you're strong so he needs to buy players. You look at that Manchester United line-up today and Aston Villa at 2.15pm when they got the team sheet, it will have given them a lift.

'And that will happen every time he plays the kids. You can't win anything with kids. He's got to buy players, simple as that. The trick to winning the championship is strength in depth and they just haven't got it.'

Paul Ince, Mark Hughes and Andrei Kanchelskis had all departed United in the summer; Ince to try his luck overseas with Inter Milan, Hughes to Chelsea and Kanchelskis to Everton.

It may have brought the club sizeable revenue of over £14.5m but Alex Ferguson hadn't brought anyone in other than the £6m purchase of Andy Cole from Newcastle United in January of that year.

The problem for Ferguson was that Eric Cantona was still suspended from football, while Andy Cole, Ryan Giggs and Steve Bruce were out injured. It wasn't solely that he thought chucking in Gary and Phil Neville, Paul Scholes and Nicky Butt (with David Beckham, John O'Kane and Simon Davies on the bench) was the right thing to do, it was the only thing to do; he had very few options.

There was a good blend of experience and talent in the Villa side that season with the likes of Steve Staunton, Gareth Southgate and, of course, Paul McGrath – still defying the years – in defence, supported by midfielders Ian Taylor and Mark Draper (who scored the first two), Andy Townsend and Lee Hendrie, while Savo Milosevic and Dwight Yorke (who got the third from the penalty spot) supplied the goals. Villa would go on to finish fourth in the league, win the League Cup and reach the semi-finals of the FA Cup that season.

Beckham did at least provide a glimpse of what was to come with a superb right-footed strike in the 84th minute from fully 35 yards out. 'After just over half an hour we're 3-0 down and it's a disaster,' Scholes told Sky Sports. 'The game's over,' agreed Butt, 'and we're thinking we've let the manager down. He's put his faith in us, we're only young and the fans are going to hate us because we're wrecking the club. In truth, that night watching *Match of the Day*, I thought exactly the same as what Alan Hansen said – that we weren't good enough.'

Although annoyed at the time, Ferguson himself has since acknowledged that as a basic principle, Hansen wasn't wrong. What Hansen didn't know, and Ferguson did, was that this particular bunch of kids were completely out of the ordinary, a totally exceptional group who broke through at the same time in a once-in-a-lifetime occurrence.

'Actually, there wasn't a lot wrong with Alan Hansen's statement,' Ferguson said in 2006. 'Teams mainly composed of young and inexperienced players rarely succeed in the toughest competitions. But at Old Trafford the Busby Babes had already proved that there can be exceptions to that rule.'

Hansen later acknowledged, 'Don't forget that the spine of that team included Peter Schmeichel, Steve Bruce, Gary Pallister and Eric Cantona. That team was a fantastic example of how to build a formidable spine and fill in everything else around it.

'The kids were great, but so were the goalkeeper, two centre-backs and the centre-forward. Even after that year when he brought those five or six sensational kids through, Ferguson always went for experience. What happened at United was a one-off, I just said it at the wrong time.'

It all changed as the season wore on. The experienced players came back, Giggs and Cole both scored regularly, getting into double figures in the league alone. And then in October the King returned.

No one knew quite what to expect from Cantona. United had played 32 matches since he had last appeared for them, and in that time they had let three of their senior players leave without bringing in anyone new. Could Cantona fill the role of elder statesman? Could he really inspire the youngsters who had looked so out of their depth in the first match of the season?

His first game back was on 1 October against Liverpool at Old Trafford. Within two minutes he had drifted out to the left flank from where he crossed for a simple goal for Butt. In truth United were second best for much of that much and a Robbie Fowler double gave Liverpool the lead, but inevitably Cantona was destined to hog the headlines.

A beautiful through ball to Giggs saw the Welsh winger pulled back and the Frenchman himself stepped forward to strike the ball firmly to David James's right and level the match at 2-2. A much more significant meeting between the two teams awaited in seven months' time.

By the time United strolled out on to the Wembley turf for the 1996 FA Cup Final, they had already regained their league title. Liverpool had finished third, which many considered an under-achievement given the strength of their squad and if United had 'Fergie's Fledglings', then Liverpool had their 'Spice Boys', a not-entirely-complimentary nickname for a bunch of players who occasionally seemed to put style before substance.

That impression was reinforced by their appearance in eye-catching cream Armani suits; there is little doubt that in John Barnes, Steve McManaman, Rob Jones, Robbie Fowler and the ill-fated Jamie Redknapp they had talent to burn, but on this day they simply did not produce it.

In fact I was lucky enough to be at Wembley that day and I don't recall Liverpool having a single shot on goal. There was a sort of half-chance just before half-time when a well-placed Redknapp blazed horribly over when reasonably set.

Not that United were very much better, but in Cantona they had a man who wanted to repay the supporters and manager for keeping their faith in him. They also had the one man who had the ability to rise above a dull game and stamp some individual genius on it.

'The young lads had always been in awe of Eric,' said Gary Neville. 'None of us got to know him well but there was a vast unspoken respect for him. We were desperate to impress him.' The Double was 'almost single-handedly down to him'.

If FA Cups are meant to be decided by fine goals, then this one was a worthy winner. In the 86th minute a punch by James from a viciously away-swinging corner from Beckham bounced off Ian Rush and into the path of Cantona. He still had a lot to do, adjusting his positioning so he could strike a thigh-high volley though a cluster of defenders. Poor James never had a chance with the ball rocketing through a sea of legs and past him before he could react.

As it dawned on him that he had won the FA Cup for United, Cantona wheeled away, his face breaking into a huge grin, and headed straight for the United fans. We acclaimed him for his genius, and for giving us the double Double.

'It is sometimes hard, when watching history in the making, to realise it,' wrote Glenn Moore in *The Independent*. 'Let there be no doubt. When Ryan Giggs is in his dotage and Eric Cantona is a grandpere, we will remember this team. It will rank with the best.'

United were the first English team to win the Double twice, and it hurt. 'I hate the fact that United won the Double,' said Liverpool boss Roy Evans. 'I could cry.'

Making Liverpool cry is always a worthwhile objective.

Just as enjoyable in the 1995/96 season was watching the Red Devils overhaul a stuttering Newcastle United side who had been ten points clear on New Year's Day and had briefly extended that to 12 points on 4 February.

Newcastle had played some swashbuckling football in the first half of the season but when the heat came on, and United used all their experience to go on a long unbeaten run – which included a 1-0 win at St James' Park – Newcastle could not live with it.

Then came Ferguson's masterstroke. Always a keen studier of people, Ferguson perceived that Newcastle manager Kevin Keegan was struggling to hold his team – and himself – together as the title race got close.

Almost in an aside Ferguson questioned whether Newcastle's opponents tried as hard against them as they did against United: three consecutive 1-0 wins, over Aston Villa, Southampton and away at Leeds had given rise to the passing comment. 'I've really kept quiet,' said Keegan during a TV interview, 'but I'll tell you something, he went down in my estimations when he said that. We have not resorted to that. You can tell him now, we're still fighting for this title and he's got to go to Middlesbrough and get something. And I'll tell you, honestly, I will love it if we beat them. Love it.'

Complete with finger-pointing, it turned into a rant which said more about Keegan than it did about Ferguson or United, 'It really has got to me.' That much was painfully obvious.

United did as Keegan had said they had to do, they went to Middlesbrough and won easily – 3-0. While Newcastle stuttered and drew both their last two games 1-1, United thrashed Nottingham Forest 5-0 then went to Bryan Robson's mid-table Middlesbrough side and won with consummate ease.

United took the field in their short-lived change strip of blue-and-white shirts, shorts and socks; with club captain Steve Bruce still recovering from a hamstring injury and fit enough only for a place on the bench, David May started alongside Pallister at centre-half while Cantona led the team out.

May, of all people, then proceeded to score the first goal, after 15 minutes, which settled United nerves. It was May's only goal of the season in any competition but when Giggs took a corner from the right it went all the way to the back post where the defender got up highest and scored from a firm header which bounced into the ground first then into the goal. May got sufficient power on his header to get it past the outstretched left arm of Gary Walsh – who had moved from United to Boro at the start of the season – and past the efforts of Branco on the line.

In the second half Cole came on in place of Scholes and with almost his first touch he found a Giggs corner, from the United right, at his feet in the six-yard box. Cole had his back to goal and the ball came in at an awkward height but with a flick of his right boot he sent it over his right shoulder and past Walsh. 'That was instinctive,' said co-commentator Ian St John. 'He knows exactly where the goal is.' With 54 minutes gone United were 2-0 up and cruising.

The third and final goal didn't arrive until inside the final ten minutes when Nicky Butt flicked a little inside pass from out on the wide left to Giggs, who was in acres of space. Middlesbrough backed off and backed off, encouraging Giggs to first keep running then unleash a magnificent shot with the outside of his left foot which gave Walsh no chance.

Game over. Title won. A light aeroplane flew over the Riverside Stadium trailing a banner reading 'Manchester United: Carling Champions', and the fans got a new song, courtesy of the legendary Pete Boyle, keeper of the United songbook, 'We won the Football League again / Down by the Riverside / Down by the Riverside / Down by the River...side'. As Boyle says, not the most lyrically challenging but perfectly capturing the joyousness of winning the league again in a season when for a long time it looked beyond United.

And an FA Cup win over Liverpool into the bargain, sealing the first double Double in history. United fans could be forgiven for wondering whether life could get any better.

v Wimbledon 3-0

32

17 August 1996
Premier League
Selhurst Park
Attendance: 25,786

MANCHESTER UNITED	WIMBLEDON
Peter Schmeichel	Neil Sullivan
David May	Kenny Cunningham
Gary Pallister	Brian McAllister
Denis Irwin	Chris Perry
Phil Neville	Marcus Gayle
Nicky Butt	Ben Thatcher
Paul Scholes	Vinnie Jones
Jordi Cruyff	Robbie Earle
Roy Keane	Oyvind Leonhardsen
David Beckham	Andy Clarke
Eric Cantona	Dean Holdsworth
Manager: Alex Ferguson	*Manager:* Joe Kinnear

AT the end of the 1995/96 season, defenders Steve Bruce and Paul Parker were allowed to leave on free transfers as a thank-you from a grateful club, Bruce to Birmingham City and Parker to Derby County. But even though Alex Ferguson still had David May and the Neville brothers fast establishing themselves as regular first-team players, he decided to move for Norwegian international defender Ronny Johnsen, who was playing for Besiktas in Turkey at the time.

Johnsen signed a five-year contract, though he ended at staying for six at United, and clocked up 99 appearances – which would have been significantly more had it not been for some bad luck with injuries.

Johnsen make his debut for United in this match, coming off the bench slightly earlier than probably even he expected when Nicky Butt picked up an injury in the 39th minute. It brought him into direct opposition with Norwegian international Oyvind Leonhardsen, who he played alongside on numerous occasions while on international duty.

United's other new boys were, in order of arrival: Karel Poborsky, the Czechoslovakian winger brought in to replace the departing Lee Sharpe; Ole Gunnar Solskjaer, the diminutive Norwegian striker bought from his home club, Molde; and Jordi Cruyff, the Dutch midfield son of the legendary Johan.

Sharpe had played 265 games for United in his eight years at the club (scoring 36 goals), but just at the moment when it looked like there might be a long-term opening for him on the right the emergence of David Beckham slammed that door firmly shut. Although Sharpe appeared in all but eight of United's competitive games across all competitions in the 1995/96 season, he knew he could not command a starting place any longer, and that realisation was confirmed in an instant when Beckham scored *that* goal.

Anyone who has ever played football knows how hard it is to strike a ball accurately from the halfway line into an unguarded goal at any sort of pace. Then fill that goal with six feet of international goalkeeper and it gets a whole heap harder.

The 21-year-old Beckham made it look easy. Yes the game was already won. Yes it was a beautiful summer's day, the first day of the new season and United started it as champions. Yes there was no pressure at all. But for all the ifs and buts it was a wonderful strike.

Eighty-seven minutes gone, United led Wimbledon 2-0 and Beckham was the beneficiary of Wimbledon substitute Efan Ekoku losing the ball about ten yards into the United half. Beckham took a couple of strides, glanced up to see Neil Sullivan off his line and hit the ball in a perfect arc over Sullivan's head and in.

Did even Beckham know what he had done? The floppy-haired youngster stood there arms aloft, just enjoying the moment. But with that one 57-yard goal Beckham launched himself into the public consciousness.

'You'll see that over and over again,' announced commentator Martin Tyler. Prophetic words about a strike which was chosen as the Premier League Goal of the Decade in 2003. 'It changed my life,' admitted Beckham.

Within a month he would win the first of his 115 England caps – a record for an outfield player – 58 of which would be as captain. He would play for England at three World Cups and two European Championships.

At club level he would make 394 appearances for United, winning six Premier League titles, two FA Cups and the Champions League. In the later part of his career he also won La Liga with Real Madrid, Ligue 1 in France with Paris Saint-Germain, and MLS (Major League Soccer) with LA Galaxy. He is the only Englishman to have won league titles in four different countries. For good measure he also played for AC Milan in Serie A, appearing on 29 occasions across two seasons.

Never a prolific goalscorer, Beckham nevertheless scored some crucial goals for both club and country – and some spectacular ones too. None more so than on the opening day of the year which was to launch him dramatically on to the world stage. 'I still remember first coming across him in the youth teams. All of us local lads, such as Nicky Butt, me and Paul Scholes, wondered who this flash Cockney lad was.' So said Gary Neville, who became one of Beckham's best friends.

The match against Wimbledon had started without any hint of the outlandish conclusion that was to come. Against a team that had finished 14th the previous season but boasted enough solid, experienced professionals to cause anyone problems on their day, United played well within themselves to carve out a comfortable victory.

Six days after they had comprehensively dismantled Newcastle United's defence to win the FA Charity Shield with a 4-0 scoreline, United quickly showed that the previous season's Double had not dimmed their competitive fires. 'Was I surprised by the scoreline?' Eric Cantona was asked after the Charity Shield. 'Well I'll say "yes" to be polite,' he memorably replied.

The first goal against Wimbledon arrived on 25 minutes from a Roy Keane excursion down the right before crossing to Nicky Butt. Butt touched it on to Eric Cantona and the Frenchman took one touch to control the ball and another to slam it home.

Although United were largely in control it wasn't until the 58th minute that Denis Irwin extended their lead. A neat one-two with Keane gave Irwin the chance to beat Sullivan at his near post, which he took. The *Daily Mail* reported, 'It was Keane who propelled United to what became a stroll when his sheer power and pace embarrassed Vinnie Jones and paved the way for Cantona's deliciously struck opener in the 25th minute.'

And then, with 87 minutes gone, came Beckham's goal. 'The goal of the season has happened already,' said a beaming Ferguson immediately after the match.

The 1996/97 season was never exactly a cruise for United, but by winning five and drawing four of their first nine they made a good start. There was a blip in October when only a world-class performance – and a string of saves – from Peter Schmeichel kept Liverpool at bay during a fortuitous 1-0 win at Old Trafford. The next two league outings saw United thumped at Newcastle and Southampton and finish the month down in fifth position. November started the same way with a 2-1 home defeat by Chelsea.

United's next league defeat came on 8 March. They went top on goal difference (from Arsenal and Liverpool) in January, and stayed there for the rest of the season. The March defeat at Sunderland was disappointing but no more than that and by the end of the season they had stretched away to win by seven points from Newcastle and Arsenal, whose challenge, not for the only time, faded somewhat in the spring.

United's defence of their FA Cup came to an early end as Wimbledon, despite losing twice to United in the Premier League, produced their best party-pooper form to beat them in a Selhurst Park replay. It was a strange tie in many ways – Wimbledon had dominated the first match at Old Trafford but had to reply on a 90th-minute equaliser from Robbie Earle to earn a replay. United won the league encounter between the two sides in the week before the FA Cup replay then proceeded to dominate the cup game virtually from start to finish only to lose it to a 64th-minute Marcus Gayle goal.

If going out of the FA Cup early had an upside, it was that it left United free to concentrate on maintaining their best European campaign for some years. Home and away defeats to Juventus weren't disastrous but it looked as if losing to Fenerbahce at Old Trafford might be. Of all the teams to lose an unbeaten home record (in Europe) to... However, that result was cancelled out by winning in Turkey, and two wins over Rapid Vienna proved sufficient to put United into the quarter-finals.

There they faced Porto, and for the first time under Alex Ferguson United produced the sort of attacking performance we were accustomed to seeing in the Premier League. Goals arrived at regular intervals, from David May (22 minutes), Eric Cantona (34 minutes), Ryan Giggs (61 minutes) and Andy Cole (80 minutes) as Porto were simply swept aside.

The Guardian reported, 'At the heart of United's success lay an inspired performance by Giggs, with Beckham, his midfield partner not far behind.'

The second leg was a formality, and after United had seen off the anticipated early assault from the Portuguese they were able to snuff out the match and return home with an accomplished 0-0 draw.

A semi-final against German champions Borussia Dortmund ended up being another important, but harsh, lesson in European football for Ferguson's young side. A 1-0 defeat in the Westfalenstadion was not a bad result, though United probably deserved a draw in terms of possession and chances created. But Lars Ricken's eighth-minute goal in the second leg made a hard task an almost insurmountable one and though United again created enough opportunities to score the three goals they needed, it was one of those nights when a combination of bad luck and bad finishing meant the ball just would not go in.

The statistics showed that United had 21 attempts on goal and Ferguson remained sanguine after the match, 'The players gave everything and I couldn't have asked for more – apart from a few goals!' Dortmund, incidentally, went on to win the Champions League, beating Juventus 3-1 in the final.

At the end of the season, with United once more champions of England, Cantona announced his retirement from football. 'I don't want to be a player who leaves a big club to play in the lower divisions,' he said. 'Manchester United will be my last club.'

Cantona further declared that his heart and legs were 'made to play British football' and that his relationship with the club was 'a love story. Old Trafford, win or lose, is a place you hate leaving. The ground and the club are like a disease – once into your bloodstream there is no escaping their charm and passion for good football.'

Perhaps Ferguson should have the last word on the player he used to call 'mon genius' as the club announced Cantona's departure, 'Eric has had a huge impact on the development of our younger players. He has been a model professional in the way he conducted himself and a joy to manage. He is certainly one of the most gifted and dedicated players I have had the pleasure of working with. He leaves with our best wishes and will always be welcome at Old Trafford, he has given us so many wonderful memories.'

The Sun journalist John Sadler opined, in the wake of the Crystal Palace incident, that Cantona should be deported forthwith. In their intemperate coverage, the paper felt that his influence was more malign than benign, but more reasoned – and reasonable – voices had prevailed. Some felt that Cantona would best be forgotten, but United fans thought otherwise and still sing his name to this day. 'I'm so proud the fans still sing my name,' he has said.

Cantona once said that, 'Those who accept being in my shadow are the most intelligent people because they know that I make them win.'

It sounds arrogant. It *is* arrogant. But it is also true because not the least of Cantona's legacy at United was a bunch of young players who would lift the club to the greatest heights it, or indeed any English club, has ever know. As Ryan Giggs said, 'When you see Eric Cantona brushing up on his skills, you know that no one can be satisfied with their standard.'

v Arsenal 2-1 (aet)

33

14 April 1999
FA Cup semi-final replay
Villa Park
Attendance: 30,223

MANCHESTER UNITED	ARSENAL
Peter Schmeichel	David Seaman
Gary Neville	Lee Dixon
Jaap Stam	Tony Adams
Ronny Johnsen	Martin Keown
Phil Neville	Nigel Winterburn
Nicky Butt	Emmanuel Petit
David Beckham	Patrick Vieira
Jesper Blomqvist	Freddie Ljungberg
Roy Keane	Ray Parlour
Ole Gunnar Solskjaer	Dennis Bergkamp
Teddy Sheringham	Nicolas Anelka
Manager: Alex Ferguson	*Manager:* Arsene Wenger

THE FA Cup semi-final replay kicks off on the evening of Wednesday 14 April and Arsenal straight away look like they are going to try to test out Phil Neville, who is deputising for Denis Irwin at left-back. Fortunately for United, and Neville in particular, Arsenal's flyer Marc Overmars is also missing the game, and Ray Parlour doesn't have the speed to get past Neville down the wide right.

The first real chances of the game fall to United; first Nicky Butt is denied what looks a possible penalty claim, then Phil Neville, getting forward well, links up with David Beckham down the left and Beckham's cross is lifted over the bar by Ole Gunnar Solskjaer.

United build a period of pressure which brings three corners in quick succession – though nothing much comes of any of them – and then a simple ball over the top looks to have caught out a rather square Arsenal back four, but Tony Adams slides in with a tackle on Solskjaer before any real danger can develop.

With 17 minutes gone, United break quickly from an Arsenal attack, Teddy Sheringham lays a ball back to Beckham. He's 35 yards out but given a little bit of time and space by Sheringham he manages to beat David Seaman in the Arsenal goal with a shot which didn't so much move as change direction in mid-air.

Although Dennis Bergkamp creates a chance for himself by cutting in from the right before shooting straight at Peter Schmeichel, it's mostly United – a Sheringham snapshot from near the penalty spot and a Sheringham header from a Beckham free kick on the left are both close, with Seaman beaten.

Gradually Arsenal fight their way into the game and by half-time it is a more even contest, but United still lead by that Beckham goal. The second half starts scrappily, though as it wears on United fashion enough good chances to be out of sight. Roy Keane puts Solskjaer clean through but with just Seaman to beat, the Norwegian drags his shot across the face of goal. A minute later Sheringham finds Jesper Blomqvist in an almost identical position and he blasts it wide.

Then Beckham is found on his own from a Solskjaer cutback and hits a chance arguably harder than the one from which he scored, high, wide and horrible. Just a minute later Solskjaer wastes a one on one by shooting straight at Seaman, Bergkamp takes a pot-shot from distance and a wicked deflection off Jaap Stam takes it beyond the reach of Schmeichel.

United almost respond instantly when Beckham slides a ball across the face of goal – Seaman can't cut it out, but Sheringham is fractions away from touching it into an empty net. Then Arsenal have the ball in the back of the United net for a second time when Schmeichel spills a Bergkamp shot, but Nicolas Anelka is offside before he picks up the loose ball and rounds the keeper.

After 74 minutes Keane hacks down Marc Overmars (on for Ljungberg) in full flight and picks up a second yellow card, having got one in the first half for bringing down Bergkamp to put a stop to a dangerous-looking Arsenal move.

Despite being down to ten men United appear reasonably comfortable in defence until Phil Neville brings down Parlour for an injury-time penalty. No complaints at the award from the United players. Schmeichel, though, using every inch of his massive frame, dives to his left and pushes it away. It's at what commentators often call 'a nice height', but it's still a fine save. Far from being pleased with himself, though, the great Dane is swiftly back to his feet and urging the team back up the field. Bergkamp, incidentally, up until then a regular penalty taker, never took another spot kick for his club.

Moments later the whistle goes for full time and we face another 30 minutes. The odds must be on Arsenal at that point: with Bergkamp and the pacy Overmars pulling the strings they are achieving some sort of ascendency, though their only clear-cut opportunity in the first period of extra time comes when Schmeichel is forced into a point-blank save on his line.

With 109 minutes on the clock the ten men of United must be tiring. One man isn't, however. Ryan Giggs, on for Blomqvist after 62 minutes, intercepts a weary crossfield pass from Vieira inside his own half. He sets off down the left wing, as he has done so many times before, but this time rather than look for an inside ball, or taking it to the byline before crossing, he decides to go it alone.

He cuts inside and weaves between four Arsenal defenders before smashing the ball past the England goalkeeper and into the roof of the net from an acute angle. It's one of the great solo goals of all time. It's probably *the* best FA Cup goal of all time. And it keeps alive the United dream of a unique Treble.

Arsenal still manage to fashion a couple of half-chances for themselves in the ten minutes that remain, but they come to nought, almost as if they themselves believe they have witnessed the winning goal. And so it proves.

'If this is the last semi-final replay goal we ever see, well it ranks with some of the greatest ever scored,' said co-commentator Andy Gray. 'He just bobbed and weaved and kept going, and when it needed a finish, my god, did he give us one. What a strike. After beating three, four, five players. Wonderful, wonderful. Fit to win any football match.'

Having already beaten Middlesbrough, Liverpool, Fulham and Chelsea in the 1999 FA Cup, United had had anything but an easy ride through to the semi-final, particularly the Liverpool match where it had taken very late goals from Yorke and Solskjaer to turn a 1-0 deficit into a 2-1 win.

And it had taken two long, hard games to get past Arsenal. The first match, a lunchtime kick-off also at Villa Park, had finished 0-0, but certainly wasn't devoid of incident. The main talking point of the first half proved to be a disallowed United goal when Keane smashed a Giggs cross in at the far post but was flagged for offside. 'He got that one wrong,' said Gray on Sky Sports.

The game remained even in the second half: Andy Cole made nothing of a one-on-one with Seaman, Ronny Johnsen just beat a speedy Anelka to a ball floated over his head, Anelka also did little with a one-on-one against Schmeichel and Arsenal required a last-ditch intervention from Adams to halt Yorke in his tracks.

Five minutes into extra time Nelson Vivas was sent off for a second yellow card, and after that it was mostly a backs-to-the-wall defensive display by Arsenal, though largely negotiated without undue alarm.

After United had edged their way past the Gunners, the final always had an air of 'after the Lord Mayor's Show' about it. Newcastle were a decent side but were several notches below the team they had been in the 1995/96 and 1996/97 seasons when they twice finished as runners-up in the Premier League. Newcastle had done well to get past Everton and Spurs in the previous two rounds but on the day they looked somewhat out of their depth.

United had the Champions League Final in four days' time and with Keane and Scholes both suspended for that match, Ferguson paired them together for the FA Cup Final.

Nicky Butt, whose role in central midfield would be crucial in the absence of those two, was omitted from the matchday squad altogether as he couldn't be risked. Top scorer Yorke was dropped to the bench for the same reason, while Stam was asked to prove his fitness after an Achilles injury, but only as a substitute.

United's plans almost went out of the window in the first ten minutes when an injury to Keane forced him off, to be replaced by Sheringham. But within two minutes of coming on Sheringham had given United the lead. A neat move between Cole and Scholes and then a one-two between Scholes and

Sheringham ended with the latter ghosting into the box and sliding a low drive under Newcastle keeper Steve Harper.

Newcastle had plenty of possession but few clear-cut chances while United, with less of the ball, did more. A glancing header from Sheringham was just wide of Harper's near post and Cole didn't quite get enough on a clever lob, allowing Nikos Dabizas to get back and clear off the line.

Newcastle manager Ruud Gullit brought Duncan Ferguson on for the second half but before the abrasive Scotsman could have an impact, United had added a second. A weak clearance by Dabizas was picked up by Solskjaer and knocked in to Sheringham on the edge of the area. His lay-off found Scholes who hammered it home left-footed from 20 yards.

A minute later Temuri Ketsbaia had a goalbound shot blocked on the line by May with Schmeichel beaten, but for the next quarter of an hour United dominated, with Yorke (on for Cole) heading a fabulous Giggs cross just over when it looked easier to score, then Sheringham came even closer by lobbing the ball on to the bar.

Newcastle sub Silvio Maric had his team's best late chance when he was one-on-one with Schmeichel but screwed his shot wide of the post.

'No disrespect to Newcastle,' said Schmeichel, disrespectfully, 'but I think they were frightened of the final. We were just steaming ahead, it was so easy for us. Even at 1-0 we started conserving energy for the next game. It was probably the most boring final ever.'

United's league campaign had been a struggle. Although they had played well, sometimes brilliantly, they had had to fight off a sustained challenge from Arsenal in particular, and Chelsea too. Although United scored 21 more goals than Arsenal, the Gunners' parsimonious defence conceded only 17 all season, 20 fewer than United so as well as falling only one point short of United's total their goal difference was only one behind also: United's +43 just pipping Arsenal's +42.

United lost just three league matches all season, as did Chelsea (Arsenal lost four) and not for the first time what swung the title in their favour was their stunning form in the New Year. All three of their league defeats – at Arsenal and Sheffield Wednesday and at home to Middlesbrough – came before the end of December. More importantly, on each occasion United bounced straight back and took maximum points from the match immediately after each defeat.

The September loss at Arsenal was followed four days later by a home win over Liverpool; a harshly awarded 18th-minute penalty was converted by Denis Irwin and a left-footed strike by Scholes in the 79th minute sealed the points. The November loss to Sheffield Wednesday was quickly followed by a 3-2 win over a decent Leeds United side, with Butt, Keane and Scholes getting the goals. The even more shocking home defeat by a mid-table Middlesbrough side on 19 December saw United hit back to beat Nottingham Forest 3-0 on Boxing Day thanks to two goals from Johnsen and another from Giggs.

It was the second league meeting of the season between United and Forest that really caught the eye, however.

It was 6 February 1999 at the City Ground, a date United usually avoid playing on for obvious reasons. A struggling Forest side – who were destined to finish bottom of the Premier League table – had conceded early goals to Yorke (two minutes) and Cole (seven minutes), although Alan Rogers equalised in between the two United goals, and that's the way it stayed until half-time.

Cole (50) and Yorke (67) each scored a second goal and with United in cruise control, Ferguson decided to give Yorke a rest and send Solskjaer on for the last 18 minutes. 'Just keep the ball and play it nice and simple,' were Jim Ryan's last-minute instructions to Solskjaer. 'We don't need any more goals.'

Needed or not, Solskjaer wasn't going to turn them down. Between the 80th minute and the 90th minute he scored four times. Ron Atkinson, the Forest manager, joked wryly after the game, 'Good job they didn't put Solskjaer on earlier. Then we'd really have been in trouble.'

United simply powered away in the springtime, going 20 games unbeaten in the league, of which they won 15. It was too much even for a good Arsenal side but that FA Cup semi-final replay was the key to so much of what followed. 'There were so many big games that spring,' said Beckham. 'But one stands out above the rest; the one that made everything possible.'

v Bayern Munich 2-1

34

26 May 1999
Champions League Final
Nou Camp, Barcelona
Attendance: 90,245

MANCHESTER UNITED	BAYERN MUNICH
Peter Schmeichel	Oliver Kahn
Gary Neville	Lothar Matthaus
Jaap Stam	Markus Babbel
Ronny Johnsen	Thomas Linke
Denis Irwin	Samuel Kuffour
Nicky Butt	Michael Tarnat
David Beckham	Stefan Effenberg
Ryan Giggs	Jens Jeremies
Jesper Blomqvist	Mario Basler
Dwight Yorke	Carsten Jancker
Andy Cole	Alexander Zickler
Manager: Alex Ferguson	*Manager:* Ottmar Hitzfeld

'CAN United score? They always score.' Commentator Clive Tyldesley's statement wasn't completely factually accurate: United failed to score in eight of their 62 matches across all competitions in the 1998/99 season, but it was rare. And even rarer on the truly big occasions.

Tyldesley says the background to that comment had been Mark Lawrenson's verdict on the FA Cup Final the week before when the former Liverpool player turned pundit had said, 'The only certainty was that it wouldn't be Manchester United nil'.

But for a long time the 1999 Champions League Final looked like becoming the ninth match in which United would go scoreless, and this time it was going to cost them the trophy that the club, and its manager, desired above all others.

United's Champions League campaign had begun with a comfortable preliminary round match against LKS Lodz, made necessary by the fact that they had finished only as runners-up in the league in the 1997/98 season. Goals from Ryan Giggs and Andy Cole had brought a 2-0 win in the home leg back in August and a solid defensive display kept the away leg goalless.

But there followed a brute of a group stage draw which pitched United with Bayern Munich and Barcelona. To make matters worse, that year not all second-placed teams would make it through to the quarter-finals – only the best two from the six groups would do so.

With Barca visiting Old Trafford on the first matchday, in mid-September, it gave United virtually no margin for error. It turned into a proverbial game of two halves with United's performance in the first half so good that the crowd were 'ole-ing'. Goals from Giggs (17 minutes) and Scholes (24) had their illustrious opponents chasing shadows. Anderson da Silva pulled one back soon after half-time and a Giovanni penalty on the hour brought the scores level, but a sumptuous David Beckham free kick on 64 minutes restored United's advantage.

A red card for Nicky Butt after he had handled in the area resulted in another penalty – this time converted by Luis Enrique – and left United hanging on rather until the final whistle.

Just four days later Butt received another red card, in the defeat at Arsenal, which constituted two of the five he received in his whole 12-year, 387-game career at our club – not bad for a combative midfielder.

The second round of matches brought another draw for United, a creditable one in Bayern Munich's Olympiastadion. United recovered well from an early goal by Brazilian Giovane Elber to lead thanks to goals by Dwight Yorke (30) and Scholes (49), but a rare mistake from Peter Schmeichel allowed Bayern to snatch a last-minute equaliser.

It all left the home and away games against Brondby as vital to United's chances of progressing. Six goals in front of the Danish side's own fans in Copenhagen would surely be enough to satisfy even Alex Ferguson. 'I wasn't overly impressed by our performance, we gave the ball away too often for my liking,' he said. 'But it's no bad thing to establish a reputation for scoring goals.'

The return fixture two weeks later merely produced more of the same – a 5-0 battering. And this time the manager was a happy man. 'It was stunning,' he said. 'Probably the best performance in the first half that I have seen in my time at Old Trafford. The movement and imagination were fantastic.'

Meanwhile, Barcelona had lost both home and away against Bayern, which meant that, heading into the fifth round of matches, United topped the group on eight points with the Germans on seven. More importantly, United were four points ahead of Barcelona and needed only another draw with the Spanish giants to ensure themselves of at least second place in the group.

It was an end-to-end affair, with United bouncing back well from a first-minute goal from Anderson to lead through Yorke (25) and Cole (53). A Rivaldo double either side of Yorke's second (68) gave cause for alarm, and the Brazilian striker almost completed his hat-trick when he hit the bar, but United survived to draw 3-3. Louis Van Gaal was the Barcelona coach at the time.

The final match of the group stages was a dull 1-1 draw with Bayern Munich. With a draw suiting both teams and – owing to results elsewhere – putting both through, they seemed to be reserving their fire for bigger challenges to come.

United soon discovered that their route to the final would demand that they navigate a duo of Italian challenges. Inter Milan came to Old Trafford on 3 March and were met with a world-class United performance. In particular Beckham, up against Argentinian Diego Simeone who had got him sent off in the previous year's World Cup finals, caused havoc down the right with his crosses. From one of these, Yorke notched United's first with a firm header after just six minutes, and the same combination made it 2-0 in the dying seconds of the first half. Inter pushed hard for an away goal in the second half, with one Simeone effort disallowed for a push.

A 63rd-minute goal from Nicola Ventola in the San Siro gave fans a few palpitations, but French referee Gilles Veissiere was strong enough to resist all Inter's increasingly shrill demands for penalties. An 88th-minute close-range goal from Scholes gave United a draw on the night and a 3-1 win on aggregate.

That was not the end of the Italian menace, however. In the semi-finals Juventus were the opposition. Not only did Carlo Ancelotti's team boast the best of Italy, it also had Zinedine Zidane and Didier Deschamps from France's 1998 World Cup-winning side and the great Dutch midfielder Edgar Davids, nicknamed 'the Pitbull' by Van Gaal.

A 25th-minute goal from Juventus captain Antonio Conte looked like it might decide the first leg until substitute Teddy Sheringham, only on for the last 11 minutes, produced a wonderful cameo which panicked the Italians until he laid on the equaliser for Ryan Giggs. It at least gave United something to build on a fortnight later in Turin.

That night started disastrously for United as star Italian striker Filippo Inzaghi scored twice within the first quarter of an hour.

Leading from the front, United captain Roy Keane almost singled-handedly dragged his team back into the match by sheer force of will and personality. He himself pulled a goal back after 24 minutes with a powerful header from a Beckham corner. Then he got a yellow card for a trip of Zidane which he knew would rule him out of the final should United get there, but he hardly let the personal disaster slow him down, let alone stop him. 'I was so much into this battle that the consequences of the card barely registered,' said Keane.

On 34 minutes, Yorke scored with a diving header to make it 2-2 and United were ahead on away goals. But they continued to press, twice hitting the woodwork, though they were grateful for a fine Schmeichel save to deny Inzaghi his hat-trick.

Halfway through the second half, Paul Scholes came on as a substitute for Jesper Blomqvist and probably wished he hadn't. A yellow card ruled him out of the final too; no doubt Ferguson was already plotting how to go about winning a Champions League Final without his central midfield.

With just six minutes of the game remaining, Yorke was hauled down when through on goal, and seeing the ball run loose to Cole the experienced Swiss referee Urs Meier played the advantage and Cole stroked it into an empty net.

United made the worst possible start to the 1999 Champions League Final, standing by as Mario Basler, who had scored the winner for Bayern Munich in their narrow semi-final win over Dynamo Kiev, opened the scoring in the fifth minute. His free kick went straight through a feeble United wall to put the Germans 1-0 up.

United were at sixes and sevens then and their performance didn't get much better. Beckham played a fine match in central midfield but bereft of Keane and Scholes, United struggled to create much, and were denied Beckham's brilliant crossing into the bargain.

At half-time Ferguson pulled his masterstroke. 'When you go to collect your medals at the end of the game, you'll be three feet from the European Cup,' he told his players. 'If you lose, you will have to walk right past it. You won't be able to touch it, you won't be allowed to lift it, and this could be your only chance. Trust me, you don't want that.'

In the second half Bayern had several chances to put the game beyond United: Stefan Effenberg, called 'the best player in the world this year' by his manager, had a decent shot, then a chip which a stretching Schmeichel just managed to tip over the bar, a Mehmet Scholl shot clipped the inside of a post and bounced back into Schmeichel's hands and a Carsten Jancker overhead shot hit the crossbar.

Sheringham and Ole Gunnar Solskjaer came on for Cole and Blomqvist, and for a Beckham corner on the United left in stoppage time even Schmeichel came up. 'Bayern had dealt with everything going into their box. The only option left was to go up and cause some havoc,' he said.

It worked. Beckham delivered it towards Schmeichel and the German defence, momentarily drawn to the goalkeeper's unexpected presence, left Yorke a little bit of space on the far side of the box to knock it back in.

Giggs helped the ball on and there was Sheringham to nudge home the equaliser.

'It's two miskicks,' said Solskjaer later. 'Giggsy miskicks then Teddy finishes with a miskick … I think, although he might not admit it! Everyone went mad except me, I headed back to the halfway line, concentrating, focused.'

Maybe not a miskick, but a scuff certainly. Sheringham didn't care, and nor did United. They all count.

'Name on the trophy!' yelled Tyldesley in the commentary box.

As the German players and coaches on both sides started talking tactics for extra time, the United players decided on an entirely different approach. They had felt the Germans rocking and decided to go for the jugular.

There were 93 minutes on the clock and another United corner came. This time it was Sheringham who helped the ball into the danger area and there was Solskjaer at the back post, losing Sammy Kuffour for just about the only time in the match, to lash it into the roof of the net. 'Manchester United have reached the Promised Land,' announced Tyldesley.

A mere 103 seconds had elapsed between 1-0 to Bayern Munich and 2-1 to Manchester United.

'It cannot be, the winners are crying and the losers are dancing,' exclaimed UEFA president Lennart Johansson in wonderment. It had taken him all that time to get down from his seat and catch the lift down to the tunnel and because he was inside that whole time, Johansson had no idea of the developments taking place on the pitch.

'Football,' said Ferguson. 'Bloody hell!'

It would have been Sit Matt Busby's 90th birthday, and with the Munich connection too it was impossible not to think there had been some form of divine intervention. 'It felt like it was meant to be,' said Ferguson.

The players partied on the pitch, then partied long into the night, but it was again Ferguson who put it most aptly, 'The celebrations begun by the goal will never really stop.'

v Leeds United 1-0

35

20 February 2000
Premier League
Elland Road
Attendance: 40,160

MANCHESTER UNITED	LEEDS UNITED
Mark Bosnich	Nigel Martyn
Gary Neville	Garry Kelly
Jaap Stam	Lucas Radebe
Mikael Silvestre	Jonathan Woodgate
Denis Irwin	Ian Harte
Nicky Butt	Matthew Jones
Paul Scholes	Lee Bowyer
Ryan Giggs	Jason Wilcox
Roy Keane	Eirik Bakke
Dwight Yorke	Alan Smith
Andy Cole	Harry Kewell
Manager: Sir Alex Ferguson	*Manager:* David O'Leary

HOW can a team top a Treble? After the trophies. After the acclaim. After the open-top bus ride. What then? It is by no means the least of Sir Alex Ferguson's many accomplishments that he is able to re-motivate a group of players who have won everything there is to win in the game, to re-energise and refresh a squad and to go again. Sir Alex most definitely achieved that over the summer of 1999.

The 1999/2000 season started with a new goalkeeper. Peter Schmeichel had announced some time earlier that the previous season would be his last with United, that he needed to move, and replacing him was the only major player issue which Sir Alex needed to address in the wake of the Treble triumph. The Australian Mark Bosnich got the nod – a free transfer from Aston Villa where his contract had run out after seven and a half years with the Midlands side – and appeared to be a good choice.

The new season started with a run of nine games undefeated. It came to a juddering halt at Stamford Bridge in October where United were beaten 5-0, but by then they had already won at both Arsenal and Liverpool and beaten Leeds United at home – the sides which were to finish second, fourth and third respectively in that season's Premier League.

United lost just three games all season and romped home by the incredible margin of 18 points. Dwight Yorke and Andy Cole got 22 goals each, while Ole Gunnar Solskjaer, Paul Scholes and Roy Keane also got into double figures.

Solskjaer repeated his trick of scoring four in one game, albeit not in ten minutes, when United beat Everton 5-1 at Old Trafford on 4 December, by which time Cole had also got in on the act by scoring four in the 5-1 win over

Newcastle United on 30 August. Yorke got a hat-trick in the 3-1 win over Derby County on 11 March and Paul Scholes did the same against West Ham United, who were beaten 7-1 on 1 April.

Arguably the most important goal of the season, however, was the one Cole got at Elland Road.

At the time of the match Leeds were lying in second place, just three points behind United. Eight days earlier, United had suffered their third league defeat of the season, losing 3-0 at Newcastle United, and Leeds clearly saw the opportunity to close the gap completely. Yorke, who had scored both goals in the Old Trafford meeting between the sides back on 14 August, started the game but limped off before the half-hour was up, to be replaced by Teddy Sheringham.

United had started the brighter of the two teams but Leeds looked dangerous from a series of Ian Harte free kicks, with Bosnich reacting well to keep out a couple of them. Scholes had probably the best chance for United when he hit a curling shot from just outside the penalty area which finished just wide.

Seven minutes into the second half, Scholes's through ball was flicked up in the air by Cole and over Leeds defender Lucas Radebe. Radebe, just back after an injury he picked up during the African Cup of Nations and himself briefly a target for United, couldn't quite recover in time to catch the speedy Cole, who gave keeper Nigel Martyn no chance with his precise finish.

Two minutes later Roy Keane struck the woodwork, and not long after that Eirik Bakke did the same at the other end from a Leeds corner. United were now content to soak up the Leeds pressure and play on the break, which their pacy front line always gave them the opportunity to do. Martyn pulled off good saves from Scholes and Nicky Butt.

Lee Bowyer missed the best chance of the match for Leeds when in the 81st minute Bosnich spilled a close-range shot, Alan Smith hit the loose ball against the post and with the ball bouncing back nicely for Bowyer he somehow managed to lift it over the bar when it seemed easier to score. 'They got the chance and took it, we had chances and we missed them,' said Leeds boss David O'Leary succinctly.

It meant that instead of Leeds closing the gap, United had extended it to six points, and thereafter they started to stretch away. There followed draws away to Wimbledon and at home to Liverpool, and then 11 straight wins which left United well clear of Arsenal in second place. United scored 97 goals in the Premier League and had a goal difference of +52.

United made a pretty good fist of defending their Champions League trophy, in what became a rather tedious four-year experiment involving two group stages.

In the first home and away wins over Austrians Sturm Graz, four out of six against Croatia Zagreb and shared points with Marseille (each side winning their home fixture) left United three points clear at the top of Group D.

They then went into Group B (of four) alongside Valencia, Fiorentina and Bordeaux.

This second group phase started badly with defeat in Florence, 2-0. Mistakes by Keane and Henning Berg cost United goals by the Italian side's two Argentinian internationals, Gabriel Batistuta and Abel Balbo. But they got back on track a fortnight later when Keane, Scholes and Solskjaer gave them a decisive 3-0 win over Valencia at Old Trafford.

The European challenge recommenced with back-to-back games against Bordeaux and as Sir Alex commented, 'We are always better in the springtime. I always prepare my teams to come strongly around March and April because that is when the moment of truth arrives and you have to win the big games. We do a lot of stamina work around the Christmas and New Year time and I think that pays off in the final two or three months.'

That proved to be the case as goals from Sheringham and Giggs brought a 2-0 win at Old Trafford, and although the French side went 1-0 up in the ninth minute in their home game, the 23rd-minute sending-off of Lilian Laslandes for two yellows in almost as many minutes turned the tide in United's favour.

It wasn't until the 83rd minute that Solskjaer grabbed the winner (Keane having equalised just after the half-hour), but it was no more than they deserved for their second-half pressure.

The fifth match brought the return of Fiorentina and an early goal for Batistuta. But United equalised in the 20th minute when Cole was given time to control David Beckham's cross and apply the finishing touch. After 33 minutes Berg headed against the bar and Keane was the quickest to the rebound for 2-1. The Italians were reduced to ten men just after the hour when Fabio Rossitto was sent off for tripping Yorke, and Yorke himself took advantage ten minutes later, stealing in to head home a Ryan Giggs cross.

The final second group phase match was far more important to their Spanish opponents than it was to United, but with news coming in that a draw would be enough for Valencia, both teams took their feet off the pedal and cruised through the last 30 minutes or so.

The quarter-final pitched United against Real Madrid, one of the giants of European football, now stirring from their slumbers. Real had won the competition in 1997/98 – their first victory since 1965/66 – and were looking for their second in three years. United returned home from the Bernabeu with a hard-fought 0-0 draw to their credit, but it all went wrong in the second leg. Keane managed to knock the ball past his own keeper in the 21st minute and as United pressed in the second half they were expertly picked off twice by one of the greatest strikers the game has ever seen, Raul.

In between Raul's two goals, Keane managed to put a sitter over the bar, but finally on 64 minutes Beckham weaved his way into the box, past a couple of attempted tackles and smacked the ball in. There were still 26 minutes remaining, plenty of time in United's playbook, but it took until the 88th before

Scholes could make it 3-2 from the penalty spot after Steve McManaman had brought down Keane, and the familiar charge came up just short for once.

Real went on to win the trophy, beating Valencia in the final. As United had unceremoniously beaten Valencia in the earlier stages, it's reasonable to believe that they might well have gone on to reach another Champions League Final had they not given Real such a big head start.

The other big story of the season was United's defence of the FA Cup, or rather lack of it. United were invited to take part in the inaugural FIFA World Club Challenge in Brazil and were encouraged to accept as many at the FA felt it would help in England's bid to bring the 2006 World Cup to England.

Sir Alex suggested that the issue of fixture congestion could be alleviated by giving United a bye into the fourth round of the FA Cup. 'We want to help the country by taking part in this event, but not if that leaves us with an impossible burden in fulfilling our domestic programme with any degree of success,' he said. 'One obvious solution would be for the FA to allow us to enter the FA Cup at a later stage.'

The FA responded by saying they would allow United to withdraw from the FA Cup entirely – they clearly wanted to have their cake and eat it, by encouraging the club to take part but without being willing to make any corresponding concessions.

It put United in a no-win situation, as chairman Martin Edwards immediately realised, 'If we don't go people will say that we are selfish and not prepared to help the 2006 World Cup bid, but it we do go we will be criticised for not competing in the FA Cup.' Edwards was spot on. United decided they would take part, and as the media storm descended on the club, the FA was notable by its absence in defending the club's decision.

Results in the World Club Challenge were mixed, at best. In the searing heat, United lost to Brazilian side Vasco da Gama, drew with the Mexicans of Necaxa and beat the Australians of South Melbourne. The four points they won saw them finish third (on goal difference) in their pool and hence not advance to either the final – won by Brazilian side Corinthians on penalties – or the third place play-off, in which Necaxa beat Real Madrid on penalties.

The warm-weather training the trip afforded Sir Alex's men was, however, considered extremely beneficial. 'It was a brilliant opportunity to relax in the sun,' said Giggs.

'We came back feeling great,' added Beckham. And that certainly showed as United ran rampant through the rest of the Premier League season and cruised to back-to-back title triumphs.

v **Arsenal** 6-1

36

25 February 2001
Premier League
Old Trafford
Attendance: 67,535

MANCHESTER UNITED	ARSENAL
Fabien Barthez	David Seaman
Gary Neville	Oleg Luzhny
Jaap Stam	Ashley Cole
Mikael Silvestre	Gilles Grimandi
Wes Brown	Igors Stepanovs
Nicky Butt	Robert Pires
Paul Scholes	Patrick Vieira
David Beckham	Ray Parlour
Roy Keane	Silvinho
Dwight Yorke	Sylvain Wiltord
Ole Gunnar Solskjaer	Thierry Henry
Manager: Sir Alex Ferguson	*Manager:* Arsene Wenger

TWO minutes are on the clock as Paul Scholes and Dwight Yorke combine for the opening goal, but Arsenal hit back and having gone close a couple of times through Sylvain Wiltord a slick passing move and a neat one-two between Wiltord and Robert Pires leads to a close-range, left-footed equaliser from Thierry Henry. The rest of the half belongs to United, however, as they simply blow Arsenal away.

After 17 minutes the vaunted Arsenal offside trap fails when Gilles Grimandi gets it horribly wrong and Yorke grabs his second of the game. His hat-trick almost follows a minute later when his header is just tipped over by England international goalkeeper David Seaman. But after 21 minutes, Yorke has his treble when a 60-yard pass from David Beckham finds him and perfect chest control coupled with a strength and determination which Igors Stepanovs never comes close to matching puts Yorke through on goal and he makes no mistake.

After 25 minutes, Yorke, who is all pace and movement, turns the Gunners' defence inside out, this way and that, destroying the floundering Stepanovs, and lays on a simple fourth for Roy Keane, charging into the penalty area and meeting Yorke's ball first time to slot it across goal and beyond the reach of a diving Seaman.

Thirty-seven minutes gone and it's Nicky Butt's turn to breeze past Grimandi down the United right to present Ole Gunnar Solskjaer with the simplest chance at the near post, and a number of Arsenal fans decide it's time to start making their way back to London.

There's just time for Seaman to make a good stop of a Scholes attempt before referee Paul Durkin brings the half to a close. Much to Arsenal's relief, United ease up a fair bit in the second half and the first quarter of an hour or so passes relatively uneventfully. A Beckham shot from 20 yards out is well dealt with by Seaman, then Jaap Stam plants a header just wide from a Beckham free kick.

Into the last ten minutes and Teddy Sheringham also goes wide with a header from a Beckham cross, then Luke Chadwick (on as substitute for Keane) weaves into the Arsenal penalty box but can't quite find the killer final ball. There's a brief flicker from the Gunners as Freddie Ljungberg, on in place of Ashley Cole, is played through by Henry, but puts it wide.

In the dying minutes of the game Solskjaer hits the post and almost immediately after that Sheringham flicks on a ball into the area for Solskjaer who in an instant returns the favour for Sheringham to score United's sixth. It puts United 16 points clear at the top of the league.

A shell-shocked Arsenal didn't even have the stomach for a fight – usually when one team is getting battered in this way, a few tasty challenges start to go in but this match didn't see a single yellow card produced.

But that more or less summed up a season in which United scored 11 fewer points than in 1999/2000 but still won the Premier League by ten. In truth, United dominated from start to (almost) finish and only defeats in the last three matches of the season took the gloss off their campaign.

The only arrival in the close-season had been that of French international goalkeeper Fabien Barthez. The signing of Mark Bosnich – which had looked a good one at the time – had never really been a success. Admittedly he was a little unfortunate with injuries when he first arrived, which made it hard for him to get a run of games, but he didn't help himself either. His eating habits in particular gave Sir Alex cause for concern and he claimed he just couldn't get his message through to the keeper.

In terms of talent, Bosnich was right up there, but Barthez quickly became a favourite of the fans. Being both French and a goalkeeper Barthez was, inevitably, a bit mad, but his athleticism and swift distribution skills were a timely reminder of the Peter Schmeichel era. 'Fabien is a World Cup winner and has not only the personality but the vast experience that is required at Manchester United,' said Sir Alex on his arrival. Barthez wasn't to prove the long-term answer, but in his first season at United he impressed all who saw him play.

There was the slight blip of losing home and away to Liverpool, but against that United averaged more than two goals per game and, in a much tighter defensive performance than the previous season, conceded an average of less than one. Yorke's hat-trick against Arsenal was only the second one of the season in the league, after Sheringham had got one in the 5-0 win over Southampton on 28 August.

There was another hat-trick in Europe, however; Andy Cole setting out United's intent in the very first match, against Anderlecht in September when the Belgian side were thrashed 5-1 at Old Trafford. After the game Anderlecht coach Aime Anthuenis said that at times United's football was from 'another planet'.

For various reasons, United were never quite able to take their dominant home form away with them, though. Despite beating PSV Eindhoven (3-1) and Dynamo Kiev (1-0), they only picked up a single point on their travels and that was in a slightly turgid 0-0 draw in Kiev against a Dynamo side that finished bottom of the group.

In the second group stage United looked to have got back to the commonly accepted way of making progress in Europe – win in front of their own fans and draw on the road. Home and away draws with Valencia looked like great results, but in the last round of matches their failure to score enough goals against the Austrians of Sturm Graz cost United a tougher quarter-final.

All looked to be going well with Nicky Butt and Sheringham putting United two goals up inside 20 minutes. Keane's 86th-minute third was the only other goal, however, and it left United one short of the number they needed to overhaul Valencia on goal difference and top the group. 'The performance illustrated perfectly where we had been going wrong,' said Sir Alex.

'Our concentration level had been wayward in our previous attempts for the win that would have moved us into the last eight of the competition but against the Austrians it was clear early in the game that there was a resolution and focus to make sure there was no slip-up. Of course it would have been nice to have won the group but that was the price we had to pay for letting ourselves down in a couple of other group games.'

The upshot of that was a quarter-final rematch with Bayern Munich, who duly beat United narrowly both home and away. A 1-0 win for the Germans at Old Trafford in the first leg – courtesy of an 86th-minute goal from Brazilian substitute Paulo Sergio – gave United a mountain to climb in Munich. And the mountain got steadily bigger throughout the first half as Brazilian Elber (five minutes) and German international Mehmet Scholl (39) increased the lead to three goals overall. Giggs pulled one back early in the second half (49) but that was all United had to show for their efforts.

'Before the game we all thought we would get through, despite the disappointing result at Old Trafford,' Keane said in *Manchester United in Europe*, David Meek and Tom Tyrrell's superbly comprehensive record of United's European campaigns between 1956 and 2001.

'But to go two goals down left us too much to do. You have to defend as a team and to lose two goals was a disastrous start for us. We had a go in the second half but that is the least you would expect from us. I don't think there are many better teams than us when we perform. But it's no good standing here and saying that – you have to go and do the business, and we have not done it this season.'

Sir Alex agreed, 'We look at Europe to measure our progress as a football team and we failed, which is a big disappointment. The experience leaves you in reflective mood, wondering what should be the next step forward. It was the kind of setback which cuts right through you and leaves you stunned. I can assure all supporters that everything is under review.'

It had begun to appear that United's comfortable demolition of each and every Premier League opponent might actually be costing them dear in Europe where they didn't have the edge, the sharpness needed to beat the very top teams.

Keane, in his usual blunt manner, said that he had seen United players getting complacent. 'All you have to do is drop your standards slightly and it's obvious, especially in Europe. It's all very well and good winning the Premier League but we need to step up to another level. We are not good enough in a lot of areas; it's hard to admit that we are not good enough but it is a fact.'

Harsh words, but it was a measure of how far United had come. For the past two seasons they had been disappointed to go out in tight ties against the teams which went on to win the Champions League – first Real Madrid and now Bayern Munich, who went on to knock out the defending champions in the semi-finals and then beat Valencia on penalties in the final to gain a deserved triumph after several years of coming close. It was clearly taking either a special team or a special performance to knock United out of Europe.

The domestic cups didn't really go United's way in 2000/01 with fourth round defeats in the League Cup by Sunderland and in the FA Cup by West Ham United but the Premier League was theirs to command.

In the build-up to the Arsenal fixture, Arsene Wenger had rather sniffily declared, 'United haven't done anything special this season.' Not for the only time in their respective careers, Sir Alex had made the Arsenal manager eat his words.

v Tottenham Hotspur 5-3

37

29 September 2001
Premier League
White Hart Lane
Attendance: 36,038

MANCHESTER UNITED	TOTTENHAM HOTSPUR
Fabien Barthez	Neil Sullivan
Gary Neville	Chris Perry
Ronny Johnsen	Dean Richards
Laurent Blanc	Ledley King
Denis Irwin	Mauricio Taricco
Nicky Butt	Gus Poyet
Paul Scholes	Darren Anderton
David Beckham	Christian Ziege
Juan Sebastian Veron	Steffen Freund
Andy Cole	Teddy Sheringham
Ruud Van Nistelrooy	Les Ferdinand
Manager: Sir Alex Ferguson	*Manager:* Glenn Hoddle

THERE are comebacks and there are Manchester United comebacks. Even before the historical night in Barcelona, United had a reputation for late goals, for turning matches around when all seemed lost and for finding the inspiration to keep fighting, somehow, anyhow.

By their own standards then, a 3-0 deficit at half-time was nothing to be unduly worried about.

United had actually been playing some decent football from the start, but Spurs were absolutely clinical with their chances. The first, on 15 minutes, was buried by defender Dean Richards on his debut for Spurs: a corner on the United left by Christian Ziege and Richards looked more determined to get his head on the ball than any of the United defenders. He made a great run at the near post and got in a stooping header to put Spurs one up.

A fine player, Richards was beset by injuries, most notably knee and back problems caused by a car crash after he had skidded on some black ice. Richards was the England under-21 captain at the time but missed large chunks of the next two seasons; an even more serious illness forced his retirement from playing and led to his tragically early death in 2011 at the age of just 36. On this day, however, Richards emphatically showed why Spurs manager Glenn Hoddle had been so keen to sign him.

Ten minutes later, a period of neat possession from Spurs ended with a cute little lofted through-ball from Gus Poyet that beat the offside trap for Les Ferdinand to run on to and bury a right-to-left shot past Fabien Barthez's outstretched right arm and into the far corner of United's net. Then on the stroke of half-time Poyet was given the freedom to run the ball down to the byline, cut back infield and deliver a cross to the far post where an unmarked Ziege helped himself to a third goal.

The Spurs fans were in dreamland. But United hadn't played badly and referee Jeff Winter said later that he sensed that a comeback might be on. 'It was the weirdest 3-0 you could ever imagine because United were on top and at half-time I said to my assistants that the game was far from over.'

In the United camp, meanwhile, the players were expecting the proverbial hairdryer treatment. Instead Sir Alex Ferguson opted for a calm approach. 'I sat down and said, "Right, I'll tell you what we're going to do. We're going to score the first goal in this second half and see where it takes us,"' he later recalled. 'Teddy [Sheringham, who had transferred back to Spurs in the close season] was the Tottenham captain and as the team emerged back into the corridor I heard him say, "Now don't let them get an early goal."'

Sheringham of all people knew the power of a United fightback, he knew that if they got an inch they could take a mile, that United could not, must not, be given a lifeline. United scored in the first minute.

United didn't have much in the way of attacking alternatives on the bench – Ole Gunnar Solskjaer had replaced the injured Nicky Butt a few minutes before half-time, and during the break Sir Alex replaced Denis Irwin with Mikael Silvestre on account of the Irishman also picking up an injury, but that was more a like-for-like switch than any profound tactical change.

His other options – Phil Neville, Luke Chadwick and Roy Carroll as the substitute goalkeeper – were unlikely to bring extra attacking threat. It was down to those already on the pitch.

Paul Scholes set Gary Neville away down the right on one of those famous overlapping runs of his, Neville crossed, and there was Andy Cole to head home the loose ball. Martin Tyler, commentating for Sky Sports, instantly asked the question as to whether it marked that start of a comeback and even at 3-1 up you could tell some of the Spurs players were wondering the same thing.

It took another 12 minutes before the next United goal, however, which came via a Beckham corner from United's right. The ball was allowed to travel a long way to where Laurent Blanc, a deadline day signing from Inter, scored with a powerful header. It was to prove Blanc's (or 'Larry White' as United fans called him) only league goal for United in 48 appearances, though he did score three more in Europe.

The equaliser came from another new signing. Dutch international Ruud Van Nistelrooy was to become a goalscoring phenomenon at United and he settled in almost instantly, scoring on his debut against Fulham. He had already notched up three in the first six matches of the season and this became his fourth in seven.

Scholes fed Silvestre and the Frenchman put in a first-time cross from the United left that was just asking to be headed into the back of the net. Van Nistelrooy duly obliged. 'Manchester United have turned things round quite magnificently,' said Tyler. 'Certainties, it seemed at half-time, to leave here empty-handed, now it is Tottenham 3 United 3. Manchester United moving in for the kill.'

Spurs were rocking and despite all the talent in their team they seemed unable to know how to prevent the United assault. It took just two further minutes for United to take the lead and this time it was their third major summer signing, Argentinian international Juan Sebastian Veron, who did the damage.

A fabulous crossfield pass from right to left by Beckham was followed by some neat touches by Silvestre and Scholes and a beautiful touch from Solskjaer gave Veron time on the left edge of the Spurs penalty area to pick his spot and beat Neil Sullivan with a shot into the corner.

United's comeback was completed in the 87th minute when Solskjaer ran at the heart of the Spurs defence and as defenders were drawn to him he found Beckham in acres of space in a central position. Beckham had time to chest the ball down and chose his spot then sent a curling, curving, left-footed shot into the corner of the net. It was Beckham's first match as captain and he crowned it with the final goal of the afternoon.

'Beckham, with time to take a touch, time to take aim... And if you give him that type of time, the outcome is inevitable,' said Tyler. 'As now is the result of the match.'

'It was probably a case of a little bit of complacency that the game was over,' admitted unused Spurs sub Matthew Etherington, 'plus Alex Ferguson's half-time talk – but United were unbelievable in the second half. You can never write them off.'

Gus Poyet, an accomplished midfielder in his playing days and a highly-thought-of coach and pundit since, said, 'It was awful, I didn't want to leave the dressing room, I wanted to hide in there. It was terrible because at half-time we thought we were one of the best teams in the league and by full time we felt like one of the worst.'

Spurs manager Glen Hoddle said much the same, 'A great game? I can't take much comfort from that because I've got to look at my own team and we're in the business of trying to win football matches.'

In spite of this result, it turned into a season which didn't quite happen for United. They beat Spurs 4-0 at Old Trafford in the March return match, with Beckham and Van Nistelrooy scoring two each, but they were arguably their best two league performances of the season. They lost nine matches, including home and away to both Arsenal and Liverpool, the two teams who finished above them.

History may judge United's two big high-profile signings differently, with Van Nistelrooy being a massive success in terms of his goalscoring and Veron being considered someone who couldn't quite adapt to the pace of the Premier League.

Van Nistelrooy's 150 goals in 219 games put him tenth in the all-time top scorers list at United, and even if there is a case for thinking that his very best days were behind him, his scoring record after he left the club suggests that he would have come very close indeed to overtaking Sir Bobby Charlton at the very top. But Van Nistelrooy was transferred out of United amid reports of a training ground bust-up with Cristiano Ronaldo followed by rumours that he had sworn at Ferguson when the latter had not brought him on as a substitute during the Carling Cup Final win over Wigan Athletic in 2006.

Veron arrived with the reputation as one of the world's leading playmakers and a range of passing beyond most of those in the game. As with Van Nistelrooy, Veron started as if he was going to pay full justice to such extravagant claims, but it never quite materialised for him. Veron played some magnificent games for United, particularly in Europe, but never mastered the Premier League.

Given sufficient space and time on the ball, Veron was masterful – which is why his performances in Europe always looked a cut above those he made in the Premier League – but he could be rattled if he was closed down quickly. Ferguson agreed this was the case, 'Veron was capable of exceptional football and was talented but he found the Premier League a bit difficult. He was a European player and that was where we got the best from him.'

Europe was again a tale of ifs, buts and maybes. Beaten home and away by Deportivo La Coruna in the first group stage, United nevertheless cruised through by beating Olympiakos home and away and taking four points out of six from French side Lille, who had finished third in their domestic league the previous season.

In the second group phase they did exactly the same to fellow French side Nantes, who had finished as champions in 2000/01, drawing away and thrashing them 5-1 at home.

It earned them a quarter-final with Deportivo and this time United emerged as victors. First-half goals from Beckham and Van Nistelrooy earned United a priceless 2-0 win in Spain and though the Spanish team fought hard, goals from Solskjaer (23 and 56) and Giggs (69) put United in control. Deportivo's only reply, apart from a Blanc own goal on the stroke of half-time, was in the final minute of the game from their Brazilian midfielder Djalminha.

A semi-final against Bayer Leverkusen appeared to hold no fears for United but they were just unable to put the Germans away. Twice they took the lead in the first leg at Old Trafford, through a Boris Zivkovic own goal on the half-hour and again when Van Nistelrooy slotted home a penalty on 67 minutes. But Leverkusen twice equalised, first through Michael Ballack (62) and then through Oliver Neuville (75).

At 2-2 United were in a perilous position, but in Germany they were again the first to score, Keane giving them a 28th-minute lead. Neuville made it 1-1 deep into added time at the end of the first half and there were no further goals in the second half, which meant United went out on away goals.

United did everything but score at the death when Scholes, Keane and Diego Forlan all had great chances to win it. To prove their credentials, Leverkusen went on to lose narrowly to Real Madrid in the final and to finish runners-up for the Bundesliga title, but that was of little consolation to a United side who had once again just missed out on a European final.

Veron seemed to bear the brunt of the criticism for United's European exit. 'I felt sorry for Seba. Cost £28m, became the scapegoat for our season,' said Keane.

Ryan Giggs later summed up the feelings of many, 'We're all still scratching our heads trying to work out why he wasn't a fabulous success.'

38

v Liverpool 4-0

5 April 2003
Premier League
Old Trafford
Attendance: 67,639

MANCHESTER UNITED	LIVERPOOL
Fabien Barthez	Jerzy Dudek
Gary Neville	Jamie Carragher
Rio Ferdinand	Sami Hyypia
Wes Brown	Djimi Traore
Mikael Silvestre	John Arne Riise
Ole Gunnar Solskjaer	El Hadji Diouf
Roy Keane	Dietmar Hamann
Phil Neville	Steven Gerrard
Ryan Giggs	Danny Murphy
Paul Scholes	Emile Heskey
Ruud Van Nistelrooy	Milan Baros
Manager: Sir Alex Ferguson	*Manager:* Gerard Houllier

UNITED went into this game against their old rivals knowing that Liverpool had won on each of their last two trips to Old Trafford and from the off appeared 100 per cent determined that the same thing was not going to happen this season.

Sir Alex Ferguson's uncomplicated advice to his team had been to make sure that they scored first. They took him at his word and tore into the Merseysiders from the first whistle, creating their first scoring opportunity after just 12 seconds when Paul Scholes threaded a ball just out of Liverpool captain Sami Hyypia's reach and into the path of Ruud Van Nistelrooy. Perhaps it was just too early in the game and the Dutchman only half-hit his shot.

The warning signs were ignored, however, and when the same United combination sent Van Nistelrooy clear, Hyypia tugged at his shirt. Possibly the offence began outside the area but it carried on inside it and Van Nistelrooy was dragged down. It looked a clear penalty – a view shared by referee Mike Riley – who also sent Hyypia off for a 'last man' foul. Van Nistelrooy got up to take the spot kick himself and planted it wide to the right of Jerzy Dudek.

When you are 1-0 down at Old Trafford, you have lost your captain and defensive mainstay and there are still 86 minutes to play, you know you're going to be in for a long hard afternoon. Both managers agreed on that, with Gerard Houllier admitting, 'Losing Hyypia was crucial to the rest of the game,' while Sir Alex Ferguson commented, almost resignedly, 'Hyypia probably had to go.'

In fairness to Liverpool, they fought hard and for an hour the scoreline remained 1-0, although there was no goal threat from them. But on the big Old

Trafford pitch, with United employing plenty of pace and width, the numerical advantage eventually told.

United's second penalty looked a little soft but Liverpool substitute Igor Biscan (brought on for Milan Baros in an attempt to shore up the defence) definitely caught Scholes inside the area having tried, and failed, to get the ball. No red card this time, rightly because Biscan was trying to play the ball but he just didn't get there quite quickly enough. Van Nistelrooy calmly converted his second penalty of the match, again to the right of the goalkeeper's dive.

Ryan Giggs made it 3-0 after 78 minutes when Van Nistelrooy held the ball up well to bring David Beckham into the game. Although his cross was just too high for a diving Van Nistelrooy to complete his hat-trick, it went through to Giggs in the middle of the goal and he made no mistake. Incredibly it was Giggs's first league goal at Old Trafford for almost two years.

Right at the death a Giggs touch found Ole Gunnar Solskjaer on the left edge of the Liverpool penalty box and he fired a shot through the legs of Djimi Traore to beat an unsighted Dudek at his near post.

It completed United's first league double over Liverpool for six seasons – they had won 2-1 at Anfield on 1 December 2002, courtesy of a Diego Forlan double. His first came when Dudek dropped a simple headed ball back to him and Forlan nipped in to tap in into an open net; the second when a Giggs run into the penalty area found Forlan on the right of the Liverpool area and he shot with too much pace for Dudek to keep out.

The league double at least made up for the League Cup Final defeat by the same opponents in March. 'If you're asked at the start of the season would you rather have two league victories over Liverpool or the League Cup, what would the answer be? It's always a disappointment to lose to them – but to have the league double is very satisfying,' said Sir Alex. 'It hurts,' said Houllier after the game, 'I have to admit that. It hurts the players, the staff and the fans.'

The Sunday Mirror the next day was emphatic in placing the result in context, 'Beating Liverpool is always a joy to behold for the boys of the Stretford End, but to send the Scousers back down the M62 humbled, humiliated and with their hopes of qualifying for Champions League [sic] hanging by a thread, really did make this a day for United fans to cherish. And if Sir Alex Ferguson's men can show the same kind of ruthlessness during the defining period of their season, there will be plenty more for those supporters to cheer in the weeks ahead.'

They was certainly plenty to cheer a week later as they destroyed third-placed Newcastle United 6-2 at St James' Park, with Scholes scoring a hat-trick. It was a game which Sir Alex described as being the sort you only see once every three years as United attacked from all areas of the pitch and were 4-1 ahead at half-time, extending that lead to 6-1 before the hour was up.

In between the big wins over Liverpool and Newcastle, United had a daunting trip to the Bernabeu for the Champions League quarter-final first leg at Real Madrid. The Spanish team's first-half performance had pundits and football fans everywhere comparing them with the great teams in history – even the Brazil side of the 1970s.

With 12 minutes of the game gone, Portuguese genius Luis Figo exchanged passes with Zinedine Zidane on the edge of the United box before curling a shot into the far corner of the goal. Just before the half-hour Rio Ferdinand lost the ball in a dangerous area and a precise pass from Zidane enabled Raul to turn, get the ball on to his deadly left foot and slot it precisely to the right of Fabien Barthez's dive. Four minutes after the break United conceded a third when a crossfield pass from Figo found Raul with the time to pick his spot with his unerring left foot.

Then United started the familiar fightback. On 52 minutes Giggs's close-range shot from Gary Neville's low cross was superbly parried by Iker Casillas, only for the ball to bounce out and up on to Van Nistelrooy's forehead. United did have chances to close the gap even further, but weren't able to do so, and the second-half bookings for Scholes and Neville ruled them both out of the return leg a fortnight later.

That return match at Old Trafford turned into an all-time classic. A Ronaldo hat-trick of power, pace and poised finishing was what eventually did for United, but that doesn't begin to tell the story of a remarkable match.

United's hard-fought away goal was cancelled out after just 12 minutes when Ronaldo smashed his first past Barthez. Van Nistelrooy made it 1-1 on the night but as United piled forward they were undone on the break and Ronaldo tapped in a Roberto Carlos cross. Almost immediately United levelled again when Ivan Helguera scored an own goal, but a third goal inside ten minutes saw Ronaldo restore Real's lead with a 25-yard strike. Not long after Ronaldo came off, to be replaced by Santiago Solari, and the Old Trafford crowd rose as one to applaud one of the great solo performances.

David Beckham was also now on the pitch, having replaced Veron, and he it was who gave United renewed hope. Beckham and Sir Alex had famously had a bust-up earlier in the year, in February, when a stray boot allegedly kicked by the boss in anger following a 2-0 home defeat by Arsenal in the FA Cup, had hit Beckham just above his left eye and left him with a cut. Although Beckham kept his counsel over the incident, he was clearly motivated in this match and his wondrous 71st-minute free kick once more levelled the score on the night. On 85 minutes, he won the game for United after Van Nistelrooy's shot had been deflected into his path and another sumptuous free kick could easily have made it five.

It was not to be. 'Can there be any doubt that the 67,000 fans packed into Old Trafford and the millions watching on television witnessed one of the greatest games of all time?' wrote *The Sun*. 'This was not a night for castigating United for their failure to reach the European Cup semi-finals. This was a night to revel in the brilliance of Real Madrid's hat-trick genius

Ronaldo, the exquisite skills of Zinedine Zidane and the amazing recovery by Alex Ferguson's men.'

The tie clearly took its toll on Real too, as they succumbed in the semi-finals to a Juventus team which United had beaten both home and away at an earlier stage in the competition.

United had restored some pride, and had played a full part in one of the great Old Trafford European nights, but now it was back down to the business of trying to win the Premier League.

As the title race between defending champions Arsenal and Manchester United went down to the wire, Sir Alex coined one of his most memorable phrases. 'It's squeaky bum time,' he said. In March Arsenal had led by eight points, but as United whittled down that lead, Sir Alex pithily conveyed the growing tension of the title race.

Four days after their destruction of Newcastle, United travelled to Highbury with a three-point lead over Arsenal but having played a game more. It was vital that they didn't allow the Gunners to make up any ground, and they duly turned in an exceptional performance to have much the better of a 2-2 draw and maintain their advantage. After the second leg of the Real Madrid tie, there were three league games still remaining; United won them all.

The first of these was a 2-0 win at Spurs – which for once the home fans might have forgiven as it extended United's lead over Arsenal to five points when the Gunners could only draw 2-2 at Bolton Wanderers. Next up was a 4-1 win over Charlton Athletic, when a Van Nistelrooy hat-trick was the team's emphatic response to a Charlton equaliser after Beckham had opened the scoring. Arsenal slipped up again, losing at home to Leeds United, and the trophy was on its way back to United.

'Arsenal, we felt, had cracked under a period of sustained pressure from us,' said Giggs. While Arsene Wenger churlishly claimed that his team was the best in the country, Sir Alex said, 'Don't believe all the stories that have come from south of the Birmingham divide – we proved ourselves as champions. I'm glad for the players and I'm glad for the fans. It's a great day for Manchester United.'

In truth while Arsenal had set the pace and looked the team to beat for much of the season, it was another of those devastating runs of form which took United to the title. Their last league defeat of the season was on Boxing Day and thereafter they won 15 of their next 18 league games – Van Nistelrooy scored 17 times over that period and ended the season with 44 goals from 52 appearances (including two as sub) in all competitions.

'I think this league win is up there with the best of them,' said Phil Neville. 'The way that we won it, the fact that we beat a great team in Arsenal, shows that we are the best team in England. Medals aren't handed out at Christmas and if you win the league it proves you are the best whatever anyone says.'

v **Bolton Wanderers 4-0**

39

16 August 2003
Premier League
Old Trafford
Attendance: 67,647

MANCHESTER UNITED	BOLTON WANDERERS
Tim Howard	Jussi Jaaskelainen
Mikael Silvestre	Nicky Hunt
Rio Ferdinand	Bruno N'Gotty
Phil Neville	Florent Laville
Quinton Fortune	Ivan Campo
Nicky Butt	Ricardo Gardner
Paul Scholes	Jay-Jay Okocha
Roy Keane	Stelios Giannakopoulos
Ryan Giggs	Kevin Nolan
Ole Gunnar Solskjaer	Kevin Davies
Ruud Van Nistelrooy	Henrik Pedersen
Manager: Sir Alex Ferguson	*Manager:* Sam Allardyce

I N the summer of 2003 the United team once again faced remoulding: Laurent Blanc had retired and David May had been released, Juan Sebastian Veron had become one of the first purchases by a Chelsea side now owned by Russian billionaire Roman Abramovich and destined to become a major force in the land, and, most incredibly, David Beckham had been sold to Real Madrid.

In purely business terms, United got a good deal for the 28-year-old, receiving around £25m. But there is little doubt that Sir Alex Ferguson was not over-fond of Beckham's celebrity lifestyle, which resulted both from his being England captain and from his marriage to Victoria, 'The big problem for me … he fell in love with Victoria and that changed everything.'

Sir Alex probably spoke more truth than he realised when he said that – it was *his* problem, not Beckham's, and his claim that the midfielder failed to become a football great does not survive even the most cursory glance at Beckham's post-United career.

Real Madrid president Florentino Perez was probably closer to the mark when he said of Beckham, 'He is a great player who is going to become part of the club's great history. He is a man of our times and a symbol of modern-day stardom. Real have signed Beckham because he's a great footballer and a very dedicated professional.'

As detailed elsewhere in this book Beckham went on to win trophies in Spain, the USA and France, to make a record number of appearances for England and is to date the only Englishman in history to have scored in three World Cups. He also has four children with Victoria. You could say that he is one of the very few people to have had the last word in a disagreement with Sir Alex, and one of an even smaller group of players whose post-United career has been as successful as his time while he was there.

'You don't realise how good David is until you play with him,' said Alan Shearer. 'He can do so much with the ball.'

But in the summer of 2003, all of that was in the future. The present was of more concern to United fans who were watching these great players leave and seeing little sign that they were being replaced.

United had a summer tour to the USA and made their way back home via a friendly with Sporting Lisbon to inaugurate their new stadium, the Estadio Jose Alvalade.

Up against United that day was an 18-year-old Portuguese winger who impressed the United players and management sufficiently for them to get in ahead of Arsenal and sign him for £12m. Three days later, on came Cristiano Ronaldo for his Manchester United debut, against Bolton Wanderers on the opening day of the 2003/04 season.

United were 1-0 up at the time, courtesy of a Ryan Giggs goal in the 35th minute, but Bolton were far from beaten. Although Jussi Jaaskelainen had had to make a superb save to deny Ole Gunnar Solskjaer inside the first ten minutes, Tim Howard had had to be just as alert to tip over a Kevin Nolan chip two minutes later. The Giggs goal, a Beckham-style free kick from some 30 yards out after Ruud Van Nistelrooy had been fouled, was sent crashing into the goal off the post. 'All those years of standing by the ball as David Beckham's decoy have just come spectacularly to an end for Ryan Giggs,' said the TV commentary.

It had put United in front but not in charge at half-time. At the start of the second half Bolton had another period of pressure: Henrik Pedersen flicked the ball on to Nolan, a striker who had a good record in recent games against United, but Nolan dragged the ball just wide. Then new goalkeeper Howard had to be alert to deal with a header; Howard was another of United's close-season signings, and another who intermingled fine performances with moments of doubt.

Sir Alex never seemed quite able to decide definitively between Howard and Roy Carroll, with the result that he switched them around and when one made an error the other got a run of games but neither was ever given the confidence of knowing that he was the first choice.

So it was that with an hour gone, Sir Alex brought Ronaldo and for Nicky Butt and told him to have 30 minutes of Premier League experience. He quickly had an impact as a trademark wriggle into the area took him past Nicky Hunt and brought a clumsy challenge from Nolan who clearly had hold of the youngster's shirt inside the penalty area and did enough tugging to warrant Ronaldo going over to win United an obvious penalty. Which Van Nistelrooy missed. Or to be fair, which Jaaskelainen saved, diving to his right to palm it away. Encouraged by that miss, Bolton pressed forward again, with Sam Allardyce bringing on Per Frandsen as a fresh pair of legs in midfield.

Fortunately it did not cost United and in the 74th minute they doubled their lead. A Ronaldo cross from the United left was overhit but found its way to Scholes on the other side of the penalty area and he instantly returned it into the six-yard box. A flick from Van Nistelrooy was well saved by Jaaskelainen, but he just couldn't hold on to the ball and Giggs was left with an easy tap-in for his second of the game.

Next on to the scoresheet was Scholes: although Van Nistelrooy was undoubtedly standing in an offside position, he didn't actually touch the through ball from Eric Djemba-Djemba (on as a substitute for Solskjaer) and Scholes was on to it in a flash to take it round the keeper and knock it calmly into an empty net.

The fourth and final goal was scored by Van Nistelrooy when a defensive mix-up left the Dutchman free with the ball at his feet about eight yards out. He didn't miss those, although the pace with which he hammered the ball into the net suggested some residual annoyance at his earlier missed penalty. In spite of that spot-kick failing, however, Van Nistelrooy still notched yet another scoring record as it was the ninth consecutive league match in which he had netted, beating Liam Whelan's previous record of eight.

That was in the 87th minute and that was how the game stayed. BBC 5 Live's Mike Ingham said, 'A bit hard on Bolton but that's life at the top,' and Sir Alex agreed, 'The scoreline doesn't really reflect how the game was going. Overall it flattered us a little bit.'

United had got off to the perfect start in defence of their Premier League title and they had found a new star.

With his floppy, streaked hair and his gold stud earring, as he took his place on the bench Ronaldo looked nothing like a Manchester United player, much less a Sir Alex player! But the moment he stepped on to the pitch we knew we had a good one.

Ronaldo's speed, ball control even at full speed, and trickery – shimmies, darts, stepovers, bursts of acceleration – were destined to make him a fans' favourite from the word go. The forums were abuzz. 'Indescribable,' said the Stretford End. 'I've never seen anything like the 30 minutes he spent on the pitch.'

Even Sir Alex was more effusive than he usually is, especially about new players. 'It was a marvellous debut,' he said. 'I thought the pace was too slow in the first half and I knew Cristiano would add penetration. It looks like the fans have a new hero but we have to be careful with the boy. You must remember he is only 18, we are going to have to gauge when we use him.'

Giggs added, 'There was a general buzz about the place when he came on, everyone had heard a lot about him and he's that kind of player who gets people off their seats and that's what this club is all about. You want players like that.

But I think he's round good people – he's at a club that knows how to handle players. The fans are bound to get excited but it is a long career and though he was brilliant, we have to look after him. I'm sure the manager will make sure that happens.'

Ronaldo himself tells the story of his signing for United and making his debut, 'Everything happened very suddenly,' he said. 'When I signed the contract with United I thought I was going to be playing in Portugal for another year before moving to England but after I'd signed, I was told United wanted me to play straight away. I asked if I could have a week because I wanted to go back to Portugal, collect my belongings and prepare everything I needed, but they said, "No, you play first and then you can go," so when I made by debut all my clothes and possessions were still in Lisbon! I only went to collect them after the match.

'It was a big, big change in my life: the language is different, the climate is different, the people are different, the food is different. All these things you have to learn about and get used to, but perhaps what helped was my previous experience of moving from Madeira to Lisbon. I was only 11 when I did that and it was very, very difficult – I used to cry every day thinking of my family. But looking back it made me learn how to survive by myself and become independent quite young. Because of football I didn't have the same childhood a normal kid has, but that has its good points as well as bad.

'I knew United was a big club and I think it's a club where you can grow as a footballer. I am not a perfectionist, but I like to feel that things are done well. More important than that, I feel an endless need to learn, to improve, to evolve, not only to please the coach and the fans, but also to feel satisfied with myself. It is my conviction that there are no limits to learning, and that it can never stop, no matter what our age.'

Sensible words from one so young. A star was born, and United had a new hero in the iconic number seven shirt, one to follow in the footsteps of George Best, Bryan Robson, Eric Cantona and David Beckham.

v Arsenal 1-0

40

3 April 2004
FA Cup semi-final
Villa Park
Attendance: 39,939

MANCHESTER UNITED	ARSENAL
Roy Carroll	Jens Lehmann
Gary Neville	Lauren
Wes Brown	Sol Campbell
Mikael Silvestre	Kolo Toure
John O'Shea	Gael Clichy
Cristiano Ronaldo	Freddie Ljungberg
Darren Fletcher	Patrick Vieira
Roy Keane	Edu
Ryan Giggs	Robert Pires
Ole Gunnar Solskjaer	Dennis Bergkamp
Paul Scholes	Jeremie Aliadiere
Manager: Sir Alex Ferguson	*Manager:* Arsene Wenger

'FOR us, winning today is imperative,' wrote Gary Neville in *The Times* on the morning of our FA Cup semi-final against Arsenal. 'There is no point in trying to play down the importance for United. Now we are out of the European Cup and too far behind in the league, it is the most important match of our season. It *is* our season. For us winning today is imperative. We have punished ourselves unbelievably on the few occasions in the past decade when we have failed to win a trophy. Finishing a campaign empty-handed is unthinkable.

'I would be surprised if Arsenal rest more than a couple of players today...it is a game they will be desperate to win. I know reaching the semi-finals of the European Cup will be their priority, but, as we know from 1999, it is all about momentum at this stage.'

Neville was right about the strength of the Arsenal squad, with arguably only Thierry Henry from their first-choice starting 11 dropped to the subs' bench, his place taken by Jeremie Aliadiere making only his seventh start for the club. 'It is ridiculous to reduce the team to one player,' Arsenal boss Arsene Wenger said later. 'I thought we created our best chances in the first half.'

He also pointed out, accurately, that United managed to cope with missing top scorer Ruud Van Nistelrooy, who had picked up a knee injury during the Premier League game between the two sides the previous weekend.

Arsenal started the brighter and in the opening minutes Dennis Bergkamp was just forced wide by United keeper Roy Carroll who got a big right hand on Bergkamp's first shot, giving Wes Brown time to get back on to the goal line and clear with a stooping header when Bergkamp did curl it in.

Almost immediately Arsenal had a corner and the ball found its way to Edu on the edge of the area; his chip beat Carroll but didn't beat the bar, bouncing off the top of it and just giving Carroll time to recover and tip over Kolo Toure's header. The second corner came to nothing.

Robert Pires had a great chance after 24 minutes when Bergkamp's cross gave him an open goal, but he managed to head the ball over the bar. Possibly still annoyed with himself for that miss, Pires was extremely fortunate to avoid a red card five minutes later when he floored Gary Neville.

United gradually worked their way into the game, testing out 18-year-old French full-back Gael Clichy who just prevented Ole Gunnar Solskjaer getting his shot away. Just after the half-hour Ryan Giggs worked some space down the right and sent a low cross into the Arsenal penalty area. Scholes met it about ten yards out and despatched a first-time shot past Jens Lehmann for a 32nd-minute lead. The move had arisen between a gang of four survivors from 1999, as Roy Keane knocked the ball wide to Gary Neville, and he found an equally decisive pass to Giggs on the right of the penalty area.

Arsenal almost got back on level terms before the end of the half thanks to a Pires free kick which was headed on to the outside of a post by Patrick Vieira.

The second half began in similar fashion but with United holding the Arsenal attack at bay fairly comfortably, Wenger brought Henry and Jose Antonio Reyes on for Pires and Aliadiere. It did enable Arsenal to up the tempo somewhat, with Reyes in particular using his pace to try to unsettle the United defence and on one occasion he did burst clear but stumbled as he was about to line up a shot.

Arsenal were still unable to test Carroll, however, until Wenger rolled the dice and brought Kanu on for Edu and switched to a more obvious 4-3-3 formation in search of an elusive equaliser. 'We lacked a bit of simplicity and vision around the box,' Wenger said after the game.

United continued to tackle, block and fend off all Arsenal's attempts and substitute David Bellion, on for Ronaldo for the last six minutes, should even have added a second when a swift counter-attack saw him somehow fail to get what would have been a tap-in at the far post.

Arsenal had one last chance in injury time when Freddie Ljungberg crossed and the ball got through to Reyes, but he could only scuff his shot into the grateful arms of Carroll.

The Gunners' dreams of a domestic Double were over, and defeat by Chelsea in the quarter-finals of the Champions League halted their progress in that competition too. United were criticised in some quarters for an overly physical approach – a Scholes challenge on Reyes, for which the United midfielder could easily have seen red, left the Spanish striker with a ligament injury while Ljungberg suffered a broken hand in the match. But by then Arsenal could easily have been down to nine men as Pires was equally lucky to receive no more than a yellow card for a challenge on Neville, and how Jens Lehmann avoided an early bath when he patently pushed Cristiano Ronaldo over, only referee Graham Barber knows.

In spite of these escapes, Arsenal still collected four bookings compared to just the one for United – Scholes – which hardly smacks of United being the primary transgressors. Lauren was booked for a scything tackle on Giggs after the United winger had got away from Vieira and was bearing down on goal, and Toure was also cautioned for illegally preventing a United move to develop.

So it was United who went on to a record 18th FA Cup Final. 'I know some will say that Arsenal against United should be the final,' said Neville on the morning of the semi-final, 'but that's the great thing about this competition. There's no seeding and you have to get on with it whether you get Arsenal or a trip to Northampton Town.'

In the final they would meet Millwall, first-time finalists and a Championship side at the time (they finished tenth), albeit one led by hugely experienced player-manager Dennis Wise who had won the FA Cup as a player with both Wimbledon and Chelsea. As his eyes and ears in the dugout Wise had Ray Wilkins, who had won the FA Cup with Manchester United. Wilkins later admitted, 'The better side won', while praising the efforts of the young Millwall side.

United seized control from the start and the result never really looked in doubt, though it did take them until almost half-time before they opened the scoring. Then a Neville cross caught Wise, of all people, ball-watching and Ronaldo sneaked in ahead of him to head past Andy Marshall in the Millwall goal.

Marshall, the reserve keeper, had already made a fine one-handed save to deny Roy Keane, and when he only half-stopped a Ronaldo shot Darren Ward got back to clear. Wise was lucky not to get sent off inside the first quarter when, having conceded a free kick by tripping Ronaldo, he pushed his hand into the teenager's face. Referee Jeff Winter, fulfilling his dream of taking charge of an FA Cup Final in his last game before retirement, clearly decided that the match was going to be one-sided enough as it was without dismissing Millwall's key player.

The second half was mostly one-way traffic as the Londoners fought a desperate battle to stay in the game. On 65 minutes Giggs went on a run into the Millwall penalty area and was brought down from behind by David Livermore. TV commentator Andy Gray said 'penalty' the instant it happened and Millwall could have few complaints. Van Nistelrooy stepped up to despatch the spot kick high to Marshall's right.

Wise then cleared one off the line before United's third and final goal came from another Giggs run down the United left which presented Van Nistelrooy with a tap-in from three yards, though he appeared to be offside. The FA Cup was won and lost and it only remained for teenager Curtis Weston to replace player-manager Wise for the last few minutes, thereby becoming the youngest player in an FA Cup Final at the age of 17 years and 119 days.

Weston later said, 'It's obviously the highlight of my career so far. I supported Manchester United as a kid so that made it even more special. I didn't get long on the pitch, but I got a few touches. I remember a sliding tackle on Van Nistelrooy and a 50-50 with Nicky Butt. I kept my shirt and I got Mikael Silvestre's.'

Ronaldo was United's man of the match, unleashing his full repertoire of tricks, not to mention his pace and showed throughout the final that he was the real deal, with a performance that was often too much for the Millwall youngsters. 'Ryan Giggs and Ruud Van Nistelrooy produced some good moments for us, but Ronaldo was particularly outstanding,' said Neville after the game. 'I think he can be one of the top footballers in the world. To come with the price tag on his head and at his age, he has been outstanding for us this season.'

It was no surprise to learn that Ronaldo was the first Portuguese player to play in an FA Cup Final, but interestingly goalkeeper Tim Howard – who had reclaimed his starting place from Roy Carroll even though Carroll had done well in the semi-final victory over Arsenal – became the first American to collect a winner's medal in over 100 years. Julian Sturgis, who played for Wanderers in 1873, had been the only previous American player to win the competition.

It was left to the two managers to pass judgement on the final. Wise rather grudgingly tried to claim that the opening goal was decisive in what was otherwise an even contest, 'The first goal killed us. We made a mistake and mistakes gets punished against these people. It would have been better if we had gone in at 0-0 at half-time.'

Sir Alex, as usual, offered a more classy summary. 'You have to respect your opponents at all times,' he said, 'and never take them for granted. It took most of the first half to open them up. We have professional players and expect a professional performance. I'm proud of everyone attached to the club. You always set out at the start of the season at this club to try and win a trophy and we've done that. I'm very pleased for the players and the fans.'

In the end, the way in which United simply swatted aside Millwall's challenge just proved what everyone suspected to be the case: that the semi-final win over the FA Cup holders had been the key contest in this year's competition. It had denied Arsenal the chance of a Double, and ensured that while the league title was lost, United would not finish the season empty-handed.

v Fenerbahce 6-2

41

28 September 2004
Champions League group stage
Old Trafford
Attendance: 67,128

MANCHESTER UNITED	FENERBAHCE
Roy Carroll	Rustu Recber
Gary Neville	Luciano Fabio
Gabriel Heinze	Fatih Akyel
Mikael Silvestre	Umit Ozat
Rio Ferdinand	Tuncay Sanli
Wayne Rooney	Mert Nobre
Ruud Van Nistelrooy	Pierre Van Hooijdonk
David Bellion	Mehmet Aurelio
Ryan Giggs	Alex
Kleberson	Deniz Baris
Eric Djemba-Djemba	Serkan Balci
Manager: Sir Alex Ferguson	*Manager:* Christoph Daum

THE 2004/05 season was one of ifs, buts and maybes for United. In the Premier League they finished much closer to Arsenal than they had the previous season, but there was a new force in the land – Chelsea won their first league title in 50 years, beating United home and away in the process and storming clear of Arsenal and United by virtue of losing just one league game all season.

United only lost five league games all season – they beat Arsenal home and away. They beat Liverpool home and away. And up until the second week of April, by which time the title race was all but over, they had lost just twice.

They also came within a whisker of retaining the FA Cup. Having already defeated fellow Premier League teams Middlesbrough, Everton and Southampton in successive rounds, they then thumped another in Newcastle United, 4-1 in the semi-final at the Millennium Stadium, Cardiff. It set up a final against Arsenal which United dominated from start to finish – and throughout extra time – but for once they just couldn't find that decisive goal. It meant the first goalless draw since 1912 (when they still had replays), and hence the first penalty shoot-out in FA Cup Final history.

Paul Scholes of all players was the only man to have his penalty saved so Arsenal somehow won a match in which they hardly had a single clear-cut chance in 120 minutes of football.

What was even more annoying was that United were clearly a better team than Arsenal that year – not only had they completed a Premier League double over the Gunners but they had also knocked the Londoners out of the League Cup. That competition had also promised much for United after they had beaten Arsenal in the quarter-finals, but again a failure to score when it really mattered cost them dear. They thought they had done the hard work in the semi-final first leg, gaining a 0-0 draw at Chelsea, but a 2-1 home defeat saw them knocked out 2-1 on aggregate.

But if goals proved rather harder to come by for United than in previous years, a solution was at hand.

When 18-year-old Wayne Rooney handed in a transfer request to Everton, the club he had supported as a boy, it began a feeding frenzy, with two knights of the realm at the forefront of the battle. Sir Bobby Robson put in a £20m bid on behalf of Newcastle United but Everton made it clear their valuation was closer to £30m. Sir Alex Ferguson stepped in and offered up to £7m more, the most ever offered for a teenager.

But as Alan Hansen told the BBC at the time, 'It is a remarkable transfer in some ways because when you pay £20m for a player, you do not buy potential, you are buying someone to go straight on to the team sheet. But then again we are not dealing with any normal 18-year-old, we are dealing with a boy who has remarkable physical and mental strength for one so young.'

As Matt Allen writes in his excellent Wayne Rooney biography *My Decade in the Premier League*, Sir Alex admitted that there were 'plenty of eyebrows raised' over the deal, but as Hansen said, 'This was a player Sir Alex was simply not going to miss out on.'

The rumours of Rooney being a special talent, a once-in-a-generation player, had been around for some years already. Everton Academy manager Ray Hall, who was in the post for 21 years, recalled his first sighting of Rooney as an eight-year-old during a game against Manchester United. 'You can picture the scene,' he said. 'There are about 150–200 parents on one side of the small field and the coaches from Manchester United and Everton on the other side, eight against eight. The ball comes across, about head height, and I'm thinking "he'll head this", but he didn't, he made a bicycle kick, straight in to the goal, a small goal. There was a complete silence, then somebody started to applaud and then everybody clapped. And the coach from Manchester United looked down the line to me as if to say, "What have we just seen here?"'

The story is taken up by Everton scout Bob Pendleton, who in his capacity as secretary of the Walton and Kirkdale Junior League went to see one of the clubs, Copplehouse Colts, about some overdue referees' fees. 'I noticed this little striker trying something different every time he touched the ball,' recalls Pendleton. 'When he got the ball, it became his and when he gave it away he expected it back.

'You hope every lad you bring in makes it, but with young Wayne you immediately knew he had something special. Coaches who'd been around for years were talking about him.'

If we didn't know Rooney was a special player before he joined Manchester United, we did when he made his debut.

It was 28 September 2004, the second match in the group phase of that year's Champions League. United had made a solid start to their latest European campaign, easing past Dinamo Bucharest 5-1 on aggregate in the qualifying round (2-1 away followed by a comfortable 3-0 at home). In the first group phase match they had draw away at Lyon, 2-2, with the goals coming from a Ruud Van Nistelrooy double. Sir Alex decided the time was right to throw Rooney in. And not from the bench, either. With Scholes out injured and Roy Keane rested, Rooney was going to start.

Inside seven minutes Kleberson skipped away from Luciano down the United left and Ryan Giggs made a great run to the near post. With nobody picking him up, Giggs was free to flick a glancing header from left to right into the far corner of the Fenerbahce goal from 12 yards. It looked so simple and was so simple.

Then the game turned into the Wayne Rooney Show. On 13 minutes he was put through by some poor defending but went a little too wide to beat Fenerbahce's excellent goalkeeper Rustu Recber. Shortly after that he displayed his phenomenal speed off the mark to scoot away from Deniz Baris and evade Recber only to lift his shot over the bar.

The Turks didn't heed the warning, however, and on 17 minutes Rooney was put through again, this time by a superb ball from Van Nistelrooy, playing deeper than usual. It was a slide-rule pass, asking to be hit, and Rooney duly did the honours with a scorching left-foot shot. 'Wayne Rooney scores for Manchester United, and it's not the last time you will hear that,' says Clive Tyldesley on the ITV commentary team. 'Wayne Rooney finds the big stage just to his liking.'

Fenerbahce briefly rallied and an Alex corner was headed home by Mert Nobre, but the ball was adjudged to have gone out of play before curving back in and a goal kick was given.

Just before the half-hour it was United 3 Fenerbahce 0 with a second for the debutant. This time Rooney did most of the work himself: Giggs slipped him a little square ball and Rooney dummied the first defender, shaped to give himself a bit of room and smacked a hard, low drive – with his right foot – across Recber and into the far corner from about 25 yards out.

Right on the stroke of half-time Rooney almost made it a dream debut when a neat interchange of passes was followed by a low cross in from Gary Neville but the teen shot just wide.

The Turkish side struck first in the second half, after just four minutes, and it was the same combination as 'scored' the disallowed goal in the first half: an Alex corner came to Nobre who finished well from about 12 yards.

A Rooney half-volley parried by Recber was United's next effort, and then came the hat-trick that had seemed inevitable for some time. United were awarded a free kick, Rooney grabbed the ball and made it plain that he was going to be taking it, then having sized up the possibilities he calmly planted it almost lazily into the far corner of the goal with a brilliant curling effort that went up and over the wall. There were 54 minutes on the clock. 'There is tomorrow morning's front-page face, never mind the back page,' enthuses Tyldesley. 'What a strike,' agrees co-commentator Andy Townsend.

Just before the hour mark, Fenerbahce somehow scored another – Rooney conceded a corner and Tuncay Sanli (later to play successfully for Middlesbrough and Stoke City) was first to a Roy Carroll parry and sneaked it inside the post.

It was the spur United needed to regain control and in the 80th minute the club's record goalscorer in Europe, Van Nistelrooy, got himself on the scoresheet when he controlled an excellent driven pass from substitute Darren Fletcher (on for Giggs) on his chest, evaded one defender and smacked the ball home.

Within a minute, Rooney proved that he could provide goals as well as score them when a carefully weighted header was directed right into the path of Bellion, who this time made no mistake for his fourth goal in seven games.

There was just time for Umit Ozat to sidefoot a volley against the United post before the final whistle went and the cameras all focused on Rooney.

'It is a great start for him,' admitted Sir Alex. 'Given that Wayne and Ruud played together for the first time the future holds great promise. As a partnership it was excellent.'

'Wayne's debut was fantastic,' said Rio Ferdinand. 'To get a hat-trick is unbelievable, fairytale stuff. I don't think he knows what pressure is.'

Still a month away from turning 19, Rooney had just become the youngest player in Champions League history to score a hat-trick. It was the start of a United career which has taken Rooney to third in the club's all-time scoring charts, and with a genuine possibility that he will top that list ahead of Sir Bobby Charlton and Denis Law before his career is finished.

For good measure he is also in the top five England scorers and could climb higher there too, where he will almost certainly become only the ninth Englishman to win over 100 caps.

Against Fenerbahce was where it all began.

v **Wigan Athletic** 4-0

42

26 February 2006
League Cup Final
Millennium Stadium, Cardiff
Attendance: 66,866

MANCHESTER UNITED	WIGAN ATHLETIC
Edwin van der Sar	Mike Pollitt
Gary Neville	Pascal Chimbonda
Wes Brown	Arjan de Zeeuw
Mikael Silvestre	Stephane Henchoz
Rio Ferdinand	Leighton Baines
Wayne Rooney	Jimmy Bullard
John O'Shea	Graham Kavanagh
Cristiano Ronaldo	Paul Scharner
Ryan Giggs	Gary Teale
Park Ji-Sung	Henri Camara
Louis Saha	Jason Roberts
Manager: Sir Alex Ferguson	*Manager:* Paul Jewell

THROUGHOUT their history, Manchester United have never been that interested in the League Cup, and under Sir Alex Ferguson in particular they tended to use it as a competition for blooding youngsters, giving squad players games and for senior players returning from injury.

There were always bigger fish to fry, at home and in Europe, and Sir Alex never denied treating it as a fourth priority. Let Liverpool concern themselves with winning it, seemed to be the message, we'll go for the bigger trophies.

Nevertheless there were times when it was taken moderately seriously. The first of those was in the early 1990s when United reached the final three times in four years, though they won only once, in 1992. The second was in the mid-to-late 2000s when Chelsea had started to dominate the domestic game.

The London club, benefiting from the vast influx of wealth from Russian billionaire Roman Abramovich and the managerial genius of Jose Mourinho, won back-to-back Premier League titles in 2004/05 and 2005/06 and won the League Cup in 2005 and 2007.

Chelsea had been able to bring in players of the calibre of Petr Cech, Arjen Robben, Didier Drogba, Ricardo Carvalho and Michael Essien and the rest of England was struggling to compete. And then they lost to Charlton Athletic on penalties in the third round of the 2005/06 League Cup.

Whether that had a bearing on Sir Alex's thinking, it's hard to be sure, but it certainly wouldn't have been lost on him – even at that early stage of the competition – that any opportunity to put a dent in Chelsea's armour had to be taken.

With Liverpool losing at the same stage (at Crystal Palace), it meant that of the 11 teams who had won more League Cups than United in history, only Arsenal, Aston Villa and Leicester City remained in the competition after the third round. And of them Villa and Leicester both fell in the next round. It looked set fair for another United v Arsenal clash as the two old rivals continued to progress – and continued to avoid each other. But it all went wrong for the Gunners in their semi-final with Wigan Athletic.

No alarm bells sounded when Arsene Wenger's men lost the first leg to a 78th-minute Paul Scharner goal, but at Highbury they could produce only a single, 65th-minute strike from Thierry Henry to take the tie into extra time. A Robin Van Persie goal shortly after the second period of extra time started looked to have sealed the narrowest of passages, but then Jason Roberts muscled his way past Sol Campbell and Philippe Senderos before forcing the ball home in the 119th minute which levelled the aggregate scores at 2-2 and put Wigan into their first major final.

United didn't have it all their own way in the semi-final either. A Morten Gamst Pedersen equaliser of Louis Saha's 30th-minute opener at Ewood Park didn't seem too damaging, especially as United had largely had the better of the contest. But when Blackburn Rovers managed the same feat at Old Trafford – Steven Reid equalising after Ruud Van Nistelrooy had put United ahead after just eight minutes – the half-time whistle went with the scores and the away goals dead level.

Saha restored United's advantage with a scruffy goal six minutes into the second half and Rovers had an inspired performance from goalkeeper Brad Friedel to thank for keeping his side in the game. 'Blackburn made us work hard and they made the referee work hard,' said Sir Alex, 'but we got there and I'm delighted. We deserved to go through.' Over the two legs that was certainly true.

Before the final, former United defender Gary Pallister pointed out, 'It's important to the players to win something. Let's not forget that these guys are professionals who are in the game to win trophies, that's what drives them. The Carling Cup might have been one of the lesser trophies that they targeted this season, behind the Champions League and the Premier League title, but it's a question of prioritising now.'

'We're not going there to be part of an occasion,' said Wigan boss Paul Jewell. 'We're going there focused on trying to win a game.'

Fortunately for United, Wigan seemed overawed by their first appearance in a major final and were never really able to get to grips with United's pace, or their extra little bit of class. In the opening seconds Wigan mounted a decent attack as Gary Teale outpaced Mikael Silvestre and got in a cross which Henri Camara headed wide from a good position. From then on, it was mostly United – Wigan were unlucky to lose goalkeeper Mike Pollitt, one of the stars of their semi-final victory over Arsenal, to an early hamstring injury and while his replacement John Filan was warming up Wayne Rooney thumped a header against the bar.

Filan was on by the 14th minute and it was only a few minutes after that when United should have opened the scoring: a powerful run by Rooney giving Cristiano Ronaldo a chance to make more of the cut-back than he did.

When the first goal did arrive, on 33 minutes, it was from a more unlikely United move. Edwin van der Sar launched a huge punt downfield, Saha headed it on and as the ball fell kindly for Rooney, Wigan defenders Pascal Chimbonda and captain Arjan de Zeeuw collided and gave the United man a clear run on goal. Rooney rarely misses such a gilt-edged opportunity, and he didn't this time, placing the ball firmly beyond the left hand of a diving Filan. Incredibly it was Rooney's first goal since Boxing Day, two months earlier.

Wigan started the second half in fighting spirit, with Roberts tricking his way past Gary Neville; Wes Brown read the play well to clear the danger. Senegalese striker Camara then displayed both skill and pace to briefly embarrass Ferdinand but Edwin van der Sar narrowed the angles and made it difficult for Camara.

United made the game safe with a flurry of goals. First Ryan Giggs picked his way through a couple of tackles in midfield before sweeping the ball out to Ronaldo. Neville made one of his famous overlapping runs and his cross was met powerfully by Saha. Filan did well to keep out the initial strike but could do nothing about the Frenchman converting at the second attempt.

Two minutes later a disastrous bit of defending from Stephane Henchoz gifted the ball to Saha who was 'spoilt for choice' as Andy Gray said on the TV commentary. Instead of firing it out to the wide areas or even back to Filan, Henchoz kicked his clearance straight to Saha. The choice he did make was to slide a pass in to Ronaldo who was in acres of space on the left-hand edge of the Wigan penalty area. Ronaldo finished with a shot across Filan, then ran over to the United fans with his top off.

'To be fair, if I had a body like that, I'd have whipped my short off by now too, I tell you,' said Gray.

And United made it three goals in seven minutes when a Giggs free kick which he took left-footed from the right of the penalty area was won in the air by Saha, then headed on by Ferdinand before reaching Rooney in the six-yard box. He spun and tucked away his second goal from close range. Rooney said after the match that he was delighted to have ended a run of 12 games without a goal, 'I was hungry because I'd not scored for a while. It was not as bad as it could have been because at least the team were scoring, but I was disappointed with the situation and I wanted to put it right. I guess there is no better time to do that than a cup final!'

Wigan boss Jewell, a class act, admitted, 'We were playing a world-class side with world-class players and we were beaten by a better side. It was like a David against Goliath match. We gave bad goals away and United were absolutely clinical. It's tough to take but we've lost to one of the most decorated sides in the world and there's no shame in that.'

His chairman and long-time Wigan fan Dave Whelan added, 'In the first minute our goalkeeper pulls his hamstring and you think, "Maybe the gods are against us." I am disappointed to say the least because if Henri Camara puts away his chance at 1-0 it would have been a totally different game. We were unlucky to go a goal down and had Camara taken that chance, who knows?'

Given how Wigan were overrun when United upped the tempo, it's hard to credit Whelan's view that it all hinged on Camara's missed chance – the Wigan defence was so shaky that United would surely have found a way past it more than once over the course of 90 minutes. And let's not forget that United did the league double over them, including a 4-0 win at Old Trafford earlier that same season.

A footnote to the League Cup Final was that it spelled the end of Van Nistelrooy's time at the club. Sir Alex had preferred Saha's pace at the start, and the Frenchman's performance in the final had done nothing to prove him wrong. But unlike Nemanja Vidic and Patrice Evra – who had joined the club in the January transfer window – Van Nistelrooy was not summoned from the bench even after the match was won. According to Sir Alex, Van Nistelrooy swore at him. 'That was the end of him. I knew we would never get him back,' wrote Sir Alex.

But the pluses still outweighed the minuses for United. The arrival of Vidic and Evra provided United with half the backline which was going to return the glory days to the club over the next few seasons, and the previous summer had seen United sign their best goalkeeper since the days of Peter Schmeichel in Edwin van der Sar.

At 34, van der Sar could hardly be called a long-term prospect, but in fact United ended up getting six years and 266 appearances in all competitions out of the Dutch international. Signed in June 2005, van der Sar had already had a successful career at Ajax and Juventus before moving to Fulham in 2001. Van der Sar had been linked with a move to United previously but ended up signing a new contract at Fulham instead in January so his switch in June, initially on a two-year deal, came as a surprise. Van der Sar had 99 caps for his country at the time of his joining United and he went on to extend that a record 130 during his time with the club.

Van der Sar won 11 trophies with Ajax and after InterToto Cup triumphs at both Juventus and Fulham, he would go on to win a further eight major trophies with United before retiring on 28 May 2011. This was the first.

43 v Liverpool 1-0

3 March 2007
Premier League
Anfield
Attendance: 44,403

MANCHESTER UNITED	LIVERPOOL
Edwin van der Sar	Pepe Reina
Gary Neville	Steve Finnan
Rio Ferdinand	Jamie Carragher
Nemanja Vidic	Daniel Agger
Patrice Evra	John Arne Riise
Cristiano Ronaldo	Steven Gerrard
Paul Scholes	Xabi Alonso
Michael Carrick	Mohamed Sissoko
Ryan Giggs	Mark Gonzalez
Wayne Rooney	Dirk Kuyt
Henrik Larsson	Craig Bellamy
Manager: Sir Alex Ferguson	*Manager:* Rafael Benitez

GOING into the vital Premier League match at Anfield on the first weekend in March 2007, United had been playing well. Since the 2-1 defeat at Arsenal on 21 January they had scored 12 goals and conceded just one in beating Watford (4-0), Tottenham Hotspur (4-0), Charlton Athletic (2-0) and Fulham (2-1).

But even though Liverpool themselves were almost out of the title race, Chelsea were still very much in it and the Scousers were desperate for ABMU – i.e. Anyone But Manchester United – to win.

The match was given extra tension, should any be needed, by the fact that the two managers never really got on.

'The advance publicity was that Benitez was a control freak, which turned out to be correct, to a point that made no sense,' Sir Alex was to write in *My Autobiography*.

The book contains a number of cutting put-downs about Benitez's lack of friends among fellow managers, his poor buying policy and his desire to defend a lead rather than increase it, though he stops short of calling Benitez a fat Spanish waiter, which is what opposing fans usually chant at him.

The main issue between them was that Benitez never socialised after a match, not even briefly, except on one occasion and also that Sir Alex felt that Benitez had made a personal issue out of professional differences.

Regardless of Benitez's bizarre 'facts' rant and his belief that Sir Alex was allowed to get away with things other managers were not, it's true that Sir Alex got into the Spaniard's head, and that enabled him to seize the upper hand in their meetings. After all, the ledger tells us that Sir Alex comfortably got the better of Benitez when the Spaniard was Liverpool manager, winning eight of their 13 meetings with one drawn.

United kicked off in a change strip of all-white and it was a scrappy, hard-fought match with Liverpool determined not to give United anything, especially as it was at Anfield, but not really having the quality to test United on a consistent basis. 'The game hasn't really settled,' said Andy Gray on Sky Sports, which as we all know is commentator-speak for 'it's rubbish'.

It was beyond the halfway point in the first half before the first real clear-cut chance occurred when from a free kick on the Liverpool right the ball was touched to John Arne Riise who drove the ball left-footed just wide of Edwin van der Sar's right-hand post. If it had curled in rather than away, it might have given more cause for alarm.

Enthused by that chance, Liverpool briefly pressed forward with Craig Bellamy robbing Nemanja Vidic and flashing a ball across the six-yard box where Dirk Kuyt just failed to get a finishing touch. Vidic continued to have trouble with Bellamy, while the Kop roared at Ronaldo for what they perceived as going down too easily, although when Xabi Alonso vociferously made the same point to the referee he was booked for his trouble.

Into the second half and Liverpool continued to have most of the play, and the chances. Steven Gerrard blasted over horribly from a decent opportunity yards out before Bellamy first forced a low save from van der Sar, then had a close-range effort ruled out for offside – correctly, but narrowly.

The biggest blow to United came not from any great play by their opponents but from an injury to Wayne Rooney. Rooney came off worse after a strong high challenge with Jamie Carragher and limped off with an injury to his left knee.

Next came a couple of penalty shouts. First Jermaine Pennant, on for Bellamy in a surprise switch given that the Welshman had looked just about the most likely player on the pitch to break the deadlock, charged into the United box but seemed to be looking for a penalty that he was never going to get.

Louis Saha, on to replace Henrik Larsson on the latter's final Premier League appearance before returning to Helsingborg, had a much better shout for a penalty after a clash with Daniel Agger, but referee Martin Atkinson was unmoved. It looked a clear penalty in real time, and even clearer on the replay, with Agger definitely catching Saha's leg.

Paul Scholes received an unfortunate red card when an ongoing series of niggles between him and Xabi Alonso saw the United player raise his hand in the vague direction of the Spaniard. No contact was made, but Alonso made enough of the incident to get Scholes sent off.

Alonso, already on a yellow card, remarkably wasn't shown a second yellow for his attempts to wrestle Scholes off the ball, particularly as Carrick had received a yellow for almost exactly the same offence in the first half.

Van der Sar then had to produce a great flying save to keep out a shot from Peter Crouch. Crouch did everything right, taking the ball down beautifully on his chest then aiming for the far corner, but van der Sar somehow dived to his left to keep it out.

Late on, though, it seemed to dawn on United that for all their huff and puff this Liverpool side was there for the taking, and they decided to take them.

Ronaldo almost scored with a header which goalkeeper Pepe Reina just about scooped away. With the fourth official just putting up the board to announce four minutes of stoppage time Giggs won a free kick on the United left. Giggs shaped to take it himself but instead Ronaldo took one that curled into the six-yard box and with Saha making a nuisance of himself Reina couldn't collect it cleanly, and it landed at the unlikely feet of John O'Shea. O'Shea had the presence of mind to smack the shot high into the net, giving Liverpool defenders no chance to block it, and the game was won.

'It is a massive three points for United at Anfield,' said Sky Sports. 'The celebrations say it all.'

Although his last Premier League game was not his best, Larsson can surely lay claim to being one of the best loan signings of all time. Larsson, who had had successful spells at Feyenoord and Celtic, appeared to be seeing out the latter stages of his career in the more sedate surroundings of his home town of Helsingborg. Then in a stroke of genius, Sir Alex persuaded him to spend three months at United while it was the Swedish off-season.

United at the time had Ole Gunnar Solskjaer injured and Alan Smith still short of full fitness, leaving their striking options down to Rooney and Saha, with no backup. 'Am I backup? Yes, at the beginning,' smiled the engaging Larsson at the time.

Sir Alex had no doubts. 'I have always admired Larsson,' he said. 'He is a great player and it's a terrific bit of business for us. We are bringing in someone who can change a game.'

In the end Larsson played just 13 times, and scored three goals, but Sir Alex said his impact cannot be measured purely in those terms. 'He's been fantastic for us, his professionalism, his attitude, everything he's done has been excellent,' said Sir Alex at the end of his loan spell. 'We'd love him to stay but obviously he has made his promise to his family, and to Helsingborg and I think we should respect that – but I would have done anything to keep him.'

In 2010 Larsson admitted that he would have loved to have stayed. 'If there is one regret I have from my career, it is that I came home to Sweden when Mr Ferguson was trying to get me to stay at Manchester United,' he told the FIFA website. 'I should have stayed at United because the whole experience was fantastic and although I was 35 at the time I still felt I had some good football in me. My time there was too short.'

Although he only made seven Premier League appearances for United, Larsson, along with Smith, was given special dispensation to receive a winner's medal at the request of the club. A fitting tribute to his influence in his short spell at Old Trafford.

The win over Liverpool, in addition to being immensely enjoyable, put United 12 points clear at the top, although Chelsea had two games in hand and United still had to go to Stamford Bridge on the penultimate weekend of the season.

Former England manager Graham Taylor called it a 'defining moment' of the season. Chelsea did their utmost, winning both their games in hand to close the gap back to six points, but United matched their victories on 17 and 31 March, beating both Bolton Wanderers and Blackburn Rovers 4-1 to maintain their six-point advantage and increase their goal difference too.

It was too much for Chelsea, who cracked in pursuit of their hat-trick of Premier League titles, and could only manage draws at Newcastle United and Arsenal, and at home to Bolton Wanderers. It meant that United were eight points clear before the trip to the Bridge, and the title was already won. Even better, it meant that the 1-0 win away to Manchester City – courtesy of Ronaldo's 34th-minute penalty – was the decider.

It was a suitable riposte from the Portuguese flyer after he had earlier been stamped on by City player Michael Ball. Ronaldo then tempted Ball into an injudicious challenge inside the penalty area and he got up to send City keeper Andreas Isaksson the wrong way.

City had a penalty of their own late in the game, from a harsh decision by referee Rob Styles, Wes Brown not seeming to make the challenge before Ball made sure he went over. In any case van der Sar saved easily and United were home and hosed.

Of the five league matches United lost, two were to Arsenal and two more, bizarrely, were to West Ham United, who added a last-day Old Trafford victory to the one they had claimed at home earlier in the season. United won't have cared about that, though. They won the title by six points and with a goal difference of +56 – 16 better than Chelsea. It also prevented Chelsea winning a domestic Treble as they claimed the League Cup and FA Cup, the latter in a less than scintillating match against United decided by Didier Drogba's 116th-minute opportunistic strike.

But the main prize, the league title, was back in United's hands.

v **Roma** 7-1

44

10 April 2007
Champions League quarter-final second leg
Old Trafford
Attendance: 74,476

MANCHESTER UNITED	ROMA
Edwin van der Sar	Doni
Wes Brown	Christian Panucci
Rio Ferdinand	Philippe Mexes
Gabriel Heinze	Cristian Chivu
John O'Shea	Marco Cassetti
Cristiano Ronaldo	Christian Wilhelmsson
Darren Fletcher	Daniele De Rossi
Michael Carrick	Mirko Vucinic
Ryan Giggs	David Pizarro
Wayne Rooney	Mancini
Alan Smith	Francesco Totti
Manager: Sir Alex Ferguson	*Manager:* Luciano Spalletti

IN 2006/07 United had made rather heavy weather of qualifying from their Champions League group. Although they had started with three straight wins – home to Celtic and Copenhagen, with an excellent 1-0 win away to Benfica sandwiched between them – they then stuttered. A 1-0 defeat in Copenhagen, courtesy of former Aston Villa striker Marcus Allback, meant United swam home still not assured of their place in the knockout phase.

Three weeks later a fantastic free kick from Shunsuke Nakamura gave Celtic victory – and another 1-0 defeat for United, with Louis Saha seeing his last-minute penalty saved by Artur Boruc. It left United susceptible to a smash and grab raid by a Benfica side who were only two points adrift and when they scored first at Old Trafford, a second successive failure to escape the group phase loomed large.

The players rallied round however, and after Nemanja Vidic had brought them level in first-half stoppage time with a typically forceful header, second-half goals from Ryan Giggs and Louis Saha sealed an ultimately comfortable 3-1 win and top place in the group.

It was one of those years when topping the group wasn't necessarily an advantage and United could have faced Barcelona, Inter or Real Madrid in the first knockout round. In the event then they must have been mightily relieved to draw Lille.

The first leg in France produced the bizarre spectacle of Lille players walking off the pitch and refusing to finish the match before belatedly being persuaded to return. Already upset that a Peter Odemwingie headed effort had been disallowed for a push, Lille players completely lost it when Dutch referee Eric Braamhaar allowed a quickly-taken Giggs free kick to stand while the home wall was still forming.

Wayne Rooney placed the ball down on the United left of the Lille penalty area and Giggs immediately struck it left-footed, curling over the wall and away to the goalkeeper's left. It was a great strike, though other officials might not have allowed it to stand.

The return leg wasn't easy but United were, for the most part, in control. John O'Shea had possibly the best chance in the first half with a header when a corner reached him, unmarked, on the edge of the six-yard box. Ronaldo could have had a penalty but instead got a yellow card for diving. Lille were mostly confined to long-range efforts and then on 71 minutes Ronaldo escaped tight down United's left. At pace he got in a good cross with his left foot and Henrik Larsson escaped his marker long enough to power home a header.

That put United into yet another Champions League quarter-final, and a match with Roma.

United certainly made life difficult for themselves in the Italian capital where Paul Scholes received his second yellow card of the game after just 34 minutes for a foul on playmaker Francesco Totti. United were down to ten and they were punished before half-time when Rodrigo Taddei opened the scoring. The midfielder's low shot took a wicked deflection off Wes Brown which wrong-footed Edwin van der Sar and rolled almost gently into the net.

Incredibly United fought back strongly and right on the hour Rooney equalised. A speedy break from Ronaldo and a deep cross from Ole Gunnar Solskjaer picked out Rooney on the far side of the penalty area, the United left, and he checked inside his marker, looked up and picked his spot to curl in a great goal.

Six minutes later, though, and only four minutes after coming on as a substitute, Montenegrin striker Mirko Vucinic put Roma back in front. A thunderous shot from Mancini was punched out by van der Sar but only into the path of Vucinic who returned it with interest, hard and low. It was great reactions from a player who had only just come on.

As damage limitation exercises go, however, a 2-1 defeat when down to ten men for almost an hour didn't seem too bad. However, United didn't have a great track record of overturning first-leg deficits and Roma arrived at Old Trafford on a ten-game unbeaten streak and boasting the best defensive record in the competition that year.

Injuries had forced United into adopting a fluid-looking 4-3-3 formation with Giggs playing in midfield alongside Carrick and Darren Fletcher with Rooney pushed out to the left wing, Ronaldo on the right and the returning Alan Smith playing as the lone striker.

On 18 February 2006, Smith, who had joined United at the start of the 2003/04 season and was being groomed for a central midfield role, suffered a horrendous injury. Playing at Anfield in an FA Cup tie against Liverpool, Smith rushed out to block a John Arne Riise free kick and broke his leg and dislocated his ankle. 'I felt my leg go from under me,' Smith told *The Sun*, 'and when I looked down the leg was lying one way and my ankle was pointing towards Hong Kong so I knew I was in serious trouble.'

Smith recovered quicker than initially thought possible and even made a cameo 85th-minute appearance against Benfica in Portugal on 26 September. However it was March 2007 before Smith made another Premier League appearance (in the 4-1 home win over Bolton Wanderers). The match against Roma was his tenth appearance of any kind since his injury.

'Some people are told they will never walk again but for 13 months I worked every day,' recalled Smith. 'The biggest achievement of my career has been playing again. It has made me realise how much I love playing football. When I look back it made me a better person. Not a better footballer – there are deficiencies in my left ankle – but understanding what I'd achieved previously and making sure I tried to prolong my career, it really made me appreciate things.'

The injury came at a bad time for Smith, and was too long-term for Sir Alex to be able to wait on his recovery. In the summer of 2006 Michael Carrick was signed from Spurs and in the January transfer window Henrik Larsson joined the club, to play in the positions which previously Smith had occupied. Smith eventually moved to Newcastle United as Sir Alex again looked to rebuild his side from a position of strength.

In the Roma game, though, with Scholes and Park Ji-Sung unavailable and Larsson's spell with the club having finished in the previous round – when he signed off with the only goal against Lille – Smith was to play a crucial role.

Inside 20 minutes, United had overturned Roma's lead as Michael Carrick (11 minutes), Smith (17) and Rooney (19) all scored.

Funnily enough the first few chances fell to Roma. Vucinic got an opening after being given far too much space by the United defence some 30 yards out. His shot went wide. Totti went even closer a couple of minutes later when he struck a low shot from distance which was closer to van der Sar's right-hand post than he might have liked.

Then Carrick, making just his 11th appearance in the Champions League, took a pass from Ronaldo, noticed Doni was slightly off his line and hit the most glorious lob for his first goal in the competition. Six minutes later a Giggs pass ought to have been cut out by Romanian defender Cristian Chivu but wasn't and there was Smith. Given it was his first goal for almost 18 months, Smith did well to keep his composure and steer it home by opening up his body and hitting a precise side-footed shot to the keeper's left.

Two minutes after that Ronaldo beat a couple of defenders deep in his own half and didn't let a foul on him prevent him from setting Giggs away down the right. As Giggs sent a ball into the six-yard box Rooney nipped in ahead of his marker to nudge the ball home.

Ronaldo then tried to get in on the act himself, cutting inside from his station on the wide right, ghosting past a couple of would-be tacklers and firing a shot left-footed across the face of the goal. It wasn't all one-way traffic, however. First Daniele De Rossi had a shout for a penalty as he was brought crashing to the ground while trying to reach a Totti cross, but was waved away by Slovakian referee Lubos Michel, then Mancini was denied a good chance by a perfectly timed tackle from Fletcher.

If Roma thought they could reach the sanctuary of half-time and regroup they were quickly disabused of the notion. Shortly after Carrick was left unmarked at the far post but finished with far less aplomb than for his goal, Ronaldo again twisted and turned, made himself half a metre of space and fired a hard, low shot that beat Doni at his near post in the 44th minute.

The second half started off the same way with United moving fluidly, their power and pace too much for the likes of Christian Panucci and Cristian Chivu – who couldn't even agree on how to spell their first name let along how to handle Rooney and Ronaldo.

The deadly duo had the first chances of the second half: Rooney cut on to his right foot from wide on the left and hit a stinging shot which Doni tipped over. Then in the 49th minute Rooney won the ball strongly in midfield; Giggs, switching to his more usual left-wing position, rolled in a cross which just eluded Smith but not Ronaldo at the far post.

Roma were in danger of being swept away as every United attack look likely to end in a goal. On the hour United made it 6-0 when Carrick was given all the time and space he needed to pick out the top corner of the net. Two minutes later it was almost seven when a cheeky Smith chip went over Doni but also, just, over the bar, then Ole Gunnar Solskjaer (on for Giggs) tried an audacious lob which Doni could only watch float over him – and over the crossbar.

Slightly surprisingly the next goal was scored by Roma. And to be fair, it was a spectacular one too as a low cross from Totti was despatched decisively by De Rossi on the volley.

Then in the 81st minute Patrice Evra, on at right-back – a position he was not going to make his own at Old Trafford – made progress up the right flank and shot low past Doni from about 20 yards out. It was 7-1 and right at the death only a fine save from Doni prevented Ronaldo picking up his hat-trick and United's eighth of the night.

Sir Alex hailed it as United's greatest European evening at Old Trafford. 'It was a fantastic performance by every one of our players,' he said. 'The speed of our play and our penetration was absolutely superb.' Goalscorer Carrick was bang on the money when he said, 'To start so well and carve out the chances and score the goals we did was a great feeling. To carry it on for the full game was the stuff of dreams.'

Some media outlets were a little sniffy about the quality – or maybe the desire – of Roma's defending on the night, but it's worth noting that the Italian side went on to finish as runners-up in Serie A for the second successive year and also won the Coppa Italia for the eighth time.

Unfortunately, United weren't able to reproduce the same level of performance in the semi-final against AC Milan and although Rooney (with two) and Ronaldo gave them victory in the first leg it was only 3-2 after two goals from Kaka.

And Kaka levelled the tie after just 11 minutes in the San Siro. Further goals from Clarence Seedorf and Alberto Gilardino took Milan through 5-3 on aggregate. The only saving grace was that a Filippo Inzaghi double in the final was enough to beat Liverpool.

v Newcastle United 6-0

45

12 January 2008
Premier League
Old Trafford
Attendance: 75,965

MANCHESTER UNITED	NEWCASTLE UNITED
Edwin van der Sar	Shay Given
John O'Shea	Stephen Carr
Rio Ferdinand	Steven Taylor
Nemanja Vidic	Cacapa
Patrice Evra	Jose Enrique
Cristiano Ronaldo	James Milner
Anderson	Alan Smith
Michael Carrick	Nicky Butt
Ryan Giggs	Charles N'Zogbia
Wayne Rooney	Damien Duff
Carlos Tevez	Michael Owen
Manager: Sir Alex Ferguson	*Manager:* Nigel Pearson

UNITED got off to a slow – for which read 'terrible' – start in defence of their Premier League title. In the first week of the new season they drew at home to Reading without scoring, then drew 1-1 away to Portsmouth before losing 1-0 at Manchester City – clubs who would finish eighth and ninth respectively at the end of the season. In those three games, their only goal was Paul Scholes's 15th-minute strike against Portsmouth.

It didn't get much better after that as four of the next five games were won 1-0, with four different players getting the crucial goals. The one shining example that maybe something better and brighter was on its way was the 2-0 win over Chelsea at Old Trafford. It was perhaps instructive that the team which most fans, and the club itself, perceived as the biggest threat to their Premier League aspirations drew United's best performance of those first six weeks. New signing Carlos Tevez got the first on the stroke of half-time and Louis Saha added the second with a penalty a minute before the end.

October saw an improvement as United strikers started to find the net with some regularity – in the consecutive 4-0, 4-1 and 4-1 wins over Wigan Athletic, Aston Villa and Middlesbrough there were four goals from Rooney, three from Tevez and two from Cristiano Ronaldo. The others came from widemen Ryan Giggs and Nani (another new singing); and Rio Ferdinand also got in on the act.

United's form was pretty good by now, though defeats by Bolton Wanderers and, in the last game of 2007, by West Ham United meant they went into 2008 in second place. Then began one of those famous United runs, the ones that occur in the cold, wet days of January and February when other teams seem to be struggling.

New Year's Day brought a 1-0 win over Birmingham City, courtesy of a 25th-minute goal by Tevez. Tevez's status was often clouded in mystery as there were doubts over who 'owned' him and officially his time at United was only a loan deal, albeit for two years. Sir Alex Ferguson's judgement that 'he'll get me 15 goals this season, and what's more they'll be important goals' was, as usual, bang on the money.

Tevez got 19 goals in his first season and a further 15 in his second for a total of 34 from his 99 appearances for the club in all competitions, many of which were as an impact sub. However, when an opportunity arose to sign him on a permanent deal, the figures being bandied about – as much as £47m was quoted at one point – were astronomical and Sir Alex decided not to pursue the option.

On 12 January 2008 came the visit of Newcastle United, a match which has had an edge since the days, long ago, when Newcastle were in contention for the title. This year they weren't, though they were to finish in comfortable mid-table in 12th.

They arrived at Old Trafford in no sort of form, having lost their previous three Premier League matches, and with Sam Allardyce having quit as manager three days earlier in the wake of a poor run of results.

They did, however, still boast United old boys Nicky Butt and Alan Smith in their ranks, not to mention experienced internationals Damien Duff, James Milner and, of course, Michael Owen.

The first half was a tale of United possession but not too many clear-cut chances, the best possibly coming inside the first two minutes when Anderson won the ball in midfield, fed Michael Carrick whose through ball sent Rooney in on goal. Opting to blast rather than chip, Rooney hit it over.

Newcastle goalkeeper Shay Given was called on to make a couple of smart saves from Rooney, and when Given was beaten Cacapa was there to clear what looked to be a goalbound header from John O'Shea.

Ronaldo could have had a penalty after 28 minutes when he went down under a challenge from Steven Taylor – Ronaldo and Sir Alex both definitely thought it should have been, but referee Rob Styles remained unimpressed, perhaps feeling that Ronaldo was looking for it a bit too much although as Taylor made no contact whatsoever with the ball, it shouldn't really have mattered whether Ronaldo could avoid his outstretched leg or not.

Then Owen raced clear for Newcastle and put the ball in the net. The 'goal' was disallowed for offside but replays were inconclusive, to say the least. If that was a lucky break for United, it was one they deserved as they continued to dominate the game. Ronaldo brought another fine save from Given and just when Ryan Giggs looked firm favourite to snaffle the rebound, Stephen Carr got in with a last-ditch block tackle.

The second half picked up in a similar vein with Taylor being called on to clear the ball off the line twice, first from Rooney, then from Tevez. It was shaping up to be one of those games when United did everything but score, but as the crowd chanted 'attack, attack, attack', suddenly the dam broke.

Smith was penalised for a foul on Ronaldo, possibly a little harshly, and the Portuguese then added insult to injury by striking the free kick under the jumping defensive wall and in. Given did well to get a hand to it but he couldn't keep it out.

Two minutes later Tevez turned provider and Taylor had to slide to get the ball out for yet another United corner. Ferdinand got up well only to head just wide of the post. Then in the 54th minute, the Newcastle defence, which had been working tirelessly to avoid being overwhelmed, suffered a momentary lapse. Cacapa played a risky ball to Jose Enrique inside the area, and he played it back to Given but gave the goalkeeper little time or options and Given's clearance rebounded off Cacapa. The ball fell nicely for Giggs who laid on an easy finish for Tevez. Newcastle briefly responded and Charles N'Zogbia hit a 25-yard strike which brought a good save from Edwin van der Sar.

But that was just about Newcastle's last word in resistance. After 69 minutes United scored a third – Michael Carrick started the move which was taken on by Rooney and Tevez to play Ronaldo in for his second.

In the 71st minute Nani came on for Giggs and almost immediately drifted in from his left-wing station and hit a cross-shot which almost snuck in. Next Carrick had a chance, but his shot was hacked off the line by Enrique in an incident which could also have led to a penalty for a clash between Carr and Ferdinand. Perhaps Styles took pity on Newcastle.

It wasn't going to save them from conceding more goals, however. In the 85th minute Ferdinand popped up at the far post to slide in United's fourth, laid on a plate for him by a sumptuous through pass from Rooney.

And on 88 minutes Ronaldo claimed his first hat-trick for United. It wasn't one of his more memorable strikes, taking a deflection along the way, but he won't have minded that; he made the space for himself by taking the ball down with his right foot, turning inside the covering defender and shooting with his left foot. It was, in fact, to be the only Premier League hat-trick Ronaldo scored for United, though his overall total of 118 goals in 292 appearances in all competitions was a phenomenal strike rate for a player who rarely played as an out-and-out striker.

In injury time, United added a sixth goal when a Tevez shot that crashed down off the bar was deemed to have crossed the line. Smith wasn't convinced and protested the decision a little too vehemently for Styles's liking. It earned him a second yellow card with just enough time left on the clock to allow him to be the first into the showers. Replays seemed to prove fairly conclusively that the ball had indeed crossed the line.

Newcastle caretaker boss Nigel Pearson said after the game that he wasn't going to make any excuses. 'It is a reality check of exactly where we are at,' he said. 'There is loads to do at this football club.'

Most of the talk after the game was indeed about the Newcastle managerial situation and who might take over, with all the usual suspects' names being bandied around. Four days after being thrashed by United, Newcastle announced the return of Kevin Keegan as manager; it was an appointment which caused a certain stir among the fans and brought an immediate uptake in demand for tickets, but had no impact on United, who had already moved on to to bigger and better things.

A little over a month after this Old Trafford thrashing, Newcastle had the chance of exacting some revenge in the return fixture at St James' Park. Again, Newcastle started well and their battling midfield held United at bay until the midway point of the first half. Then on 25 minutes Rooney stole in at the far post on a fabulous ball from Ronaldo for an easy finish.

As United started to switch the ball from wing to wing, Carrick was pulling the strings in the middle and from one of his passes, Ronaldo got United's second on the stroke of half-time. The quality of Carrick's through ball was matched by the quality of Ronaldo's run and after that a goal was never in any doubt.

Newcastle actually had the first chance of the second period, Duff forcing van der Sar into a good save. Ten minutes into the second Ronaldo was at it again: rounding the keeper easily and firing into an open net. Senegalese defender Abdoulaye Faye, a favourite of Allardyce whom he played for at Bolton, Newcastle and West Ham, pulled one back at the second attempt from a Milner corner. There were only just over ten minutes left at that point, but if Newcastle had visions of a late comeback, they were swiftly put to bed by an unstoppable Rooney curler.

Despite being on a hat-trick himself, Rooney unselfishly played in Saha for a rare right-footed finish in the final seconds. 'The match was decided by the front players,' said Sir Alex later. 'They were just magnificent.'

Despite their 11-1 aggregate hammering of Newcastle, United nevertheless ended February still second behind Arsenal. However, March brought five consecutive victories – 3-0 away to Fulham, 1-0 away to Derby County, 2-0 at home to Bolton Wanderers, 3-0 at home to Liverpool and 4-0 at home to Aston Villa. Thirteen goals scored, none conceded. It broke Arsenal's spirit and left Chelsea as their only challenger.

United's 2-1 defeat at Stamford Bridge at the end of April was a setback, though mostly I remember that game as being a wall of sound from United fans from start to finish. Didier Drogba, as ever, was an absolute handful throughout and goals in each half from Michael Ballack against Rooney's 57th-minute strike gave Chelsea what was just about a deserved win in the lunchtime kick-off.

It kept the two sides level on points but United's massively better goal difference – helped in no small part by the two big wins over Newcastle – effectively meant they had to drop points in one of their last two games. They didn't, beating West Ham 4-1 at home, then Wigan 2-0 away. Chelsea's failure to beat Bolton at the Bridge gave United a two-point margin of victory.

Between New Year's Day 2008 and the dying days of the season, United lost twice (once when it didn't matter) and drew three times, winning the other 13. United scored 43 goals and conceded 11. No wonder no other team could live with them.

v Chelsea 1-1 aet

46

(United win 6-5 on penalties)
21 May 2008
Champions League Final
Luzhniki Stadium, Moscow
Attendance: 67,310

MANCHESTER UNITED	CHELSEA
Edwin van der Sar	Petr Cech
Wes Brown	Michael Essien
Rio Ferdinand	Ricardo Carvalho
Nemanja Vidic	John Terry
Patrice Evra	Ashley Cole
Owen Hargreaves	Claude Makelele
Paul Scholes	Michael Ballack
Michael Carrick	Frank Lampard
Cristiano Ronaldo	Joe Cole
Wayne Rooney	Florent Malouda
Carlos Tevez	Didier Drogba
Manager: Sir Alex Ferguson	*Manager:* Avram Grant

U P STEPS John Terry to take the fifth and final penalty for Chelsea. Already Michael Ballack, Juliano Belleti, Frank Lampard and Ashley Cole have scored theirs. Carlos Tevez, Michael Carrick, Owen Hargreaves and Nani have scored for United, but Cristiano Ronaldo's miss with the third penalty has left their team at the mercy of Terry.

The rain is bucketing down on a sodden Moscow pitch and Terry's standing leg slips away from him slightly. As a result his penalty, which goes to Edwin van der Sar's left while he dives right is just very slightly mishit. It clips the outside of the post and stays out.

It's back on. But now it's sudden death. Anderson steps up and despatches his penalty calmly and coolly; Salomon Kalou does the same. Then it's the turn of Ryan Giggs, who tonight made his record-breaking 759th appearance for United.

No problem. Nicolas Anelka, on as a 99th-minute substitute for Joe Cole, is the victim of some gamesmanship from van der Sar as the Dutch goalkeeper points to his left but chooses to dive to his right. That's where Anelka hits it and van der Sar saves. It's what is often referred to by commentators and pundits as 'a nice height for the goalkeeper', but it's a decent penalty from the Frenchman and van der Sar has to get across briskly and get a strong punch on it.

United are the champions of Europe for the third time in the club's history.

Van der Sar is buried beneath a mound of United players: 13 years after he won the trophy with Ajax, the 37-year-old keeper has done it again. It brings to mind Martina Navratilova's comment that she wanted to be the youngest winner of Wimbledon, not the oldest. But van der Sar doesn't care. He's later voted man of the match by UEFA and praised by Sir Alex Ferguson as a 'vital, vital player. His calmness, composure and presence is phenomenal.'

'It's the first penalty shoot-out I've ever won in a big game,' exclaims Sir Alex. 'I thought we were fantastic in the first half and should have been three or four up and then they got a lucky break right on half-time. It gave them impetus and I thought they were the better team in the second half, they had more power than us. Actually I was quite glad to get to extra time so I could change the formation a little and then I thought in extra time we were the better team.'

'I missed my penalty and it felt like the worst day of my life,' said Ronaldo. 'I thought we were going to lose. Now it's the happiest day of my life.'

The 2008 Champions League Final probably wouldn't feature on anyone's list of classic finals but United won't mind about that. They started the final the stronger and after some initial sparring United began to take a grip on the game.

A quick one-two between Wes Brown and Paul Scholes – with BBC Sport's Jonathan Stevenson describing Scholes's flick as 'absolute genius' – gave the right-footed Brown a little space on the wide right and Brown cut in to deliver a left-footed cross perfectly on to the head of Ronaldo to head home the game's opening goal in the 26th minute.

Rio Ferdinand then nearly scored with an equally impressive header seven minutes later – but at the wrong end, a bizarre incident which required a great save from van der Sar.

United went back on the attack. In the 33rd minute Wayne Rooney found Ronaldo with a raking crossfield pass and the Portuguese flyer's cross was delivered to Tevez whose close-range header was somehow blocked by Petr Cech. The Chelsea keeper then did even better to keep Carrick's side-footed follow-up out. Tevez missed an even easier chance shortly after when he couldn't get a firm enough touch on a wicked low cross from Rooney.

On the stroke of half-time, Essien's speculative effort took deflections off Nemanja Vidic and Ferdinand before falling right into Frank Lampard's path. They had van der Sar diving all over the place, in the wrong direction and he had no chance to recover in time to stop Lampard's effort. Lampard took full advantage of Chelsea's stroke of fortune to level the match, and they took their improved form into the second half, beginning to assume a measure of control with Ballack in particular producing some strong runs and dangerous passes. Their only clear-cut opportunity, though, was when Drogba curled a shot against van der Sar's post.

The game moved into extra time, and the late-night drama carried on. Lampard picked up a ball inside the United penalty area and planted a left-footed shot against the bar, then it was United again as Patrice Evra cut a ball in from the left to Giggs whose shot was headed behind for a corner by the covering Terry.

In the teeming rain, with players struggling for a foothold and the ball skidding off the sodden surface, the second half of extra time produced little of note in terms of goalscoring opportunities. There was a bizarre flashpoint, though, which ended in a red card for Didier Drogba. A nothing argument between Tevez and Terry and then a whole group of players saw Drogba hit Vidic right in front of the referee and get a straight red.

And so to that dramatic penalty shoot-out…

'The feeling of saving that last penalty, that's immense,' said van der Sar, 'immense. We got a bit lucky with the slip from John Terry but you could say they got lucky with their goal because the ball changed direction and I tried to change direction also and slipped. The pitch was a bit slippery, other players were sliding too.'

Anelka later said he hadn't wanted to take a penalty as he felt he wasn't warmed up enough as he had only been on the pitch for the last ten minutes of extra time.

But if there was a Chelsea 'fall guy' after the match, it wasn't one of the players – Avram Grant was sacked three days later.

It had been an impressive European campaign from start to finish for United – especially as they were also contending for the Premier League title, which they ultimately won. It began in Group F, alongside Roma, Sporting Lisbon and Dynamo Kiev: a reasonable draw but by no means an easy one. But they built impetus right from the first match when they won in Lisbon, a 62nd-minute header from Ronaldo being the only goal of the game.

Ronaldo, who had been at Lisbon as a youngster and had made 25 appearances for the first team before his big-money transfer to United, refused the celebrate the goal, but it was an important one for United.

In the second match United beat Roma, who were probably thankful to escape with a 1-0 defeat (courtesy of a 70th-minute Rooney goal) after their embarrassment of six months earlier. Back-to-back matches against Kiev were safely negotiated as United won 4-2 in Russia through Ferdinand, Rooney, and two from Ronaldo, then 4-0 back at Old Trafford in the first week of November. On that occasion Gerard Pique and Tevez gave United a comfortable half-time lead; further goals in the second half from Rooney and Ronaldo helped the goal difference.

The fifth round of matches saw a second win over Sporting Lisbon, though United had to come from behind at half-time to do it – Tevez equalising on the hour after Sporting had taken the lead midway through the first half. Ronaldo snatched a late, late winner two minutes into time added on.

It left United and Roma already through to the knockout stages so they played out a fairly tame 1-1 draw in the Stadio Olimpico.

United drew Lyon, one of the harder opponents they could have got from the group runners-up, and were relieved to snatch a 1-1 draw in France via Tevez's 87th-minute equaliser of an earlier Karim Benzema goal. The away goal just swung the tie marginally in United's favour, although they only scored once in the second leg – through Ronaldo just before half-time. In was one of those situations where the goal didn't actually change what the visitors needed to do: they still only needed to score once to tie everything up, and they did hit the post on one occasion but for the most part United held them at bay without too many alarms.

The quarter-finals had promised another titanic struggle with Real Madrid, but the Spanish giants were surprisingly beaten both home and away by Roma. United were in no mood to let the same thing happen to them and taking full advantage of the injury-enforced absence of the totemic Francesco Totti from the Roma line-up they scored goals in each half through Ronaldo and Rooney to grab hold of the tie by the scruff of the neck.

The second leg was a closer affair, but after Daniele De Rossi missed a first-half penalty the Italians never seemed to believe they could score the two goals which would put them back on level terms. Tevez's 70th-minute headed goal removed any remaining doubt.

Three English teams made it though to the semi-finals – United got the other qualifier, Barcelona. Would they have preferred Liverpool or Chelsea? It's a moot point, but United set about their task with relish in the first leg in the Nou Camp. Ronaldo inexplicably fired a penalty wide in the third minute but United coped well with the Spanish team's movement and tiki-taka possession football to keep the tie goalless.

Scholes's early goal in the return gave United a lead on the night and in the tie, but it was a precarious one as a Barca reply would have put them in front on away goals. That ensured the game remained tense, but United were able to see it out and make their plans for Moscow.

'He has given Manchester United fans the most fantastic ride,' said Sir Bobby Charlton after the final. 'We have had fantastic players who have come and gone and he has made Manchester United what we always thought it was – number one.'

v Chelsea 3-0

47

11 January 2009
Premier League
Old Trafford
Attendance: 75,455

MANCHESTER UNITED	CHELSEA
Edwin van der Sar	Petr Cech
Gary Neville	Jose Bosingwa
Jonny Evans	Ricardo Carvalho
Nemanja Vidic	John Terry
Patrice Evra	Ashley Cole
Cristiano Ronaldo	John Obi Mikel
Darren Fletcher	Michael Ballack
Ryan Giggs	Frank Lampard
Park Ji-Sung	Joe Cole
Wayne Rooney	Deco
Dimitar Berbatov	Didier Drogba
Manager: Sir Alex Ferguson	*Manager:* Avram Grant

UNITED got off to a slow start in the defence of their Premier League title, and that's probably being kind. A 1-1 draw at home to Newcastle United on the opening day of the season was followed by a narrow win at Portsmouth, the only goal coming from Darren Fletcher just after the half-hour.

Then defeat at Liverpool, despite Carlos Tevez opening the scoring after just three minutes – the first Premier League loss to the old enemy since 2002, and in the year in which United were bidding to equal Liverpool's record of 18 league titles. A 1-1 away draw at Stamford Bridge was a good result, particularly as Chelsea didn't find an equaliser to Park Ji-Sung's opener until ten minutes from time. Nevertheless it left United in 15th place after four games, hardly what we were used to seeing.

October brought an improvement but still United were never placed higher than third in the first half of the season, and that is where they finished the year. New signing Dimitar Berbatov at least sent the Stretford End off for their New Year's celebrations in reasonable spirits after scoring the only goal of the game at home to Middlesbrough on 29 December.

With the FA Cup third round taking place on the first weekend in January, and the League Cup semi-final first leg taking place in the following midweek, it was an unusually late resumption of the Premier League season on 11 January.

Chelsea were still a place ahead of United in second but had played 20 games to United's 18, and they were about to become the victims of the start of one of those runs which carries all before it. 'Historically, we're always strong in the second half of the season, and we've got the squad to make it a good run-in for ourselves, we've just got to go out and perform,' said Ryan Giggs.

The opening minutes were mostly United as Giggs crossed for Jonny Evans to head weakly and then Petr Cech dropped the ball under no pressure at all and was relieved to see that there were no United players around to snap it up. Rooney powered into the box but was well handled by Ricardo Carvalho before Frank Lampard picked up the game's first yellow card when he missed the ball and cleaned out Rooney.

Gradually Chelsea worked their way into the game, though the only half-chance they had came from a set piece which Michael Ballack struck under the wall Ronaldo-style but he failed to catch it cleanly and it was cleared easily.

Midway through the first half United were back on the attack when they got a free kick for a handball by Ashley Cole about 30 yards out. Ronaldo's kick took a deflection and went for a corner which Giggs took but though it bounced dangerously around the Chelsea box no United player could quite get a clean shot at it.

A good run by Rooney was stopped illegally by Jose Bosingwa, and then Rooney laid on a good chance for Berbatov but the Bulgarian couldn't get his feet sorted out and Cech made the save. The United pressure was building, though, and Chelsea, who went into the game on the back of three draws from their past four league matches, were hanging on a bit.

Chelsea managed to get in a series of blocks to potentially dangerous looking United moves, firstly when Park Ji-Sung's shot beat Cech but was beaten away for a corner by John Terry, then when Darren Fletcher's shot met the same fate.

Just as the game moved into time added on at the end of the first half, United had yet another corner and this time Berbatov flicked it on and at the far post was Nemanja Vidic to bury a header and open the scoring.

United probably just about deserved the half-time lead – they had plenty of possession, lots of corners and a couple of decent, if not totally clear-cut, chances. But it remained a precarious advantage.

The second half started off with United still on top and one ball from Giggs to Park would have led to a goal if the Korean had been able to control it first time. Then a Ronaldo cross just evaded Berbatov at the far post. Chelsea were restricted to long-range efforts for Cole, Didier Drogba and Nicolas Anelka (on for Deco at half-time).

On the hour a United free kick from about 35 yards out had Giggs and Ronaldo over it but in the end it came to nothing as Ronaldo took it but hit the wall. But a couple of minutes later United had their second – and some breathing space.

Patrice Evra and Ronaldo combined well down the left and although the Frenchman's cross just went over Berbatov's head, Rooney was there to tap it in through Cole's legs. Evra picked up a knock somewhere along the way and limped off to be replaced by John O'Shea, but Park and Fletcher worked hard to prevent Chelsea taking advantage and Gary Neville was once again in fine form, reading the danger before it materialised and intercepting or heading it away.

And United remained deadly on the counter-attack with precision passing from Berbatov and Rooney and Ronaldo always looking to get in behind the defence. As the match moved into its final ten minutes, United pressed again. A Ronaldo free kick cannoned off the wall and almost caught Cech out, then a brilliant through ball from Berbatov for Ronaldo saw the offside flag wrongly go up.

Ronaldo had a pop from distance and made the ball move and sway, but it went wide. Then from another run down the left Ronaldo was fouled and he jumped up to take the free kick himself, swinging the ball into the Chelsea penalty area where Berbatov's run gave him half a yard on Franco Di Santo (on just a couple of minutes earlier in place of Joe Cole) and he put it past Cech for 3-0.

There was a nice assist from Vidic who planted his big frame in the way and prevented any Chelsea defender getting to Berbatov. Game over. And action over for the most part.

Some of Chelsea's sluggishness could be attributed to the fact that they were woken at 7am by the fire alarm in their hotel going off – no doubt attributable to an over-zealous United fan – but they never really seemed 'up' for this game. United were marginally the better team in the first half but in the second they just rolled over Chelsea: Fletcher, Park and Giggs got a hold on midfield, Berbatov made some fabulous passes and Rooney and Ronaldo's runs took them into dangerous parts of the pitch time and time again.

If United needed a kick-start to the season, this was it. Berbatov ultimately wasn't to prove the long-term solution to the striking dilemma but there were times when he was coruscatingly good, particularly in this first season. He was certainly sufficiently successful to persuade Sir Alex to allow an increasingly grumpy and frustrated Tevez to leave. 'I don't think Dimitar was a failure here,' said Sir Alex in 2013 ahead of the Bulgarian's return to Old Trafford as a Fulham player. 'He is a very talented player and he had a decent goalscoring record here.' If a goal every three games is what is expected of a top-class striker and a goal every two games is the mark of a truly exceptional goalscorer, then Berbatov's 56 in 149 games puts him somewhere between the two.

A bigger issue was that Berbatov's languid style tended to slow play down when Sir Alex always preferred his teams to speed things up, and play at pace. 'The problem for him was the way we wanted to play,' confirmed Sir Alex. But Berbatov was the undisputed man of the match in this particular game.

It was a victory which took United within five points of an increasingly nervous looking Liverpool side, and with two games in hand. Two games later, United hit the front.

A first-minute winner by Rooney at home to Wigan Athletic and a 90th-minute winner by Berbatov away to Bolton Wanderers overturned

Liverpool's advantage and United remained in first place for the rest of the season.

A 4-1 defeat by Liverpool in mid-March was an irritating blip but of no wider relevance in the championship race; defeat at Fulham a week later was bizarre. But wins in nine of their last ten games – the other being an unusually tame 0-0 draw with Arsenal in the penultimate match – was more than enough for United to secure the title. They became the first, and to date only, club to win three consecutive league titles on two separate occasions. They also equalled Liverpool's haul of 18 so next they wanted the record.

Winning the previous year's Champions League qualified United to take part in the FIFA Club World Cup, for the winners of each of the six continental confederations, held in Japan between 11 and 21 December. Apart from there being some handy prize money on offer ($5m for the winners), it was felt that United taking part in the competition would be 'a good thing' for English football to be seen to do, so they went with the FA's blessing.

Because of the structure of the competition, United entered at the semi-final stage where they met Gamba Osaka from Japan. The Japanese side struggled to contain United's power and first-half headers from Vidic and Ronaldo opened up a 2-0 lead at half-time. Although Gamba pulled one back early in the second half, United restored then increased their lead through Rooney, Fletcher and Rooney again. The game won, United eased up and conceded two late consolation goals to the battling Japanese side.

The final pitched United against LDU Quito of Ecuador, to be played at the International Stadium in Yokohama. United were mostly on top in the first half – although LDU did miss an open goal – but couldn't make the breakthrough their play deserved. A series of good saves from LDU's veteran goalkeeper Jose Francisco Cevallos and a couple of occasions when Park could have done better kept the score at 0-0.

Shortly after half-time they were reduced to ten men after Vidic had been sent off for an elbow on Argentinian forward Claudio Bieler. Bieler had fallen right on top of Vidic and made no effort whatsoever to avoid landing on him, but there was enough deliberate movement of his elbow to warrant Vidic's red card.

In spite of that, United coped pretty well and on 73 minutes a pass found Ronaldo on the edge of the area. The LDU defenders were so busy watching Ronaldo and wondering what he was going to do it gave Rooney just enough time and space on the left-hand side to curl a shot beyond the keeper and into the net.

LDU did start to show a bit more attacking intent after that, but their only really good chance came in the final minute when Edwin van der Sar was forced to tip over a swerving long-range shot.

In the cannon of United trophies, it is clearly a minor one, but another box to tick nonetheless, and one which made them the first English club to win the event in its new format. It gave us a new chant, too, 'We're champions of England, champions of Europe, champions of the world.'

'We're the best team in the world,' grinned a delighted Rooney, who was top scorer in the competition and named player of the tournament. 'It's a great achievement for the team and something we're all really proud of.'

v Aston Villa 2-1

48

28 February 2010
League Cup Final
Wembley
Attendance: 88,596

MANCHESTER UNITED	ASTON VILLA
Tomasz Kuszczak	Brad Friedel
Rafael	Carlos Cuellar
Jonny Evans	James Collins
Nemanja Vidic	Richard Dunne
Patrice Evra	Stephen Warnock
Michael Carrick	Ashley Young
Antonio Valencia	James Milner
Darren Fletcher	Stiliyan Petrov
Park Ji-Sung	Stewart Downing
Michael Owen	Emile Heskey
Dimitar Berbatov	Gabriel Agbonlahor
Manager: Sir Alex Ferguson	*Manager:* Martin O'Neill

TURN the clock back 12 months and United had won through to their first League Cup Final for three years. Winning the Premier League title and the Champions League in 2007/08 had persuaded Ronaldo to give the club one more season and United came very close to matching – or even surpassing – their spectacular exploits of 1998/99.

Ultimately they lost in the semi-finals of the FA Cup (to Everton on penalties) and the final of the Champions League (2-0 to Barcelona), but as detailed in the last chapter they retained their Premier League title and added a first Club World Cup.

Their route to the 2009 League Cup Final had taken in wins over Middlesbrough (3-1), Queens Park Rangers (1-0) and Blackburn Rovers (5-3), all at home. The semi-final pitched them against Championship side Derby County but any thoughts of a comfortable passage to Wembley were swiftly removed when Derby won 1-0 at Pride Park on 7 January.

United did quickly overturn the deficit through first-half goals from Nani, John O'Shea and Carlos Tevez. A penalty from Giles Barnes put Derby back in the game with just over ten minutes to go, but Cristiano Ronaldo, on as a substitute, restored the three-goal advantage with a penalty of his own. Barnes scored a second with a free kick, but too late to affect the course of the game which United won 4-2, and the tie 4-3 on aggregate.

The final, against holders Tottenham Hotspur, was an entertaining affair despite the lack of goals with chances at either end throughout the 90 minutes. United started the brighter with efforts from Darron Gibson and Rio Ferdinand beating the Spurs keeper Heurelho Gomes but also just clearing the bar and Nani, whose effort was well saved by Gomes. After those initial flurries by United, Spurs got into the game a bit more, mainly through the pace of Aaron Lennon.

Ten minutes into the second half Sir Alex Ferguson decided to shore up his midfield by replacing Danny Welbeck with Anderson, and the tactic worked well with United assuming a measure of control in that area. Ronaldo, who had earlier been booked for diving when he could just as easily have been awarded a penalty when Ledley King appeared to stand on his foot, had the best chance of the game in time added on when his shot crashed off the inside of the post with Gomes well beaten.

Extra time brought a drop in tempo on the big Wembley pitch as United brought Giggs on for Gibson while Spurs replaced an exhausted Lennon with David Bentley and Jermaine Jenas with Gareth Bale. A winner for either side never looked that likely in the extra half an hour so the League Cup Final went to penalties for only the second time in its history.

For the neutral, the penalty shoot-out was something of a disappointment as Spurs managed to score only one of their first four kicks while United notched three. Giggs took the first, going in off the inside of the post to Gomes's left. Jamie O'Hara went for the same spot but didn't get quite enough angle on it and Ben Foster made a superb block. Carlos Tevez buried his, low to Gomes's left and already Spurs were under huge pressure.

Vedran Corluka scored his comfortably enough, but Ronaldo kept United in the driving seat, again low to Gomes's left. Bentley, who hadn't been on the pitch that long, hit it wide of Foster's right-hand post and it was left to Anderson to apply the *coup de grace* with a calm left-footed strike to Gomes's right.

Foster was chosen as the man of the match on the basis of a solid performance throughout the two hours of normal play and his great penalty save from O'Hara.

Although United were to narrowly miss out on the other two trophies for which they were in contention in 2008/09, it was still a fabulous season with victory in three competitions. The 2009/10 season was less successful as the club adjusted to life after Ronaldo, but the opportunity to become the first team to retain the League Cup since Nottingham Forest managed it in 1990 was seized with both hands.

United's progress to Wembley in 2010 had come via a 1-0 home win over Wolverhampton Wanderers, courtesy of a neat Danny Welbeck goal, followed by a 2-0 win at Barnsley through Welbeck again and Michael Owen. Next up were Tottenham Hotspur who were sent away from Old Trafford well beaten after two first-half Darron Gibson goals.

The real drama was saved for the two-legged semi-final against Manchester City. It was almost inevitable that Carlos Tevez would score – and he did, twice, in the first leg as City overturned an early Giggs tap-in from a great ball into the City six-yard box by Rooney to win it 2-1. It is a bit of a mystery how City won, frankly, as they were comprehensively outplayed for most of the game.

United were confident but in the return leg at Old Trafford, it took until the second half before Paul Scholes cancelled out the City lead with the sweetest of low strikes from right to left; then Carrick put United ahead on aggregate by seizing on a loose ball, only for Tevez to make it all square again.

But in a typical United surge they flooded forward and only a top-class save from Shay Given kept City in the contest. Then a Giggs cross in stoppage time was buried by Rooney, who put in what Sir Alex later described as a 'wonderful performance' and celebrated with an impressive cartwheel/flip. And who can blame him? It is always nice to get one over on the old enemy, especially in a major cup semi-final, and even more especially when City have in their ranks a former United player.

No team managed by Martin O'Neill can ever be taken lightly. A team which had taken four points off United in the Premier League (drawing 1-1 at Villa Park earlier in the month having won 1-0 at Old Trafford in mid-December) even less so. United went into the 2010 League Cup Final as marginal favourites, but the emphasis was very much on the word 'marginal'.

That 10 February draw at Villa Park had cost United in other ways, too. Ryan Giggs had broken his arm in the match, forcing him to join Anderson and Rio Ferdinand on the injured list, while Nani had received a red card for a two-footed challenge on Villa captain Stiliyan Petrov which had resulted in a three-game suspension. Rooney had a minor knee injury which prevented him from starting so in came Owen who had joined United in the summer from Newcastle United.

On a cloudy but dry day, United got off to the most disastrous start possible. Three and a half minutes in, as Ashley Young hooked a ball cleverly down the inside-left channel Gabby Agbonlahor got the better of Nemanja Vidic who was always struggling to get back and get a challenge in, and when he did referee Phil Dowd had no hesitation whatsoever in awarding the penalty.

United waited with bated breath to see if a red card was going to follow but not only did it not, not even a yellow was brandished – which was just as well for Vidic and United as he did get a caution midway through the second half. 'We got a lucky break there,' admitted Sir Alex later. 'He could have been sent off.' 'It's not a good decision by an otherwise fine referee,' said O'Neill. 'It's poor.'

They still received their punishment, however, as James Milner hit the penalty right-footed low to Tomasz Kuszczak's left as the goalkeeper went right and the scoring was opened.

It proved to be one of those occasions, however, when it might have been unwise to wake the sleeping giant. Roused by the need to respond, United broke into their free-flowing football and end-to-end play was always unlikely to favour Villa in the long run. In fact, there was no 'long run' about it; it only took United until the 12th minute to get back on level terms – Dimitar Berbatov robbed Richard Dunne of the ball and burst through with a great run which carried him into the penalty area. Dunne recovered well to get a challenge in but the ball rolled right into the path of Owen, following up, who struck a firm first-time shot from right to left past Brad Friedel's outstretched arm.

From that point, the game was quite an open one for some time, but gradually Villa were pushed deeper and deeper as they tried to defend. Park had a fine chance which he managed to hit against the post while Milner almost got his second with a 20-yard piledriver which Kuszczak did well to get to.

After half-time Carrick had a shot well saved by Given, and Rooney, on as a substitute for the injured Owen shortly before the break, nearly scored with an audacious near-post flick. Friedel made a great save from Carrick after the midfielder had been set up by a clever back-heel from Berbatov.

Villa had their moments too, with a couple of great runs from Young, and when he knocked the ball beyond Fletcher then turned on the after-burners his cross almost picked out the waiting Agbonlahor. Then Young got another chance when a Villa corner was headed out to him but he hit his volley slightly down into the ground and the lush Wembley turf took all the pace off it.

The winner came from Rooney, in the 73rd minute. Antonio Valencia, who had transferred from Wigan Athletic for around £16m almost eight months earlier, led Villa a merry dance down the right-hand side before chipping it back from the byline. That sort of cross still requires a fair amount of work from whoever is heading it in order to generate sufficient power to beat a Premier League goalkeeper, but Rooney demonstrated the technique – and the neck muscles – to execute that skill. It was a perfectly-directed header which looped up and over Friedel, whose half-step to his right made it impossible to get back to his left where Rooney directed his header.

'Another day, another goal, another reminder that Wayne Rooney is head and shoulders above every other player in the country,' wrote the excellent Henry Winter in *The Telegraph* the next day. *The Guardian*'s Kevin McCarra sounded a similar note, 'Rooney was initially among the substitutes because he was tired, affected by a heavy cold and carrying a minor injury. Still he was nowhere near handicapped enough for Aston Villa's liking.'

Three minutes later Rooney almost got another when, from another ball in by man-of-the-match Valencia, he smacked a powerful header off the post. O'Neill changed things in an attempt to get back into the final by replacing Carlos Cuellar with the giant John Carew and from Stewart Downing's cross Emile Heskey's header bounced off Vidic's shoulder and on to the bar, but no one could deny that United were worthy winners.

United, who had previously thought of the League Cup as good experience for younger or newly signed players, have now won it on four occasions. That is more than any club except Liverpool, who have always valued it more than most for some reason, and Aston Villa, who have five wins but none since 1996.

v Blackburn Rovers 7-1

49

27 November 2010
Premier League
Old Trafford
Attendance: 74,850

MANCHESTER UNITED	BLACKBURN ROVERS
Edwin van der Sar	Paul Robinson
Rafael	Christopher Samba
Rio Ferdinand	Ryan Nelsen
Nemanja Vidic	Michel Salgado
Patrice Evra	Phil Jones
Michael Carrick	Pascal Chimbonda
Nani	Brett Emerton
Anderson	David Dunn
Park Ji-Sung	Herold Goulon
Wayne Rooney	El Hadji Diouf
Dimitar Berbatov	Jason Roberts
Manager: Sir Alex Ferguson	*Manager:* Sam Allardyce

WITH one minute 43 seconds on the clock, Wayne Rooney got up at the near post to flick Nani's cross on to Dimitar Berbatov who got a foot ahead of his marker and volleyed in from close range. Anderson arguably clattered Paul Robinson chasing a ball moments before Nani hit his cross, but whether it should have been penalised or not, the Rovers keeper clearly hadn't recovered either his footing or his composure before the ball came over.

Even before the second goal arrived, Nani missed a decent chance at the near post, Berbatov headed wide from a corner and Christopher Samba almost scored an own goal, albeit under huge pressure.

On 23 minutes the inevitable happened and a beautiful one-two between Ji-Sung Park and Rooney left Park though on goal with only Paul Robinson to beat – which he did with ease.

Samba perhaps should have cut the final ball out, but it was a precision pass from Rooney and all Park had to do was lift it over the goalkeeper, and then avoid landing on him when he came down.

With United attacking from all angles and all areas of the pitch it was no great surprise when they added a third, though this time they had a huge helping hand from the Blackburn defence as Pascal Chimbonda played a blind pass back to his goalkeeper. Berbatov was lurking, for once his lack of movement off the ball proving a help rather than a hindrance, and he intercepted to blast the ball high into the Rovers goal. To be fair to Chimbonda, it did appear that he was being advised to knock it back to Robinson, but a quick look up might still have been advisable.

Seeing easy pickings, Nemanja Vidic decided to get in on the act and came storming forward for a Nani free kick on the edge of the Rovers penalty box. A well-flighted ball was asking to be headed home but Vidic missed just about the easiest chance of the match. Berbatov was then denied what looked an obvious penalty – perhaps referee Lee Probert could see the way the game was going already and was feeling kindly disposed towards Blackburn.

It was 3-0 at half-time and it could have been six, but United didn't waste any time in putting that right at the start of the second half. Berbatov finished off a move he had started inside the United half with a simple side-footed finish from about ten yards out. These were the Bulgarian's first goals since the match against Liverpool two months earlier, when ironically he had also scored a hat-trick. Going ten matches without scoring was not the sort of form either United or Berbatov would have been hoping for but he made up for it in this match.

Barely a minute later Nani made it five, getting a deserved goal of his own having created several for others. After a great run down the wide right channel, the Portuguese winger stormed into the Rovers penalty area before cutting back inside to rifle home a left-footed curling shot for 5-0 – and still no Rooney on the scoresheet; he made a great run into the penalty area but Nani delayed his cross just long enough for Robinson to make a good block with his legs.

Berbatov was not done yet, though. Shortly after the hour he found the ball landing virtually at his feet after a great run from Rafael followed by a bit of pinball in the area. A Park shot was blocked and fell to Berbatov, who had little more to do than fire it in from just outside the six-yard box.

To say that Berbatov can look a bit languid is like saying Peter Schmeichel was an extrovert, but with his minimal backlift and precise finishing the Bulgarian could make the act of scoring look very simple indeed, and he did just that again when his attempted cross bounced back off Ryan Nelsen and right into his path. With Robinson having taken a step or two to his right in anticipation of the cross, there was just enough room for Berbatov to slot it inside the near post.

Another United break saw a combination of a quick throw from van der Sar, even quicker passes from Anderson and Patrice Evra, an early ball to Rooney and an even earlier ball from Rooney to substitute Gabriel Obertan (a winger, signed from Bordeaux, who always promised slightly more than he managed to deliver in his two seasons at United). The Frenchman should have done better than hit it straight at Robinson, though to give the former England keeper his due, he came out quickly and spread himself well.

Slightly bizarrely, not to mention somewhat against the run of play, Samba pulled one back for Blackburn with seven minutes remaining, with a towering header from Josh Morris's left-footed cross which under other circumstances might have received more than a passing mention. There was still time for

Robinson to deny Berbatov his sixth goal of the game with a great tip over from a header.

The win had huge implications for United as it was the day they went top of the Premier League, and they stayed there for the rest of the season. 'We were completely outplayed,' confessed Allardyce. 'We're extremely disappointed with our performance and the result, and I'd like to apologise to Blackburn fans. Unfortunately we caught United at their best.'

In a reversal of United's normal style, they played the first half of the 2010/11 season in storming fashion, not recording their first league defeat of the season until 5 February when they lost at Wolverhampton Wanderers. For all that, though, a record of seven wins and seven draws prior to the Blackburn game had kept them in second or third place through the first half of the season.

They had ratcheted up the goals themselves but had been unable to prevent their opponents scoring plenty too. A couple of defeats in March, to Chelsea and Liverpool, were cancelled out by an unbeaten April when they won three and drew one of their four games.

It all meant that by the time they travelled to Ewood Park for the penultimate match of the season, they knew a draw would secure them another title. The big one.

Allardyce had departed in the middle of December 2010 and Steve Kean, the first team coach brought in by Big Sam, was placed in temporary charge, then a few days later given a contract until the end of the season. A proud Blackburn team were absolutely determined not to be rolled over on their own patch in the same way that they had been at Old Trafford and they fought United every inch of the way in the early kick-off on 14 May.

Again United looked to get off to a dynamic start and put pressure on the Blackburn defence, but Nani was unlucky to do no more than hit the crossbar after four minutes from a Rooney cross; he wasn't quite able to direct the header downwards enough. Blackburn were briefly the better team – Samba had sliced a volley when well placed on 11 minutes, and he did put it in the net seven minutes later with an overhead kick but there was a foul on Vidic in the build-up. Brett Emerton finally gave Rovers a deserved lead just before the midway point in the first half.

Tomasz Kuszczak was never entirely convincing in this game, which was a shame for him as he was in pole position to seize the goalkeeping slot when van der Sar retired at the end of the season. Instead, his shaky form persuaded Sir Alex to cast his net further afield, eventually bringing in young Spanish keeper David de Gea. De Gea endured a rocky start to his United career, possibly because he wasn't physically robust enough to withstand some of the Premier League-type challenges on him which would probably have been penalised for foul play in Spain. Now de Gea has put on some more muscle and is more confident than he was initially in coming for crosses, without losing any of his shot-stopping capabilities, he is looking like the keeper we all knew he could be.

With Blackburn scrambling to cut out or block anything and everything, United didn't have many clear chances, and in fact Rovers had arguably the best chance to score when Jonas Olsson headed against the woodwork with Kuszczak beaten. There was a half-hearted shout for a penalty when Antonio Valencia went down under a Gael Givet challenge, but referee Phil Dowd decided that the Ecuadorian was looking for it a bit too obviously.

United's equaliser finally came from a Rooney penalty after Javier Hernandez had been brought down by Robinson. Blackburn felt it was a harsh call as it appeared that the speedy Hernandez was running the ball out of play, but he had just got a toe to the ball before Robinson caught him.

From that point on both teams seemed content with the draw which would suit both their purposes and not too much energy was expended in the search for a winner in the final 16 minutes. United were content to pass the ball among their back four, from side to side without feeling the need to go anywhere, and when Blackburn did recover possession, they seemed happy to do the same. More by luck than judgement, Nani had a good chance to take all three points, but that would have been hard on a feisty and determined Rovers side who deserved the point in their ultimately successful battle against relegation.

'My greatest challenge is not what's happening at the moment,' Sir Alex Ferguson had said during the 2002/03 title-winning campaign. 'My greatest challenge was to knock Liverpool right off their f***ing perch. And you can print that.'

Media all round the world did precisely that. No wonder the Scousers hated Sir Alex – not only did he say quite clearly what his intentions were, he went out and accomplished exactly what he said he would. Even back then he had been playing the long game. This was United's 19th title, the 12th under Sir Alex himself, and the moment couldn't have been any sweeter.

'We have won the FA Cup more times than anyone,' said Sir Alex. 'And now we have won the Premier League more times than anyone. It's not so much passing Liverpool, it's more important that United are the best team in the country in terms of winning titles.'

For once, I have to disagree with Sir Alex – it *is* about passing Liverpool. As Ryan Giggs said, 'It means a lot, especially for the older supporters who through the 1970s and 1980s watched Liverpool win everything.' Bang on, Ryan, that's me!

'Now obviously the tables are turned. We've done so well over the last 20 years to overturn that sort of deficit, to get to 19 titles is special, and the fans know that.'

v Aston Villa 3-0

22 April 2013
Premier League
Old Trafford
Attendance: 75,591

MANCHESTER UNITED	ASTON VILLA
David de Gea	Brad Guzan
Rafael	Ron Vlaar
Phil Jones	Joe Bennett
Jonny Evans	Nathan Baker
Patrice Evra	Matthew Lowton
Michael Carrick	Charles N'Zogbia
Antonio Valencia	Ashley Westwood
Ryan Giggs	Fabian Delph
Shinji Kagawa	Gabriel Agbonlahor
Wayne Rooney	Christian Benteke
Robin Van Persie	Andreas Weimann
Manager: Sir Alex Ferguson	*Manager:* Paul Lambert

IT'S a long ball into the Aston Villa penalty area from the United right by Rafael. It's not even a particularly dangerous looking one, being slow and loopy, but the goalkeeper doesn't come for it and the uncertain young Villa defence let it go all the way through to the far post where Ryan Giggs is standing. Giggs simply cushions the ball back into the Villa six-yard box, causing mayhem and panic.

As the Villa defenders dither in getting the ball out, Robin Van Persie does not and he decisively sticks out a foot. United are ahead. There are 80 seconds on the clock. As ways to start a potentially championship-winning match go, this is hard to beat.

A minute later an Antonio Valencia cross takes a deflection and Van Persie twists to get in a volley on his favoured left foot which flies narrowly over. The way the Dutchman contorts to get the ball on to his foot at a height where he can strike it is the mark of a world-class striker, but on this occasion he just isn't able to drag the shot down under the crossbar.

The United siege continues as Villa just aren't able to clear their lines. A Giggs ball in is knocked down by Van Persie for Shinji Kagawa to hit from close range, but Ron Vlaar somehow gets in an excellent block.

Next Rafael hits a sweet right-footed strike from right to left that beats Brad Guzan but smacks off the inside of the post and to safety.

A quick-fire Villa passing move out of defence brings a chance for their top scorer Christian Benteke. He perhaps should have hit it from left to right with his left foot but instead tries to open up his body and lofts a right-footed curler but just gets too much elevation on the shot.

But despite the threat of a breakaway goal from Villa, United keep applying the pressure at the other end, and on 13 minutes, Van Persie got his, and United's, second of the evening. Wayne Rooney, playing in a deeper-lying role with the freedom to take up positions all over the pitch, hits a 40-yard pass to Van Persie who just about stays onside, then lets the ball fall over his shoulder and hits a dipping left-footed volley past a bemused and stranded Guzan. It's skill and technique of the highest order, and yet Van Persie makes it look like he does it every day. He probably does.

'How do they do that?' asks the guest I was watching the game with. Damned if I know, but it's spectacular to see, and it got the Old Trafford crowd on its feet, acclaiming the Dutchman, and the Englishman, and the whole United team.

Then comes almost 20 minutes of calm before, shortly after the half-hour, Kagawa's through ball sends Giggs into the area, once more ensuring panic among the inexperienced Villa defence. If you look at the numbers there are actually four Villa defenders in and around the six-yard box but Giggs still has time to select his option, choosing to lay the ball right-footed across to Van Persie. RVP has enough time to take a couple of touches before slamming it high into the net for a first-half hat-trick.

Paul Lambert had taken over from the sacked Alex McLeish on 2 June, signing a three-year deal. Most of the season was a struggle against relegation for a young Villa side who spent a large proportion of the season in, or close to, the bottom three before finishing with a comparative flourish to garner 41 points and end up in the relative calm of 15th position.

Against United, Lambert fields more than half a side of players in their early 20s, and they are simply no match for the power and pace of a determined United side who know they will tie up the title with a win.

But for all their difficulties in defence, Villa look good, and occasionally threatening, going forward. Even at 3-0 down they show some spirit, Gabby Agbonlahor taking Benteke's pass and sending a swerving shot not far past David de Gea's post shortly before half-time.

Not content with getting the goals, Van Persie pops up at the other end early in the second half to clear an Andreas Weimann effort off the line after the young Austrian gets in a good looping header which is bound for the net.

Benteke's snap shot brings a good low save out of de Gea who then tips over a decent long-range effort from substitute Karim El-Ahmadi (on for Charles N'Zogbia at half-time).

United's first good chance of the second half doesn't arrive until the 71st minute when Ashley Westwood clears a Jonny Evans flick off the line, and five minutes later Kagawa should score United's fourth when a wonderful shimmy and switch of feet leaves him unmarked in front of goal, but he spoils the moment by blasting high over the bar.

And Valencia, who had laid on that chance for Kagawa, himself should wrap things up a couple of minutes later but Guzan makes a smart save.

So 3-0 it remained and United won their 20th league title. They had started the match comfortably clear of the rest and that was still the position at the end of it. With four games to play the gap was big enough after defending champions Manchester City had lost at Tottenham Hotspur the day before.

City are obviously a growing force in the land, with their huge investment following the 2008 takeover by the Abu Dhabi United Group. So far they have won two Premier League titles, an FA Cup (2011) and a League Cup (2014) as a return on that investment, which the *Manchester Evening News* recently estimated at over £370m on players.

They had snatched the 2011/12 Premier League title from under United's noses with virtually the last kick of the last game but were unable to mount a sustained challenge the following year. Despite what a number of critics dubbed an ageing team not comparable with the great Sir Alex Ferguson sides, this United team regained the Premier League title by nine points – a win, two draws and a defeat in their last four games allowing the chasing pack, headed by City and Chelsea, to close the gap slightly long after the title had been won.

Old Trafford has now seen the Premier League title decided there on four separate occasions – 1999, 2002, 2009 and 2013 – which is more than any other ground. United are by some margin the best supported club in the country so it seems fitting that they should witness these occasions.

'It is sweet,' Sir Alex told the BBC. 'They're a great bunch of boys, great staff, fantastic support. We have all the ingredients to win the title. They focused on the challenge of City and came up trumps. Our consistency for the last 20 years is unbelievable. This club never gives in. From Sir Matt Busby, the Munich disaster, to rebuilding and to win the European Cup, that tells you the history of this club – every player who comes to this club has to have that ingrained.'

Was the signing of Van Persie the key to United reclaiming the Premier League? By modern standards the £22.5m (plus a further £1.5m which has already become due as it was dependent on United winning the Premier League or the Champions League) United paid for a striker who was almost certain to net them 20 goals a season if fit was a gimme. 'I remember Arsene Wenger saying to me "he's better than you think" when we concluded the deal,' said Sir Alex. 'He was right. In terms of impact he has had as big an impact as anyone I can imagine. He has been unbelievable and tonight he was unstoppable.'

Former United coach Rene Meulensteen told the BBC that the reason Van Persie chose the number 20 for his shirt when he joined United was that Meulensteen convinced him he would be responsible for bringing home United's 20th title. Even allowing for a slight dip in form in the 2013/14 season, Van Persie has scored 48 goals in 76 appearances for United (13 of them as a substitute) by the summer of 2014.

It is an even higher conversion rate than he enjoyed with Arsenal and the way new manager Louis Van Gaal set the team up to play in 2014/15 – with Rooney and Van Persie playing up front and a number ten, most likely Juan

Mata, in the hole behind them – there was every likelihood of Van Persie being able to maintain his scoring rate.

'It didn't really matter who scored as long as we won this game – and we did,' said a smiling Van Persie. 'It's a great feeling.'

'When you lose it in the manner that we did last year, it's always special to win it back,' said Giggs. 'We did it in style.'

They certainly did. United fought back brilliantly from the shock of conceding the Premier League the previous season. Although they lost at Everton on the opening day they then won four in a row – including beating Liverpool 2-1 at Anfield, courtesy of a stunning Rafael strike and a late penalty from Van Persie. Another hiccup followed when they lost at home to Spurs, which cost them a slip to third in the table. Then came a second fine run of wins, this time five in a row, which included beating Arsenal 2-1 at home and then claiming a 3-2 victory at Stamford Bridge.

One of the season's more noticeable results came on 17 November when United lost at struggling Norwich City. Whether that resulted in the hairdryer treatment in the changing room in Sir Alex's last season, we'll never know, but United then embarked on a run of 18 games unbeaten – 16 wins and two draws.

That included a win away to Manchester City thanks to two first-half goals from Rooney and a 92nd-minute winner from Van Persie. It also included doing the double over Liverpool, always worthy of more than a passing mention; Van Persie and Vidic got the goals.

It meant that by the time City came to Old Trafford and snatched victory, it was no more than a minor blip on the road to the 20th title. United won at a canter, by 11 points, and with a goal difference of +43 – by a strange piece of symmetry scoring exactly twice as many goals as they conceded, 86 to 43.

It was a fine note for Sir Alex to retire on – 27 years in charge, 21 domestic trophies and six more in Europe or worldwide, United taken to the very pinnacle of the English game. 'It is the right time,' he said. 'I would like to thank my players and staff, past and present, for a staggering level of professional conduct and dedication that has helped to deliver so many memorable triumphs.'

The Sir Alex Ferguson years will never be forgotten by the fans.

Manchester United move on into a new era, hopefully one which will be just as successful and produce many more greatest games for someone else to write about in the future.